OPEN

AN ADOPTION STORY IN THREE VOICES

ALAINA O'CONNELL
ALEX PORTER
&
SARA O'CONNELL

BALBOA.
PRESS

A DIVISION OF HAY HOUSE

Balboa Press books may be ordered through booksellers or by contacting:

Balboa Press
A Division of Hay House
1663 Liberty Drive
Bloomington, IN 47403
www.balboapress.com
1 (877) 407-4847

Because of the dynamic nature of the Internet, any web addresses or links contained in this book may have changed since publication and may no longer be valid. The views expressed in this work are solely those of the author and do not necessarily reflect the views of the publisher, and the publisher hereby disclaims any responsibility for them.

The author of this book does not dispense medical advice or prescribe the use of any technique as a form of treatment for physical, emotional, or medical problems without the advice of a physician, either directly or indirectly. The intent of the author is only to offer information of a general nature to help you in your quest for emotional and spiritual well-being. In the event you use any of the information in this book for yourself, which is your constitutional right, the author and the publisher assume no responsibility for your actions.

Any people depicted in stock imagery provided by Thinkstock are models, and such images are being used for illustrative purposes only.
Certain stock imagery © Thinkstock.

Print information available on the last page.

ISBN: 978-1-5043-8047-8 (sc)
ISBN: 978-1-5043-8049-2 (hc)
ISBN: 978-1-5043-8048-5 (e)

Library of Congress Control Number: 2017907594

Balboa Press rev. date: 05/11/2017

For my four children, my true legacy.
Alaina O'Connell

To my three daughters. I love you.
Alex Porter

To my big, unique family.
Sara O'Connell

ACKNOWLEDGEMENT

We want to thank our family and friends for supporting us in our desire to bring this story to light.

A special thanks to Sherry Simmons for her meticulous proofing when we could not see straight anymore, and gratitude to Jessica Vineyard of Red Letter Editing for her excellent editing skills and critical questions so that the reader could follow a story that spanned twenty-six years. We also want to thank Shelley-Ann Hincks who told us that this story simply had to be shared with the world.

Finally, we want to thank our children, who lived this story and taught us so much about what love really is.

PREFACE

This is a true story, and like many true stories, it does not follow a scripted format. It began as a gift to my daughter Sara. I wanted to tell her the story of her adoption, of how she was loved, wanted, and valued. I enriched the story with photographs of smiling faces and happy endings. It was to be my gift to her when she came of age, before she met her birth mother.

Actually, I began writing it before she was born. I would stand beside her little crib and pray for her spirit to hear mine and respond to my voice through the firmament. I wanted her. I would be a good mother. My husband dreamed of having his own child. It was a prayer—a prayer that was answered.

After Sara came into our lives, I began writing nightly entries into a journal, chronicling the rollercoaster ride of the adoption process. I softened some of my feelings because I wanted to protect her from all the grown-up happenings surrounding her life. My journaling was truthful, but it left out much of the story. Maybe it left out most of the truth.

When I finished my story, I sat for months pondering the impact of my own writing and the love that poured onto the pages that Sara would one day read. However, with time, I realized that only half of the story had been written. One half had not—her birth mother's half. We had been in communication throughout the adoption process, so it was easy for me to call one evening and tell her what I had done. I asked her if she was ready and willing to tell her story, too, so that Sara would have the whole legacy of her beginning. Alex, her birth mother, wholeheartedly agreed, and within a few months, she sent her half of Sara's story. I was awestruck by the simple, healing honesty of this young woman, who had given my husband and me such a wondrous gift at a great cost to her. She had no idea what the cost had been to us.

The journal sat in a box for several years as we added to our story: the changes in our lives, our fears for the future, and how to tell Sara about her adoption. In the course of time, there emerged another story within the one we had written: the unique relationship between Alex and me. Most of my friends who had adopted wanted nothing to do with the birth mothers; there was a sense of ownership, a territorialism, toward the child. By not allowing birth mothers into their lives, the birth mothers didn't exist. But Alex did exist. I saw her every time I gazed into Sara's eyes. I did not own Sara.

Our story is real. It was sometimes tragic, like life. Yet, on some level, the guts of our story had been left out of the journal. Finally, eight years after we began, in a conversation as casual as one over a cup of coffee, Alex and I decided to rewrite it and tell the whole truth—the real story. And so, what began as a journal for Sara evolved into a journey of two women whose love for one another grew over the years and who promised each other to do the right thing for the child they both loved. This is that story.

All names have been changed to protect the privacy of the people involved. We hope that we have done that respectfully; that was our intent. The story meanders at times because we must tell you who we are. We must show you where the scars are hidden. We must say it straight, without sugar or manipulation.

This story is for every woman who considers adopting a child or who considers giving her child up for adoption. It is about how complicated life is and how destiny plays a great role in each of our lives. It is about a windy road that leads to a salvation of sorts. This story will never end. It was written for the love of Sara and for what it means to be truly O P E N.

~Alaina O'Connell

§

Daughter

Some daughters are born of
The flesh,
The mysteries of their bond
Written indelibly and forever
Upon every cell.
Some daughters are born of
The spirit,
The mysteries of their bond
Written quietly
Upon the heart.

§

CHAPTER 1

Alaina

How did a forty-year-old woman who had been married for twenty years, had raised three great children, and had vowed never, ever to remarry wind up married again and adopting a baby at age forty-five? Who would have thought, twelve years earlier, that I would one day divorce my husband, marry my children's piano teacher, and adopt a child, much less *want* to adopt and raise another child? I stand in awe at the power of this love stuff.

I witnessed myself fall in love with this man—I literally fell under a spell, which I truly believe he did not consciously cast. He was just as surprised as I was by our love, our unfathomable attraction to one another, and our sense of cosmic destiny, though God knows he would never have used those terms.

I had known Jason for five years as "the piano teacher." I wrote a check once a week for my three children's piano lessons. I would run into the living room, scribble a check, and disappear into my room to correct papers for school. He would be cordial, smile, and leave. After my separation from my husband, Jason and I would chat after the kids' lessons for a moment or two about kids, life, and his desire to find a young woman to marry and have a family. I matched him up with a couple of my best friends who were anxiously seeking husbands, and he even took one out, only to return with shrugging shoulders. "No, too wild. I actually want a simpler woman—soft, nurturing . . . you know, special!" Maybe if my children hadn't insisted that we invite him to dinner one night, I might have successfully escaped into blissful singledom, a place I truly longed for after twenty years of trying to please a host of people. But no. Instead, I said, "Sure. Ask him over." I had no clue what was to happen.

That evening, I volunteered to play a game of stare-down with him since he was beating my children handily, round after round. They would sit across from one another on the floor and try to make the other laugh. As a normal, red-blooded Leo female, I couldn't resist the game and wanted to prove my regal standing by showing this guy what I could do with my eyes. Thus, I stepped into destiny's web, totally unsuspecting. I sat down in front of this man whose athletic body, muscular and trim, seemed almost boyish next to my motherly figure. I crossed my legs and intended to have some fun with him. I fixed my green, feline eyes into his black-brown ones and waited. What happened was extraordinary. I was trying to think of something else so as to not start laughing or giggling, when suddenly my entire being was swept up into his eyes, and I felt myself being dragged into them. I tried to look away but was helpless, truly paralyzed. I whirled and whirled into the darkness and observed how he was not the person I thought he was. I felt naked and sexual, primitive and vulnerable, trapped, and even a little afraid. I used all my strength to exit his grasp on me. The kids were laughing and egging me on to win, but I had lost. More precisely, I *was* lost. Suddenly, the spell was broken when he blinked and pulled away sheepishly. "That's not fair!" he said.

From that night on, my life changed. Months later, when we were in love and there was no going back, I learned that he had felt the same thing but had thought I was doing it to him. Soon I was standing on a mountaintop stark naked, screaming about the wounds of my life and claiming freedom from the past. Some months after that, I discovered that part of me had been asleep before I met Jason, and his stubborn love was forcing me to face every demon I had ever created. One year after our stare-down, I was standing in my backyard reciting wedding vows I had written. I began painting for the first time, and I dreamed that with this man I could adopt a child and begin another family, despite the incredulous reactions of most of my friends. "What has happened to Alaina?" What, indeed!

We couldn't have been more different from one another. He was neat; I was messy. His toothpaste tube was always rolled up tidily; mine was, well, messy. He lived in shorts and tennis shoes; I liked to dress up. He was a spendthrift; I was a spender. I would have never picked him out of a lineup of possible suitors, or he me. He was darker than my type, shorter than my type, too alternative a lifestyle for my type. I always played it safe. After my childhood, who wouldn't? No, this man was not for me. I was too old for him, too tall for him, and I couldn't have any more children, the main item on his list. I was definitely not the Miss Right you take home to Mama: "Oh, Mom, I want you to meet this nice middle-aged woman I met at work and her three teenagers." No, I was definitely not the pick of the week. But what I was, was the best woman in the world for this man—well, maybe not the man whom the world knew: carefree-cute, tennis-playing, piano-playing Mr. Charm. But I was the right woman for the real man: brooding artist, secret-keeping man whose world lay deep within him and whose heart was wounded and vulnerable. I was the woman for that man. Or so I thought.

In our own way, we brought to one another a first-time quality: first conscious commitment, first transparency of the soul to another soul, first union of the spirit. These things could not be seen with the naked eye, and they certainly defied what everyone who knew us could see, but we knew what no one else could know: that it is very dangerous to get into a stare-down contest. Very dangerous, indeed!

But that's not really where this story begins.

§

CHAPTER 2
Alaina

I am in a hospital. Many people are milling around whom I do not know. I feel a compulsion to go to the bathroom. Alone in the stall, I suddenly feel that undeniable feeling of giving birth. There, all alone, I deliver a baby girl. She does not cry, and I notice that her face is very mature. Her eyes, green like mine, look up at me trustingly. I am afraid she might not survive. She seems so serious for a baby.

A stern nurse comes in and shouts, "Have you not cut the cord? You idiot! The child will die." She hands me a scissors, and I try to cut the cord. Tiny filaments separate from the main cord, but the cord will not break. The baby seems weaker, yet she looks so trustingly into my eyes that I must proceed. After much effort, the last filament is broken through. The baby is now separate from me. Suddenly, I am alone with her in front of a large mirror. I place the child's face next to mine. To my utter amazement, our faces, hers and mine, become one.

Wasn't this the dream that started my journey to Jason? Wasn't this the dream that placed my unsteady feet on the path of awakening? As the resistant filaments of my past clung tenaciously to my unconscious mind, I knew that I, the real me, was yet to be born. I had no way of knowing then that this self-discovery would destroy my marriage to Johann, hurt my children terribly, and strike a death blow to the family I called my own. In the years to come, I would break all the rules: divorce my husband of twenty years, defy my family to marry Jason, unearth family secrets that lay asleep in my cellular memory, and blame everyone for my pain. I would also send three children off to college, adopt a baby, be forced to choose between Jason and my family of origin, and ultimately begin to put the pieces of my life back together.

When I was finished (although I doubt that one ever is), there was a new person staring back at me in the mirror—a stranger, an artist, a poet, a woman. Somewhere in the pit of my terror, I knew that my dream was a prophecy of the future that lay ahead. I had to make that journey because the newborn in the dream trusted me to. If there had been any way to avoid the pain of growing, I would have taken the easier road. I didn't realize it at the time, but a more authentic part of me was emerging.

I suppose I was remembering all of this because of Jason's and my decision to adopt. Adoption meant motherhood. Motherhood meant mother. Mother meant that I would finally have to come to terms with the woman who had governed my actions in life and haunted me in death. Mother meant I had to begin to unravel a puzzle that was complex, buried, and lost to my conscious self. How could I become a mother again if I didn't find the mother I had lost so long ago? I used to believe that it was my hatred for her that fueled my desire to live. I used to think a lot of things, most of them myths of my own making

I was born in 1945, just after the big bomb. I think my spirit didn't want to surface with the world at war; it waited until the war was officially over. On August 16, with my father in the Navy somewhere in Hawaii, I entered the cold world and was placed into the hands of a woman who loved me but didn't love herself, a woman who had been given nothing as a child yet was determined to give her children everything. Unfortunately, she had to take me home to her parents' house.

My mother's father, a womanizing, alcoholic gambler, loved my mother, hated his sons, and disdained the mother of his children, whom he had not married. I remember only terror in that house. I remember the indescribable feeling of secrets too awful to speak screaming through the rooms and waking me in the darkness of my tiny crib. I always knew I was not safe there. That house and all the pain that dwelled there haunted me for the next forty-two years.

When my nineteen-year-old father returned from the war, instead of coming back to Indiana and his basketball scholarship, his childhood sweetheart and his betrothed, and a neat little life on the farm, he came home to a beautiful, hot-tempered wife whom he had impregnated after he had known her but a few weeks. She loved him fiercely but had no tools to enter an intimate relationship with. He also found an eight-month-old daughter who resented his intrusion into her life with her mama.

My father's dreams ended that day. He would not be a basketball star. He would not be a doctor. He would not be happy. Instead, he would be tied down to me and the responsibilities of fatherhood. I thought he blamed me; I've lived my life in pursuit of his approval. Instead of becoming a doctor, he became an alcoholic, and for a very long time I thought that was my fault, too. It was my mother, however, who cared for me, sewed all my clothes, and did all she could to be the mother she never had.

I have no memories from most of my childhood. They are buried somewhere deep within me as a protective barrier against the parts that I don't want to see or feel. I grew up a good girl, trying to please everyone, hiding the secret of our family's troubles, and battling my mother. She loved me passionately, but there was one big proviso: I couldn't grow up! To Mom, that would have been betrayal. I loved her. I hated her. I needed her. I wanted to escape her. I learned to lie early to hide what little of my true self existed. I had to lie. What I felt or wanted was not heard. I developed a woman's body, but I was nothing more than a scared little girl looking for sanctuary. I sought love, yet when I got it, I ran away like hell. I never understood why I did this; I simply accepted the family's verdict that I was fickle.

As soon as I could muster the courage, I fell in love with a family in the church I was attending. They had a son who was going off to Viet Nam, and I adopted him—and them—as my road to salvation. Since "good girls" wouldn't think of having sex before marriage, I flew off to Hawaii to meet him for his R&R and we got married. Much to my naïve dismay, he had already been with many prostitutes and asked things of me I couldn't even pronounce, much less contemplate doing. My young husband took pity on me, and I managed to escape my honeymoon without consummating the marriage.

I returned home, angry with my father for not stopping me from going. He was too drunk to care. I buried myself in my studies at the university and began to experiment with my sexuality. My god, I was going to know something when that guy returned. When he did return, though, I packed him off, confused and befuddled, to his mother. I met Johann within a week.

Johann represented everything I lacked: stability, solidness, salt-of-the-earth kind of stuff. We dated for one year. Naturally, I couldn't tell him that I was still married, so the lies began. I wanted to be perfect for him. It never occurred to me to ask if he was perfect for me. All I knew was that I wanted him to give me a home and children. Children! Children were what I really wanted. They would make everything OK. They would make me OK.

I didn't tell Johann I was already married until the night he proposed. By that time, my guilt was so great and the shame so overwhelming that I practically begged him to forgive me. For what? What had I done? I was a lost child in a woman's body. I was unconscious. I needed him to give me definition, and that's exactly what happened. After I divorced the Navy man and Johann and I married, I made my well-being his job. It wasn't his job, but I didn't see that for many years. I never considered my first union a marriage, since we actually spent a total of only two weeks together. We were two lost kids caught up in the confusion of our generation's first war. My first true marriage was to Johann.

Things were rocky from the start. I didn't know how to be married any more than I knew how to feel worthy of life. But Johann was a patient lover, and I learned what I thought love was about. I polished his shoes and car. I cooked three meals a day. I bargained for our first child, begged for the second, and defied him for the third by getting pregnant without his permission. His ardent command that I couldn't have any more children after the first two was incentive enough to defy him, and I was pregnant a month later. He was furious and told me to get an abortion. I said no. I went home to my mother until he came around. He was a good man; I was a little girl.

Motherhood was the only thing in the world that made me feel complete. I was whole with my three babies. I was somebody. I loved being pregnant, and I loved giving birth. I loved holding and hugging my babies. I was in love with my children. Johann was in love with his desire to climb the academic ladder at the university, where he was a talented professor. We both had what we wanted, and yet we didn't.

The truth was, everyone thought we had it all. I was beautiful when

I was young—that is to say, my mother thought I was beautiful, and men were drawn to me, though I really didn't know why at the time. Johann was successful and reliable, and we had these three beautiful, smart kids. But I didn't know what a healthy relationship looked like; I could have tripped over one and not recognized it.

Sometime in the ensuing years I began to suffocate. I was teaching at an elite high school in our town and beginning to think that I was smart and competent. I was also starting to realize that I needed to return to the spirituality I had enjoyed as a child. I ignored it on the surface, but a tiny voice in me continued to guide me back to God, back to myself. My mom, though flawed in many ways, had given me a simple faith that had sustained me throughout my life. Johann thought Christianity was "kitsch." I didn't know what that meant, but in time I realized it meant I wasn't good enough or sophisticated enough for him. When I began reading books on spirituality, he summarily threw my books away, thinking that would end the nonsense. It didn't. Instead, it went underground, where most of my life was lived, aside from raising the children. I continued to search, but I didn't always search in the right places.

Eventually, I realized that our relationship felt suffocating. There was always a teacher-student dynamic between us. I wanted to be separate, not just his underling. This, of course, ignited in him an almost compulsive need for conquest, but I was rebellious. No one would control me! I didn't have a clue where any of this was coming from. We started couples therapy to bring me back under control, although it would turn out to be the beginning of the end of our marriage.

During this time, my mother was dying; she had been ill for a very long time. The doctors had initially given her six months to live, yet she had lived eleven years. She was stubborn, too; that's where I got my rebel attitude. When my kids were little, she experienced a series of strokes, which turned my strong, feisty mother into another person, someone she would not have wanted to be. We spent days, weeks, months rushing to the hospital after working all day, only to sit helplessly by her bed and watch her fade from this Earth.

The week before she died, she was in a coma after a recent stroke and had been moved to a nursing home because my parents had no insurance. When I entered the room, I smelled death. The beds around her were occupied by skeletal figures, barely visible under their sheets. I approached her bed, and a myriad of feelings engulfed me. All the years of fighting this powerful woman struck me like a blow to the gut. It would be many years before I was able to see her for the scared little girl she was.

We were alone on that particular afternoon. Johann waited in the car with the three kids bouncing in the back seat. My mother's hair was greasy and unkempt, which would have killed her vanity to know. But she was beyond vanity now. I felt deep in my heart that she was holding on for all of us. I touched the blanket but never let myself touch her. "I think your work here is over, Mom. I think Jesus wants you to come home. It's OK. We're all OK." I noticed a single tear trickle down her cheek, and a chill ran through me. She had heard me. She was listening. I couldn't say I was sorry for all the things I had done to hurt her. I was angry with her for leaving me. I was thinking of me, not her. I had so much to learn, so much to learn about us both. *Mother.* The word itself had power over me.

I returned to the car, strapped the seatbelt across my lap, and announced, "Grandma will die this week. She's ready to let go." But was I ready to let her go? Those words I couldn't say aloud.

As I now contemplated motherhood again with the idea of adopting, I tried to remember the times when my mother touched me. I recalled a letter I had written. I finally began to decipher the pieces of my mother and my relationship with her.

Dear Mom,

I am trying to remember the times that you touched me. I observe myself touching my own children— hugging and caressing them—and for the life of me I can't remember you touching me in affection. There are times that stand out strongly in my memory, though, really big times for me.

You touched me when you did my nails on Sunday afternoons. Yes, and when you set my hair, or cut it. It was great having a hairdresser for a mother. But why did you always cut my hair so damn short? Linda got to have the long, beautiful hair, but I always got that "Shinseki," as you used to say. Come to think of it, Linda got to be the sexy one, too. I was supposed to be the "good" one—you know, proper. I didn't want to be all that proper, but somehow my role was being shaped for me. Oh yes, I rebelled, but there was always the prude somewhere close—the one with the short hair.

You touched me when you hemmed my dresses. Remember? You'd stick me with one of those pins. I'd look down and watch the top of your thick, auburn hair, your hands always busy at work with some project. "Stand up straight!" you'd say, and of course, I would. I always wanted to please you and Dad. But during the hemming, your rough, busy, capable hands would accidentally brush against my leg, and I would feel uncomfortable with the touch. It came so seldom, you see.

Yes, those hands made quite an impression on me. As you filed and beautified my lovely long nails, I'd think how ugly your hands were. I always got compliments on mine. Now I look at my own hands and I see yours, and I now know that the reason yours were so ugly was because of all the work you did for everyone else. Life makes ugly hands. Now I understand.

But the most powerful memory of all was the smell of Vicks VapoRub. Whenever I got sick as a child, you'd come into my room and rub Vicks onto my flat little chest with those rough hands of yours. The strong vapors would signal me that all was OK—my mom was there. Dad may be out in the garage, drunk, but my mom was there. The slow, circular movements across my chest would lull me back to sleep, all thoughts of illness fading into slumber. That was love to me.

I didn't wonder about this until Johann asked me incredulously one night why, when I couldn't sleep, I would rub Vicks on my chest whether I had a cold or not. I felt better, that's all. Loved. Comforted. For that was the only time you touched me. Just the smell of Vicks today reminds me of you, and I feel mothered. Funny, yes, but also sad. How I must have longed for just a simple hug, not to mention a kiss. You know, I can't remember one kiss that you ever bestowed on me, not one natural, spontaneous kiss.

I smell your wonderful dusting powder now in my memory. Every day at four o'clock you would emerge from the bathroom bathed, combed, and perfumed for Dad to come home. I would stand in the hall just to get a breath of you. How I longed to cuddle, although the word "cuddle" doesn't quite fit at all, Mom. You were definitely not a cuddler. But I am. I know that now. I like—no, need—to cuddle. Skin is so wonderful. Why was yours so strange to me? Why were our skins strangers to each other? Mom, your skin was always so remote. Cold.

My thoughts return to the night you died and to the many nights when I stood at your hospital bed, thinking that the end had finally come. Linda would hold your hand. Dad, like me, would stand off at a distance. I felt so guilty because I thought I should want to touch you. I longed to touch you, but I didn't want to. I felt oddly repelled by the touch, the very touch I needed so much. Does that make any sense? But the truth is, we had never touched in life, and I didn't know how to touch in death. I stood there transfixed by your blue fingernails and rough, work-worn hands, and I wanted them to finally take me in your arms and hug me. How dare you die without ever doing that? How dare you?

All I have of you is the memory of Vicks VapoRub. I guess that was your only way of touching me. I ask myself now, who touched you? I ask myself now why I couldn't have been wiser then to see what life had been like for you.

As for me, I had to learn to touch from scratch. First I learned from the kids. They taught me. It felt good. But it wasn't until much later that I learned to allow myself to be touched by an adult. That was much, much harder. *That* took trust. And to think that I deserved it was even harder.

You know, Mom, I discovered that I am a very sensual woman. I live for touch. I could wallow in touch. But there are still times when a new feeling rises up in me. I can't quite explain it. It's new. It's strange.

If I ever see you again, I hope that I can embrace you. I will throw my arms around you and bury my head into your powdered chest and just feel you, be close to you. It's what I always wanted, and I want to believe that you wanted that, too.

Years passed before I would confront those feelings again. I had to be brought to my knees by life before I began to see the woman who was my mother. Years and years went by before I started asking different questions, before I saw how frightened she had always been. Mother. Motherhood. Becoming a mother again! I sought a salvation that could only come through forgiveness and seeing my wild mother in all her facets, the way I wished to be known. Actually, it was exactly ten years later.

§

CHAPTER 3
Alaina

J didn't begin the affair until after my mother had died. The sheer force of her wouldn't have allowed me to cross that line of desperation. It was brief, a futile and desperate attempt to awaken, show Johann how angry I was, and destroy my life. I didn't care who knew at work that I was flirting with one of the teachers. I felt suddenly attractive and dangerous. Home was work and responsibility. Johann was a success. The kids were all smart and successful, yet I was empty, and so I did what so many have done: I tried to fill a hole that could not be filled by another human being. A little kindness, a compliment, and a note in my mailbox seduced me. My mother was gone, and I felt that, finally, my life was mine to lead as I wished. I gave no thought to the lives my decision would hurt.

The affair didn't last long. I was much too guilty to sustain that kind of deception. My marriage was coming apart, and I was making it happen.

I entered individual therapy and began to unravel my fractured life. That was when the dreams began. Feelings and images were surfacing that frightened me. I shared them with my sisters, but they did not want to hear about them. I was finishing my counseling degree, beginning a new career, and I hated myself. I couldn't look Johann in the eyes. I slept on the floor. I couldn't bear to see my children's faces when Johann and I fought. I had to get out of the marriage, and this was the way I chose. It played out the way I created it: disastrously. An affair is not about two people. It is two stones thrown into a pond; they may touch the bottom but not before their ripples reach everything.

When I finally finished my counseling credential and became a school counselor, a new woman was emerging. My children were wounded, and I had caused that pain. I had broken all my own rules. On the one hand, I was growing, but on the other, I was destroying everyone in my path.

As the dreams increased, I began to remember the incidents of molestation at the hands of my grandfather. Once I confronted this, the tightness that had always sat in my throat was gone. I bore him no hatred; that wasn't the point. But remembering allowed me to see why I feared my own sexuality and escaped any attempt at intimacy.

All the pieces began to fit. I was finding myself but losing my family. They all thought I had gone mad, and sometimes I agreed with them. It was a lonely time—a dark night of the soul. I don't think any of it would have happened had my mother lived. I used to think that if she were gone, I would be free of the power she had over me. I was wrong—and right. I was wrong in that she was within me and I carried her pain into the world. I was right because with her gone, I could begin the process of birthing myself.

About this time, Jason entered my life. The rest is history, as they say. But falling in love and offering oneself up to another human being isn't idyllic, either. His love for me awakened a deeper pain and longing. I felt all the good, but I also felt the demons catching up with me. I wanted to please him, so I lied a lot. We battled together, at each other, for each other. I became fearful that I would lose him. I was insanely jealous. I felt inadequate and unworthy. Too much was happening, and there was still this unresolved thing with my mom.

Ten years after her death, I began to see that my healing was inextricably tied to my understanding of our relationship. One day, I left work in the middle of the day and drove to the cemetery, which I had not visited since her death. I found her headstone and fell like a rock upon her grave, heaving sobs of anguish and regret. I lay on the damp grass like a child who is falling asleep in her mother's arms and wept. "Hold me, Mama. Help me find my way. Help me heal." A wonderful calm embraced me. I sat up and grabbed my journal and began to write.

Mama,

I know that you can't hear me and that it's been ten years since I said goodbye in that cold hospital; however, I feel it is finally time to put it together and make some sense of my life with you.

I remember so vividly the night you died. I was standing there holding your cold, withered hand, watching the life-support machine verify what I already knew—that you had gone, were finally free from the enslavement that was your short, violent life. While Linda stood on one side of your bed and I on the other, Dad lingered in the shadows, passively acquiescing to the finality of it all.

Funny, how powerful an experience death is. I recall only one other feeling like this: the times that I gave birth. It's ironic that we, you and I, should be together at the end as we had been at the beginning: linked for all times by our ambivalence and pain and love.

As I walked away from your room knowing that you were lost to me, I felt both numb and free. How many crises had we survived, how many false alarms? Now I felt my life would be my own and that you could no longer control me. How wrong I was!

Of course I cried—because I loved you—but did you know that I have never been able to visit your grave? For the last ten years, I have tried to rid myself of the chains of our past together. However, the other day, on a mountaintop, I stood face to face with me—and thus, face to face with you. I must stop running away, for I am weary.

No one on Earth had the effect on me you had. All that is good about me I got from you, and all that is evil and afraid I got from you. But today I must ask for something that I never asked you for when you were alive: your forgiveness. Forgiveness, because high atop that mountain, I saw you; not the volatile, angry, confusing giant of my childhood, but the frightened, lost child who was my mother.

All these years, I have kept the old hatred alive, recalling with flamboyant animation all your crazy doings. Perhaps if I hated you enough, I would not have to face the overwhelming loss I felt from being abandoned by you. To remember your goodness would be to acknowledge how much I always wanted your love, a love you were incapable of offering. I hated you because you would not give it to me, but then, how could you? Who had loved you, Mama?

When others remember their childhoods, they recall vacations spent in happiness or moments of great joy at a simple dinner. But when I recall my childhood, I recall being awakened in the darkness of the night by screams and threats. "I'm going to kill you, you dirty son of a bitch!" rang so long in my small ears that I came to believe everyone lived like we did. Then there were the attempted suicides, coming into your room to find you tied to the door knob with one of Dad's church ties, only to find you the next morning busy at work making a wonderful breakfast or sewing me a new dress. The attempts were feigned, of course, but I did not know it. They were real to me. This was not half as confusing, however, as your words, "I'm a happy woman, yes, I'm happy!" God, how confusing you were. I didn't realize the effect of those words on me until I was a woman myself. Even years of studying psychology and counseling did not penetrate the system of defense I had so skillfully created from feeling that confusion and terror. Yes, I wanted to hate you, Mama.

The other day I was on a great hike in "God's country," as you would say. My fears and exhaustion from the exertion triggered an attack on Jason that would have made you proud. I was saying, " I don't trust you! Leave me alone!" but I was feeling, *I am afraid you'll leave me like my mother did.* I was crying, "Go ahead and leave. I don't give a rat's ass!" but I was crying inside, *I need you so much, Jason. I'll die if you leave me.* I meant nothing I was saying; in fact, the more afraid I got, the more hostile and irrational I became. I was so close to having it all—Jason loved me and we were happy—but I couldn't handle it. The prospect of loving and being loved was intolerable. For one instant, I wanted to throw myself down the cliff and die. The pain and fear were too great.

In that moment of possible annihilation, I saw. I saw you, Mom, screaming horrible things at us that I believed you meant, threatening to kill yourself so many, many times, and for the first time in my whole life, I understood you. I shuddered and fell to my knees and cried the anguished cry of a child weary of longing and needing that which she could not have. I saw the poor child you were and the life you had grown up in, how brave you were to overcome an alcoholic, unpredictable father and brothers. You were abused in some way by all of them, and yet you dutifully accepted all the responsibilities of caretaking. I became aware of the madness and chaos you endured and how you wanted it to be different for your three daughters. You cooked and cleaned, sewed all of our clothes, and held the chaos and terror inside of you with the sheer force of desire to create a better life for us. You were not educated enough to know that so much pain can not be contained without great cost to one's inner self. You fought the demons alone, as you had always done. You viewed anyone who dared to love you with skepticism and destroyed anyone who tried to get close to you. If I had only known sooner that your viciousness was a feeble attempt to mask the fragile, soulful child who needed to be held and protected.

In that moment of awareness, I began to forgive you. I laughed at myself—a professional counselor who knew full well the dynamics and pathology of families but had not been able to stop myself from enacting the inner torture that had become part of me. The wind was pounding my tear- and dirt-stained face, and I stopped. For the first time in my life, I let some truth in. I saw anger for what it was: fear. I tasted it. I wanted to run, to escape rather than face those feelings I had spent my whole life avoiding. Suddenly I was drained and without power to move or feel or fight.

I felt the beginning of hope standing alongside the despair. I knew then that you had lived and died without ever having felt that hope, and I wanted to hold you and take the fear out of your heart.

A great rage has lived in me for so long that I scarcely know how to live without it. But I must give it up. The demons are not gone, but there is a single crack of light and love showing me a way out. Mama, I will no longer think of you in anger but in love and forgiveness. If you are out there and can feel me, know that my struggle with you is over. I hope you can forgive me for not seeing you as you really were: just like me.

Love,
Alaina
August 1990
P.S. I know now that you really did want to hug me.

§

Reconciliation

Gone forever
Sleeping in that grave so cold
Alone in death
As in life
How I long to touch you
Finally

Breathe in the good that
You were, and
Soothe the fears that
Tormented the pages of
Your fate
Mother
I am like you
Your good and your evil
Flow through my veins
And color what I see
At long last I see you
At long last I can say
"I am your daughter"
You gave me your fears
And your heart
I no longer feel shame
I feel compassion for you
And love
And so much love
Goodnight, my strong, fragile
Mother
My passionate, wild, and frightened foe
I accept the you in me
You have forever a place of peace
Within my heart
Remember me in yours

§

I rose from her grave and noticed the imprint of my presence now resting above my mother. I knew I didn't have to return to this place again, because she would always be with me. My step quickened as I returned to my car. Things would be changing now. I felt a new beginning; little did I know it would be a child.

§

CHAPTER 4
Alex

I was born in Germany and came to the States when I was very little. My father was killed in Viet Nam in 1968, and my mother was left alone with five small children, whom she raised all on her own. She never let anyone see her pain and anguish when my father was killed. She was a strong woman, but she had a hard life, beginning when she was a little girl in Germany.

When I was a little girl, she would tell me stories about her childhood. She and her family would run from one bomb shelter to another during the raids in World War II. She said she saw many of her friends die before her eyes. Those experiences affected her all her life.

When she was nineteen, she had her first baby and married a man who did not love her and treated her badly. By age twenty-five, she had three babies and had divorced her husband. She raised her little ones on her own and worked three jobs while her mother took care of the children. Then she met my father and had my brother and me. Eventually, she left Germany to come to America. When she first arrived, she could not speak much English or drive a car or even write her own name. When my father was killed, she had to learn to do all of those things. She began cleaning other people's houses.

My mother was a great woman. She worked her whole life and always provided us with unconditional love. We grew up never wanting for anything because our mother gave us all that she had.

She never dated or remarried; she lived only for her children. I got into theater and music when I was in high school, and she always came to see me perform. She often said she was proud of me and loved me. She was such a strong force in my life. She never let anyone see her cry or show weakness. I don't remember there being a man in the house. My grandmother, whom we lovingly called *Oma*, was also an indomitable figure. She cooked and cleaned and took care of us while my mother worked.

After I turned seventeen, my mother became very ill with cancer. My whole family was devastated, for she was our rock. My world turned upside down, and I became her caregiver. I fed her, cleaned her, and gave her medicine while my friends were dating and having fun. Now my mother was dying. My senior year was spent in the hospital, night after night, beside my mother, watching her slip away more and more every day. I would hold her hand while she cried because of the pain. I was helpless; there was nothing I could do for her. I had no one to comfort me. My older brothers and sisters had moved away and had their own families, so my little brother and I were there for her. We had to grow up fast.

On my graduation day, I came to the hospital to show my mother that I had done it—I had made it through high school—but she never knew I was there. I just sat beside her and held her hand and talked to her so she would know that I loved her and so she would be proud of me. On August 25, 1984, the Angel of Death came to take my beloved mother home.

Now I was completely alone. The person who loved me the most was gone, and I had no place to call home. I had to grow up and face the world on my own. I was lost for a very long time. I had no direction. I had no one to turn to for help, no one to talk to about the pain I was suffering. Where was my life going?

I met a girl in town who was moving to Washington to start her life over. I had nothing to keep me where I was, so I went with her. Once there, I met, fell in love with, and married a young man who I thought I was in love with. We were married after knowing each other for six months. I thought I had love in my life again and that I wouldn't be alone anymore. Within a year, I found out that he was cheating with someone at work. He left me four months later, and I was once again alone. All of this happened before my twenty-first birthday.

I moved in with some friends I had met at work, and I quickly learned to keep my sorrows deep inside. I would show the world I was a strong woman who could not be defeated. I would be wise about men and not fall in love so quickly. I could not get hurt, and I did not need love; all it had gotten me was pain and loneliness. I would only work hard and stay strong.

I didn't want to be the little girl lost anymore. I wanted to make my mother proud of me. I would not depend on anybody for anything. I promised myself that I would make my way in the world on my own terms and never look back. My mother did it with five children; I was going to do it all by myself. I didn't want to be the victim anymore. I went back to school to learn German and maybe even become a teacher. That was my goal. Then I met Duncan.

I was working at a hair salon in southern Washington, and about twenty people were waiting in the lobby to get their hair cut. When I looked out toward the lobby to call my next client, I saw a young man with round glasses, a black-and-white T-shirt, blue jeans, and long, one-length hair. I thought, *What a great-looking guy!* He was different from any boy I'd ever met in Washington. I hoped I would get to cut his hair. Fate stepped in, and he took a seat at my station.

Duncan was not the kind of man I was usually attracted to. He was shorter than me, had a very small frame, and my friends thought he looked like a computer nerd. But to me, he was beautiful. I liked him the moment I saw him.

While I was cutting his hair, he told me that he was going to Germany for six months to travel and see his sister and brother, who worked there. Since I was from Germany and had been raised by two German women, I was interested in his travels. Before he left the salon, I gave him my grandmother's address in Germany and said if he was ever close to the town where she lived, he could look her up. He told me he was studying German at the university and he could speak it very well. I had learned German from my mother and grandmother and spoke very little, but I understood it well. I gave him my address and asked if he had time to please write me from time to time and tell me what was going on in Germany. He left. I was blown over.

Time passed, and I hadn't heard from Duncan for a long time, so I was surprised when he sent me a German magazine that November, the same one that my *Oma* would read to me when I was little. It brought back many good memories.

Duncan returned from Germany in December 1988. He called me and asked if I wanted to go see a concert with him. It had been six months since I last saw him, and I had almost forgotten what he looked like. At first I thought no, but since I hadn't been on a date in a long time, I thought, what the heck. He picked me up at my house, and when he walked in, he took my breath away. He had changed since we last met.

We went out that night, and that was when I fell in love. I can't explain it; there was something about him that just attracted me. He was kind and sweet and different from any other man I had ever met. He brought me all kinds of German Christmas chocolates, nuts, and cookies from his travels in Europe. We spent countless hours with each other, and he would even come over to take care of me when I had a cold, bringing me vitamin C. We made love for the first time close to Christmas, and it was truly wonderful.

I started to admire him a lot because he was so smart and worked hard in college. He had a great relationship with his family and loved his brothers and sisters. He became my friend and my lover, and I was able to tell him things that I told no other human being. But since I had some learning disabilities, I always felt a little ashamed. I tried to hide this from him and would use the dictionary to help me with spelling and writing so that he wouldn't notice. I wanted to be the perfect girlfriend.

Even though I told him a lot about me, I kept my short-lived marriage from him because I didn't want to be carrying a lot of baggage. That was when the lies started to grow. I wanted to show him that I was a strong, loving, caring, take-charge woman who could do anything. I didn't want this relationship to be like any other, and it wasn't. He treated me very well, and I couldn't get enough of him.

I met his friends from high school, and we would party with them. They were all nice, and they accepted me. Everything was going so well; then, in early March, something happened that I wasn't prepared for.

I was taking a German class at the local college, and Duncan was helping me. I didn't get my period after my twenty-fifth birthday but thought nothing of it at first. After a week passed and it still didn't come, I got a little worried and took a test. The stick turned blue, and so did I. I realized I was pregnant.

It was a total shock. We had used protection, but something had gone wrong. I didn't know what to do. I didn't want anything to mess up our relationship. How was I going to tell Duncan? What was he going to say? What was I going to say? How would he take it? I hoped he wouldn't think I did it on purpose, because truly I did not.

I just pushed it out of my mind and decided to deal with it later. Everything was going so well. He loved me. I knew he would not blame me for this.

As soon as I saw him the next day, I knew I had to tell him. As we sat down in my empty German classroom, he knew something was wrong. I was a wreck, with tears running down my face. I told him I was pregnant. At first he said nothing. Then he said that he had to think it over. I wanted to say that I was happy and that I really wanted this baby with all my heart; the more I thought about it, the happier I got. A baby! My mother did it with five babies, and we all turned out OK. But I kept silent because I wanted to hear his reaction first. I knew that he wanted to finish school, and a family was not what he wanted right now. Sometimes things don't always happen the way they are planned. I thought he could still go to school and I would raise the baby. We walked out of the classroom in silence, and I knew that my inner happiness must be quieted. He said he needed time to think, that he wanted to discuss it with his mother.

As we left each other, my heart started to sing. I began to plan how I would take care of this baby. I called my family and my best friend to tell them the news. I knew Duncan loved me, so he would surely come to love and accept the baby; it was just so new to him. He would come around.

A week later, he called and asked me to have dinner with him so we could talk. He said he had talked to his mother, and she agreed with him that I should get an abortion. An abortion? That had never even crossed my mind. I didn't want one. I started to plead with him and beg him to understand that this was something wonderful, that I wanted this baby more than anything. He didn't. He kept repeating that we were both too young. He still had a year of college, and fatherhood was not on his mind.

I called my family that night and asked for help and advice. They said they couldn't help me with my decision, but they did think that I was too young and should be married before having a baby. I knew Duncan didn't want to marry me. What was I going to do? I wanted this baby, but under all the pressure from Duncan's family and my own, six weeks later I let them talk me into ending my baby's life.

I cried so hard the night before it happened, trying to understand that it was best for everyone. Knowing what I was about to do, my heart cried for my baby. I asked God for forgiveness, because this was not what I wanted. But since everyone else thought that this choice was best, and because I loved Duncan so much, I went ahead.

We never did talk about my abortion afterward, but it left a deep hole in my soul that would never go away. I kept the pain hidden deep inside so no one would know what I did. If people did ask, I just said that I had lost the baby.

My feelings for Duncan changed that day. I still loved him, but a little part of me died with my baby. I realized that Duncan was not that perfect, after all. I had put him on a pedestal high above me, which was not where he belonged. Then he told me that in the fall he was going back to school—without me. Now I was going to lose my baby and the man I loved.

In June I went back home to see some of my family and everything I had left behind. I wanted to see my old house where I had grown up. Maybe I would find the little girl who once was so happy and loved by her mother. I needed my mom more than I ever had before. Now, standing and looking at my childhood house, all the old memories flew back. Even though we children never had much, what we did have was a lot of love and happiness. Looking at my old house now, I realized that I had no home anymore. I had no mother to call or to go to. A place that I once knew to be safe was now empty and cold. I wanted my mother back. I wanted my baby back. I wanted to feel safe in my mom's arms just like I wanted my baby to be safe in my arms. I felt so lost, so very lost.

§

A few months passed. Duncan and I never spoke of my abortion again; we just pretended it never happened. I didn't tell him about how much it affected me, and I was trying hard not to let the sorrow overwhelm me. I tried to be positive about everything.

Duncan was getting ready to go back to school in August. As the month grew closer, I grew more and more depressed. I knew I was losing him, this man who was the love of my short life. I could see how eager he was to return to school. I felt that what he was most eager to do was get away from me and all that we had gone through. I was insecure and questioned him about where our relationship would go from here. He finally confessed that he wanted to end our relationship when he went back to school. He always seemed to know what was good for us. His reasons confused me, and maybe he was confused, too. Maybe he just wanted an excuse to get away from me.

One afternoon in July, as the sun was going down, he turned to me and said, "We should just enjoy the time we have left and not dwell on my leaving. Just try to remember the good times." Those words made me angry. How very *male*. It was so easy for him to turn his back on me. I had truly believed that Duncan was my soul mate. I had never opened to another human being as I had with him. Now he was going. I couldn't understand how it was so easy for him to let go. I couldn't understand how he could not be in love with me as much as I was with him.

At work, no one knew what was going on in my relationship. *Don't let the world in*, I reminded myself. I was such a great actress; I only let the world see the happy Alex, the Alex who was all together. *That* Alex didn't have any problems; she was always the happy-go-lucky one. I always had a smile on my face and acted positive. My depression never showed because I hid it. I kept everything nice and quiet and never let any of my co-workers or family know how Duncan or my abortion had affected me. But inside, I was screaming in silence. I felt totally isolated.

In the summer of 1990, I came up with a plan. Desperate, I felt my heart couldn't lose anything more. I wanted to be pregnant again with Duncan's child. I thought that if I could have his child, I would never, ever be lonely again. This child would fill up all of the empty spaces in my heart, fix all the demons that plagued me. I loved this man and thought that if I had his child, a small part of him would always be with me. It was a desperate thought, but I was a desperate woman who needed help and was taking the wrong road to my salvation.

I put my plan into action. First, I threw away my birth control. Then I started trying to get pregnant before he left for school. I had no intention of entrapping him; all I wanted was his sperm. In my mind, I wanted this baby for myself. I knew what I was doing was wrong, but my heart felt it was right. I would question myself a hundred times a day, and guilt haunted my every move. Each day that I missed a pill, my guilt compounded. I was ashamed, but I couldn't tell a soul.

My plan was to not tell Duncan until the baby was born. I would keep the pregnancy a secret from him and from my own family. He would be hundreds of miles away, and I wanted to take back what I had lost, what he and his family had taken from me. I realized that this was crazy, but I was trying to make up for being deserted and left behind. I didn't consider the impact of this on my life, my baby's life, or Duncan's life. I didn't care about anything but getting my baby back. I was trying desperately to make the pain go away.

In the middle of August, I missed my period and knew my plan had worked. At first I thought, *Oh, God! What have I done?* Then jubilation overwhelmed me. *I'm going to have a baby!* Then guilt. My mind screamed, *Alex, you did this the wrong way!* But my joy outweighed my guilt. The day Duncan left for school, I knew that his child was deep inside of me. My heart sang for joy.

On the morning of his departure, the guilt weighed heavily on my chest as I looked into his eyes. Silently I kept saying to myself, *He may be leaving, but I have a part of him with me. The pain of our separation is bearable.* We said our goodbyes at his house, and tears ran down my face. I really did love him, yet deception was written all over my face. He kissed me for the last time, and I pressed my body to his, wanting to tell him that our love was growing inside of me, but I said nothing. As I drove away from his house, I looked at myself in the rearview mirror and did not like the person staring back at me. What had I become?

Four months after Duncan left, a friend of mine called to say he and his new wife were coming to Washington to live. They wanted to stay with me until they could get jobs and afford their own place. I had known Randy for a long time and trusted him completely. We had grown up together. I was more than happy to help them as much as possible.

When they arrived, his wife seemed very nice, and we all got along well. At the time, I was living in a single-room apartment, so there wasn't a lot of room for us. After a month of looking for work, they found jobs and suggested that we all find a bigger apartment and live together, and they would help me with the baby. At first I was reluctant, because I wanted to do this on my own—I didn't need anybody. But they convinced me that it would be good for everyone, so eventually I agreed. We found a two-bedroom apartment, but since they had no credit, I put everything in my name—the apartment, the phone, and the electricity. They picked out furniture for the apartment, but because they didn't have cash, I lent them money to furnish the place.

I started working longer shifts and saved as much money as I could. I was getting excited about my baby's birth. Randy's wife and I went out to look for baby clothes. I purchased a baby crib and a changing table. I was getting the baby's room all ready.

When I saw my first sonogram, I cried. I wanted to share my happiness with Duncan; he was such a part of this miracle of life, and yet he knew nothing about it. I knew he would find out about it sooner or later, but at the time, all I was concerned about was taking good care of myself and making as much money as I could to save for the baby and me. I joined a support group of young women at a church who were also having babies. I prayed to God for forgiveness for all my sins in conceiving this child. All the ladies in the church group were much younger than me. We would come together every Monday night and talk about what to expect after our babies were born and how to handle a newborn. We would talk about our fears as new parents-to-be and how to support each other and ourselves.

Since my family lived far away, I knew that I would be doing this on my own. How was my family going to react? I had kept them in the dark about this pregnancy because of their reaction to my first one. I couldn't bring my family into this right now. I would wait until after the birth.

Everything was going well, and I was falling in love with my expanding belly. I felt the very first kick. Soon I was not able to get into my regular clothes and happily went shopping for maternity clothes. I would take long walks and talk to my baby. What was he or she going to look like? All my conversations with my clients were about babies, and I started reading baby books and buying baby supplies.

During my prenatal visits, my doctor said I was gaining a lot of weight in too short a time, and she was concerned. She wanted to monitor my weight gain every week, but all I cared about was that I was happy; all the guilt I felt was buried inside. Nothing was going to spoil this for me.

Duncan called in November and started asking questions. "What have you been up to? How are things going?" He had called before, but since our relationship was over, we didn't talk much anymore. I could tell by the sound of his voice that he knew something, though I didn't know exactly what he knew.

After a lot of questions, things grew silent. Suddenly, my heart was pounding. Then he said, "My friend John saw you the other day." I knew my secret was out. He continued, "He said he noticed your big belly." I didn't know how to respond. There was an unbearable silence that seemed to last forever. Suddenly, without notice, all the guilt and rage rose up from inside me, and I screamed, "I didn't want to be left alone!" He blew up. "You're ruining my life! How could you do such a thing to me?" I tried to explain to him through his screaming that I was going to do this all by myself. I wanted nothing from him—no money, no support. I just wanted this child for myself. "How could you have kept me in the dark for so long?" I couldn't find the words to explain myself. I felt helpless and small. I didn't want to hurt him or ruin his life or his college career.

He finally calmed down and said that when he returned for Christmas break, we would sit down and talk about everything. *Now* he wanted to talk about everything! What about everything from a few months ago? I said I was sorry, but my words fell on deaf ears.

When we hung up the phone, I felt small and worthless. I just hurt the most important person in my life, and I pushed him over the edge. He hated me and I hated myself. It seemed that the walls were tumbling down all around me. Not only had I hurt Duncan, but also things at home were getting bad.

Randy and his wife had started fighting a lot about everything, and it was getting hard to live with them. They weren't paying back the money I had lent them. I needed the money now, but they kept making excuses, saying that they would pay me when they got their next paychecks. They also promised me that they would have their relatives send it, but nothing ever came.

They took off in early December for a trip to "help their relationship." Two weeks later, Randy's wife showed up alone and said that they had decided to move back home and were leaving in a week. She started packing, taking everything I had bought with my money. First I was in shock, then disbelief. What was I to do? I called the police, but since I had no receipts, they wouldn't do anything. I begged her to at least pay part of the rent until I could get a new roommate; she told me she would mail it to me.

I now lived in an empty apartment and had to pay the seven-hundred-dollar rent. The phone bill was a hundred and ten dollars, and the electric bill was seventy-five. Most of the food was gone. This all happened in two days. I knew that I would never get back the money I had lent Randy and his wife.

All the money I saved up working those extra hours was gone. I got very scared. I had enough money for one month's rent, and then I would be broke. "God, what am I going to do? What is happening to me?" Was I being punished for my sins? I had trusted Randy and his wife and never believed that this could happen. I didn't know what to do. I called social services and made an appointment to see what help I could get. After going over my budget with me, the social worker said I made too much money to qualify for food stamps, and I would have to wait for the paperwork to kick in to get financial help. Until then, I had to rely on friends and family.

Now I was forced to tell my family about my pregnancy, but before I did, I heard about an organization that took women in when they were pregnant and helped them. I thought this would be my salvation. I found their number and called. I told the woman about my situation, and she said I could come and stay with them until I was back on my feet. My heart started to rise in hope. Then she asked me how old I was. When I said that I was almost twenty-six, she grew silent, and a heavy dread enveloped me. She told me that I was too old, that they only took women in from sixteen to twenty-three years old. I asked her if she would make an exception; she said she was sorry, but she was only following protocol. She suggested that I consider an open adoption or a women's shelter, then just hung up the phone. I started to cry. This could not be happening. Everything I had planned was falling apart.

"God, please! What am I going to do?" I called Duncan and told him what had happened, but he said that he had no money to give me; he didn't offer any help, and I couldn't blame him. I knew his family wouldn't help me because they knew that I had deceived him. I knew then that I had to call my family, but I didn't want to call them in defeat like this; I felt like a failure. Reluctantly, I dialed my oldest sister's number with trembling fingers and waited. *What would she say?* I wondered. Ever since my mother had died, my older sister had taken charge of the family. We all went to her when we needed help. I thought that after telling her what had happened, I could live with her until I got enough money together to get back on my feet. When she answered the phone, I just started to cry. I told her my story between sobs and held my breath.

After hearing what I had to say, she was silent for a long time. Then what she said sent my world crashing down: she would not take in me or the baby. She felt that I had to deal with this myself. She wouldn't offer me any help at all.

Now everything was lost. I had no one to turn to, nowhere to go. The one person who loved me and would have helped me the most was dead, and I needed her now more than ever before. "Mommy, Mommy, I need you, and I'm scared. I'm alone. I am afraid."

I didn't have an alternative plan and was at a total loss. I was going into my sixth month of pregnancy, and I wasn't sure if I was going to have a home to take my baby to. I just cried and cried until there were no more tears. Then I began to get angry.

I got angry with God for doing this to me. Was it because of all the lies I had told and the secrets I had kept? Was I being punished for them? I wanted this baby so much, and now everything I had planned had gone wrong, and my savings were gone.

Then I got angry with myself. Why had I put myself into this situation? I was so selfish, thinking only of my own needs. I hadn't thought about Duncan or this baby I was carrying. I was so stupid—and scared. I had high blood pressure because of the weight I had gained during the pregnancy. I tried to pull myself together and sat down to calm myself, fearing that the extra weight might hurt the baby by toxemia or preeclampsia. I called my group counselor and told her what had happened. She told me she would find me a roommate and do all she could to help. I thanked her and knew that I had to figure out where to go from here. I started to pray very hard and asked the Good Lord for guidance. I prayed a whole lot that night.

When I returned to work, I kept silent about what had happened with Randy and his wife and my money problems. The following weeks were hell not knowing what to do or how to fix things, not knowing what lay around the corner.

Even though it rains all the time in Washington, people continue their lives as if the sun were shining. In early January, I took a lunch break and sat and watched children in the park laughing, smiling, and screaming with joy. I put my hands on my stomach and thought about what I had to give this precious child. I was living from paycheck to paycheck, and standing on my feet all day was getting harder and harder. I sat on that bench and watched how happy the children were as they played with each other. I wanted that for my child. I remembered what the lady had said to me about putting my baby up for adoption.

I wanted a home with two happy parents, not with someone who had to worry about where the next paycheck was coming from. I wanted my baby's life filled with laughter and sunshine, music and art. Sitting on that bench, I knew that I had to give my baby a better life, and that life was not with me. Adoption seemed my only hope. This child deserved it. I brought her here to Earth on purpose for my own selfish reasons. Now I had to be unselfish and find her the best parents I could.

I slowly walked back to work, my head down. I had a very heavy heart. That night I took a pen and scribbled some words to my unborn child. It was to be a promise I would keep, no matter how difficult.

> Today I am making a promise to you, my beloved child. I will go out and find the right family to raise you. I will search this whole world if I have to in order to make sure you have the best mother and father any child could want. I will look for a home filled with love, music, and art, because these things matter to me. I want your world to be filled with song and dance and lots of sunshine.
>
> When you look into your mother's face, it will not be mine, but a woman's who will love you as much as I love you now. When you wake up in the morning, her hands will hold and care for you. When you stumble and fall, she will be there to help you back on your feet. And when you cry, she will be there to wipe your tears from your eyes.

I will find this woman for you. I will always know where you are and how you are doing. I want you to know that even though I will not be there when things happen in your life, I will never be far from you. I will carry you with me always, until one day you will come to see me and know that I did it all for *you*.

Just know I love you with all my heart and soul. And I will keep my promise.

Alex Porter

§

Now that I had made up my mind to give up my baby for adoption, I had the hard task of finding the right parents to raise my child. First, I had to figure out where to start. Who was I looking for? What kind of people did I want? *I want someone like me*, I thought. I wanted someone who believed in the things that I believed in: music, art, dance, and unconditional love. I wanted my child to have the best that two parents could give.

I picked up the phone book, looked through the section of lawyers in the Yellow Pages, picked out a female lawyer's name, and called. The attorney said she didn't handle adoption cases, but she gave me the name of a lawyer who did. I called him, and we spoke for half an hour; he seemed eager to help me. This is how my journey began.

I knew there was no turning back. I thought that if I got the ball rolling, I would feel better about my decision. When I talked to Duncan at Christmas about an adoption, he thought it was the right thing to do. He wasn't ready to be a father, and he wanted to stay in college. He went back to school at the end of December and asked me to keep him informed about everything. I was shocked when he said he still loved me and wanted to have a relationship, especially after what I had put him through. Maybe our love could survive this.

As I drove to the lawyer's office, I felt unsure and very scared. What was I, at almost seven months pregnant, going to tell this man about why I didn't want my baby? The truth was, I did want my baby, but I thought

I couldn't tell him the true story, so I decided to say that I wasn't ready to be a mother and hoped he wouldn't question me further.

When I walked into his office, his secretary looked up at me and then looked away. She knew why I was there, and that made me feel worse about my decision. Then the attorney, a large man with gray hair and a wide smile, came out and greeted me. We went into his office, and I told him my story about not being ready. He never questioned me. He showed me all the forms that I would have to fill out and how the process of open adoption worked. He also told me that if I changed my mind during the process, I could go to jail. I didn't know anything about adoption, so I believed him. It was all so overwhelming.

Now I knew I couldn't turn back. We talked about how I could pick out my baby's parents and get pictures and letters from them about how my baby was doing. We made an appointment for the following week go through some portfolios of potential parents. I could look at them and decide which of them I would like to meet. We said our goodbyes, but I was left with a feeling that something wasn't right. Something just didn't feel right about this man. I didn't trust him.

That night, I went to my church group meeting and told the leader that I had decided to give my baby up for adoption. She started to cry, and I immediately joined her. She was incredibly understanding and said that before I made such a decision, I should seek the help of a counselor. She gave me a card with a woman's name on it and said this decision would affect the rest of my life. I wanted to tell her right then that I really wanted to keep my baby but that I had no money, but I was too ashamed. My tears were mistaken as being from the difficulty of making such a choice, but in truth, it was all about my sorrow.

I went back to the lawyer the following week, and he brought out seven portfolios of families. I hadn't realized how many people wanted babies. There were all different types of families. Some had adopted before, and some were childless. They all had nice homes, and their lifestyles were pretty much conservative. Each family wanted a baby to fill their home with love. I looked through the portfolios, but no one stood out for me. However, I agreed to meet five of the couples and get a feel for them. We set appointments with my choices for the weeks ahead. I was getting a little excited because I was hoping I would find my baby's parents among these five couples. It was a very long week.

I was nervous on the morning of the first meeting, and getting dressed was nerve-wracking. What was I going to wear? How should I act? I had never done this before. What would they think of me, a twenty-six-year-old woman, giving up her own child? I just wanted the week to be over with so I could find my baby's parents and go on with my life. That's what I thought, anyway. When I arrived at the lawyer's office to meet the first couple, I thought, *Okay, Alex, smile big, and be happy!* With this mask on my face, I walked in.

The first couple were in their forties. She was a housewife and he a businessman, and they lived on the Columbia River. They were quite nice and had adopted once before. They had a four-year-old, but they had not brought her along; I understood why. Actually, I would have very much liked to see her and how she interacted with her parents. The couple seemed kind of boring and a little strict but wholesome in their lifestyle. They had a big, beautiful home and a dog. Our conversation was strained, and I didn't feel comfortable with them. They wouldn't tell me exactly where they lived, which seemed a little strange. After they left, I felt in my heart that this was not the right couple. As it turned out, all the other couples I met had something I didn't like about them. They were too strict, boring, or religious.

When Friday came and went with no results, I started to think that maybe this baby was meant to stay with me. Maybe I could do this on my own, after all. When I walked out of the lawyer's office, I reached into my pocket and found the card of the therapist that my group leader had given me the week before. It was not working out with this lawyer, so I called the therapist and made an appointment to talk to her. I needed help, and maybe she would be my savior.

I went to see her but was feeling uncertain about talking to a stranger about my sorrows and losses in life. But I needed help. I had no one else to turn to. I was going into my seventh month of pregnancy, and I had gained eighty pounds already and was not feeling very beautiful—or strong.

The therapist was a nice woman. We spent time getting to know each other that first day, and after I told her about the meeting with the attorney and the couples, she suggested that I might have the wrong attorney. She gave me the phone number and name of a man whom she had dealt with before in an open adoption. I called and made an appointment to see him that following Tuesday. I felt good about this therapist, and talking to her about my decision about open adoption had made me feel better about it—and she was willing to help me find the right parents. I finally had a friend on my side.

I met the new lawyer, Jack Hartnell, on an unusually cold but sunny day in January. I instantly liked him. He made me feel important. He was caring and told me that I should keep going to the therapist to make sure that what I was deciding was the right thing for me. The other lawyer had never suggested that I seek help. Jack was different, and I told him how the other man had scared me into thinking that I could get into trouble if I changed my mind.

Jack said that when I was ready, he would help me find parents for my baby. He was an adoptive parent himself, had a really good relationship with his baby's birth mother, and felt strongly about the benefits of open adoption. When I left his office, I felt in my heart that this was the man who could help in my search. I began to feel hope.

I continued to go to the therapist's office for weekly sessions, and Jack paid for them. I was able to express a lot of the sorrows and tragedies I had experienced in the past and the hopelessness I was now feeling. I talked about all the things that had been haunting me. We talked about why I was giving this baby away, and I came to peace with my decision.

I met with Jack in the following weeks, and we started to look through portfolios. He showed me twenty or more, but none stood out until I came upon the O'Connells. Something hit me; their portfolio was different. The woman was a teacher. She spoke German, and she had taught it in school. She already had three children. The man was an artist, a musician, and worked with children. He also wrote music. Both their hobbies were painting. They had their wedding pictures in the book, and they looked very happy.

I felt strongly about this couple; I wanted to meet them. Jack set up a meeting for February 14, the day of love.

§

Chapter 5
Alaina

$\mathcal{I}$ had been very nervous for a few days. Something was brewing inside; I could feel it, and I had learned that my intuition was usually correct. This antsy, edgy feeling had permeated my Christmas shopping and preparations. I got this way when my unconscious mind grappled with something important. Seeds planted months or years before choose their own time to be born, and I was learning to listen to the inner voice that ran parallel to the waking notes of my physical voice.

I busied myself with Christmas tree lights, wishing that the uneasy feelings would be overshadowed by the spirit of the season. No go! *What was coming?* I wondered silently as the room lit up with holiday colors. The season always brought me joy and fear. Ever since I was a child, I both looked forward to and dreaded Christmas because my parents were especially volatile at that time. Their anniversary was on December 24, and my father's drinking and my mother's disappointment and rage always ruined it. It seemed that I had inherited this trait to spoil the moment, and I feared myself a little, especially after all the stresses of the last year.

I made my way up the stairs to Jason. "I want us to adopt a baby!" I blurted out the words as if from nowhere. Jason looked up from brushing his teeth, mouth foamy with toothpaste. "We'll talk about it," he said calmly.

"No, we have to start now. I have this feeling that our baby has been conceived already, and we need to find her," I said.

I had no idea what prompted this outburst. Just a few weeks earlier, we had agreed to not adopt, that we were OK as we were. I had had a hysterectomy when I was thirty-one and had told Jason about it on our very first date. It had been a sensitive point for both of us from the very beginning. Wasn't the fact that I could no longer have children ostensibly been the reason for our breakup after a year of dating? When Jason's mom realized that Jason and I were going to marry, hadn't she said to me, "Now I will never be a grandmother!"? Hadn't the issue of children poisoned every walk in the park, where young mothers strolled their babies as a blatant reminder of my own infertility? Hadn't I learned over the last two years what infertile women must feel every time they hear that another friend is pregnant? The mixture of joy for the friend and burning envy and inadequacy made the situation easy to avoid. After having been so fertile as a young woman, I had never understood the plight of infertility . . . until now. Suddenly I, too, dreaded the happy faces of expectant mothers, for they reminded me that I could not give Jason a baby—the one thing he wanted. When we first got together, my dream was that my three children would be enough for him. It was their dream, too. However, that was not to be.

In the months after our wedding, we wrestled with whether or not to introduce another child into our already complicated family life. There was also the fact that, emotionally, I needed to feel that I was enough for Jason. No woman wants to feel inadequate, and the scars from our many talks about babies had left their mark on my fragile ego. This "not enough" feeling ran deep in my veins, since as a child I always felt that I could never be good or nice enough for my father to stop drinking or my mother to be stable. I tried to be enough for Johann, but I picked a man from another culture and set myself up to be just a little different, just a little less than ideal. The depth of my own *Weltanschauung*, or worldview, permeated every act, and now to feel inadequate as a woman, too, was almost too much.

I don't know when it changed, but sometime during all our trials and tribulations of beginning a new life with three grown, beautiful, wounded teenagers and a lot of unfinished stuff of our own, I slowly began to believe that Jason did love me and that he was not going anywhere. The night I actually heard the words, "We don't need a child, we need each other. You are all I really need," was the night that my inner attitude began to change. Now it was safe. Now that I knew I was enough, I could give him this gift. I could see adopting a child as an enrichment to our lives and not a prerequisite to our happiness. Many years would pass before I would know if Jason loved me for real, but at the time, I had convinced myself that I was healed. I now thought how foolish my words were as I wrote them down.

Months had passed since this conversation, and a gestation had needed to take place in me. I was not to bear him a child, but inside me grew the willingness to love again, to commit to another human being, to be a mother. "I want you to call an attorney tomorrow. Let's get started right now."

"OK, but are you doing this only for me?" he asked honestly.

"Yes—and no. Yes and no," was all I could say. The truth was that I *was* doing it for him, to hold him, to please him, to give him what he wanted. *I* surely didn't need a child; I had already raised three. I was done, out of the woods, so to speak. If I had said that I was doing it for him, he would have declined—I knew that. Yet, what was wrong with wanting to give your mate what he wanted? My motives were muddled and unclear, but my heart was open. The rest I would work out later: the fear of starting over, the envy of having to share him with someone else, and the very act of bringing in a perfect rival for his attention that I longed for. But those thoughts were hidden, even from myself.

We began the networking process that other couples embark upon when they want to adopt. We quickly learned about the best attorneys, the ones with a high success rate in placing babies. We didn't care what it cost. Within twenty-four hours of agreeing to move forward, we made an appointment with a prominent attorney in Seattle. He was known as a real bastard but was successful in the business. The thought of the "baby business" was repugnant to me, but it was the price one paid for a child.

I went to the attorney's office to pay the retainer for an initial consultation. His office was opulent and trendy. When the elevator door opened to his floor of suites, I felt that it was all wrong—not the idea of adoption, but the attorney. This was a high-class baby mill. It was cold. But I paid the fee and left with the first available appointment in hand, two months later.

This feeling of "wrong" stayed with me all day. The decision was right, but something was wrong. What was it? Everyone assured me that this attorney was the best; he knew how to find babies, and we wanted a baby.

That night, I was overwhelmed by a strange feeling inside of me. It was so strong, as if my cosmic inner voice had grabbed me by the will and shaken me. "Jason, this man will not find us our baby. Our baby is about ready to be born. I feel it. She's out there. We have to find her." Poor Jason, who was very down-to-earth and not at all susceptible to voices from the cosmos, humored me. "No, I'm dead serious, Jason. We must find another attorney. I don't like this bastard. He's wrong for us."

"OK, OK, we'll keep looking."

The next day Jason spoke to a client of his whose son was adopted. She recommended that he speak to a woman friend of hers who had successfully adopted a baby the year before and was impressed with the attorney's humanity. Jason's conversation with the young woman led us to Jack Hartnell, who worked fifty miles from our home. Jason absolutely hated to drive long distances, and it was unlikely that I could cajole him to drive out of town on a workday and then return home and go to work. But he liked the man's voice, and he could see us in two days.

To say that we were nervous would be the understatement of a lifetime. I primped for an hour, a change from my usual ten minutes. We drove the long distance, then sat before Jack, ready to sound like the best possible parents in the whole of human history. He was sensitive and noted our fears. He went through the rundown of adoption: his fees, the process, and the chances; our chances were not good. First of all, I was forty-five and Jason was forty. We were hardly the sweet, young couple that would be attractive to a young girl giving up her child for adoption. Second, I already had three children—a big no, since most prospective birth mothers wanted to give their baby to a childless couple. The list was endless. Jack didn't try to discourage us, but he was realistic. We left with guarded optimism, ready to wait the usual six months for a bite.

Our next task was painful: we had to put together an album to sell ourselves, which made me so uncomfortable. We raced home with a sense of urgency that Jason caught from me. "We have to do it today and send it tomorrow! We don't have much time!" I couldn't get the thought out of my mind that time was important and that we were running out of it.

But how do you present yourself to someone in a way that would tell your story in one page and make her want to select you? I felt rejected before I began, but we compiled a series of pictures, I wrote our story, and Jason wrote and recorded a song for the baby, a touching, sweet lullaby calling the baby to our hearts. In less than twenty-four hours, we had sent it by Federal Express to Jack's office, then told ourselves to forget the whole thing so that we wouldn't go crazy waiting for a call that might never come.

What I hadn't expected was the reactions from friends and family. The comments ranged from "That's wonderful" from my best friend to "You're crazy!" from most of the others—including myself in my quiet hours alone. Sometimes I saw myself as an ancient woman pushing a stroller; other times I was in a state of total invigoration, hope, and energy. I was in the grey area that I eventually came to see as life. No decisions were easy. There were prices to be paid—payoffs and consequences.

Jason assured me that our sex life would not diminish. "Right, Jason, but then you haven't had a kid, either." My jadedness tarnished the anticipation at times, and other times I radiated joy. I knew in my heart that I didn't want to share Jason, though. I had always longed to be number one in a man's life.

The kids were less than enthusiastic. At a meal one Sunday evening, when we broke the news of our decision to them, they accosted us. "How will this affect our college financing?" and "Well, now Jason will get his real baby!" and finally, "I don't want it; I won't like it; I won't babysit for it." That pretty much summed up their feelings. They were threatened as hell, and who could blame them? Still reeling from my divorce from their father, they, like me, vied for Jason's attention and a special place in his heart.

§

It was a Thursday afternoon. I had returned from work and was lying in bed for ten minutes, trying to rally my strength and spirits after a stressful day, when the phone rang. I always hesitated to answer it. First, I hated to talk on the phone, especially since I did it all day. Most of those calls were from angry or unhappy parents who wanted to blame a teacher or me or anyone about something their kid had done or failed to do, so

I avoided the phone. Second, if it wasn't for me, it was for the kids. That day, for some reason, I broke my cardinal rule and picked up the receiver.

"Congratulations, Alaina. You've been selected by a birth mother, and she wants to meet you and Jason right away!" Jack's voice was jubilant. What a wonderful job it must be to make calls like that. It was almost enough for me to change my opinion of the phone.

Through a sudden flow of tears, I managed to say, "But it's only been two weeks. How can this be?" I was shaking so hard that I fumbled the receiver, and it crashed onto the floor.

"Well, the birth mother has been to several attorneys and interviewed several couples, but she's decided on you two."

"When is the baby due?" I asked sheepishly, still not believing my ears.

"In seven weeks. Can you come on the fourteenth? We don't have much time for the home study and all the legalities."

"Yes, of course. But why did she pick us? You said yourself that we were poor bets because of our age and stuff."

"Well, you know, life is just that way. It takes the right person at the right time. But to answer your question, she wanted someone who could give the baby music and teach her German. Her mom was German and died young, and she feels nostalgic about that. She wants to be a German teacher."

"Jack, did you know that I had been a German teacher? I didn't mention it in our album because I am a counselor now. I only said that I *spoke* German. In fact, that sentence wasn't even in my first draft. I didn't know if that information would hurt or help our case. Some people don't like Germans."

"It was the first thing that caught her eye. When she learned that Jason was a musician, she was sold."

An incredible feeling swept over me. All the feelings of the past months began to fit. Our baby was out there. She was searching for us, and we had found her. I silently thanked my cosmic inner voice for forcing me to act quickly. If we had waited, she would have been gone.

"Oh, Jack, I am so happy. Forgive my tears. I can't seem to stop them." I could hear that he was tearful, too, and I knew that we were not just a business to him. The whole thing was just so right, so very right.

"OK, we'll see you on February 14 at three o'clock," he said.

"That's Valentine's Day. How appropriate!"

After we hung up, I sat for a long time. Within me grew a child now, and I felt its spirit move inside me as my own children had so many years before. "Don't worry, little one," I said aloud to the child who would soon be cradled in my arms. "I have found you. You are safe."

That night, I awoke with a poem in my mind. I got up and jotted it down. I didn't know this young woman, but I wrote on a small piece of paper the words that were in my heart as they came to me. I put the paper in my purse. I would know when I met her if I should give it to her. I would know. My heart would lead.

§

The truth is a funny thing. Jason and I did meet the way we described in our portfolio, but Shakespeare wrote that the course of true love never runs smooth. Our sojourn into married life with children was a nightmare at times. We agreed on nothing around raising my children. Now we were faced with the task of writing a letter to the birth mother explaining our life and hoping that something we wrote would interest her. It was an awful process. So much was riding on what I wrote, and I was really afraid, yet I couldn't appear to be so.

I thought of all the couples who were doing this project, too, laboring over old photos, trying to decide which ones would best fit an album for a birth mother. Each couple would then have to sit down and tell their story, and of course, the story must be good enough to capture the eye and heart of a panicked child who is pondering a major life decision. I thought I understood how teenagers thought. First, I had been one. Second, I had three. Third, I had taught and counseled hundreds of these kids. Because I knew so much, I was terrified, and I should have been. Teenagers are an unstable lot, which is an understatement just as "dysfunctional family" is an oxymoron. One never knows what teens are going to do, because they themselves don't know what they're going to do, or why. To think that someone in such an unstable state would have the power to grant or withhold from us a child was frightening at best and infuriating at the very least.

I sat before the computer and stared for what seemed like hours. What could I tell a person whom I had never seen about my life? What should I tell? What should I leave out? That was probably the most important part: the part I should leave out. I saw Jason's and my life together as a magical love story, but do I tell her that everyone in the family rejected our love, our union? That because of our love and desire to love one another, I had lost the love of my entire family? Do I tell the prospective birth mother that I was a counselor and that I worked with kids like her, or do I tell her that I had come from a wounded past myself and therefore understood the darkness and aloneness of families?

Would the truth frighten her off? How could I win her over without telling her who I was, where I came from, that I had almost no memories of my childhood and had to ask my sisters because large parts were just a blank? Do I say that I can remember no joy, no laughter, no carefree drives as a family? That instead, I conjure only flashes of horror and fear and have decided that it is better to remember nothing? Do I say that when I attend professional conferences and we break out into groups, I begin each introduction by saying, "I come from the other side of the tracks. My sisters and I were the only white girls in an all-Black school, and I made it out!"? Do I say that the next emotion is shame—shame for revealing my identity? Shame that instead of the educated, refined, professional woman they think they see, I am nothing but "white trash," as my father used to call my mother when I was little. Do I tell her that I feel shame for the fact that my real language is not proper, educated English but Black slang? That nothing about me was what it appeared to be? Do I relate my history that I lived in the garage behind my grandparents' home, which had one tiny bedroom and one pot for us all to pee in? That I was afraid that anyone who spent two minutes with me could see my past oozing out of my pores and reject me as I had rejected myself? Do I confess that I was ashamed of my mother because she used bad grammar and couldn't pronounce "oregano" and "wash rag"? That I was ashamed of my alcoholic father, who used to stumble into the church pew and glance at me with bloodshot eyes as I turned away? That I tried to ignore the fact that I was most of all ashamed of myself because, no matter how hard I tried, I would never be like the others?

Or do I simply say that I made it out of the ghetto, denying my origins every inch of the way, and that I have made it to some semblance of middle class in the material world? Do I expose myself and tell her that within me lives a frightened child of emotional abuse and terror and that some nights I lie in a fetal position and dream of the warmth of the womb of a mother who could not show her love for me? Do I tell this birth mother that I have grown up to become a committed mother who has learned much from her children, or do I tell her that sometimes I hear my own parents' shrill voices scream in fear at their children's stirrings of independence? Do I, in short, tell the truth?

I longed to tell this young lady, who might give me her child, that this baby would complete us, would make Jason and me a real family. I wondered if I should tell her that I was afraid that if we couldn't adopt, Jason would leave me and find a younger woman who would give him a child. I wanted to tell her that I was articulate, strong, and kind but also confess that I was fearful, insecure, and not always certain that I was enough, for both were true. That's the problem with truths: there are so many of them.

I was still sitting in front of the computer as my children strolled by—angry, beautiful teenagers who loved me but also hated me, too, for I was responsible for breaking up the family by divorcing their father. I wondered if I should tell the birth mother that as a woman, I was proud that I had chosen to be happy, to find love again, and be myself, or whether to tell her that in order to do that, I had sacrificed my three children's security and threw them into the whirlwind of a second marriage. I wondered if I should tell her of the nights that I cried myself to sleep in guilt that I had broken their hearts.

Do I tell her that Jason loves my children and wants them to be his own, or do I tell her that his idealism of being a stepfather was over after week two of the marriage? Marriage can be so complicated. Perhaps I should tell her that the kids couldn't wait for a new sibling. Or should I tell her the other truth, that they are threatened by the thought that they will be displaced by this new baby and their needs will be put on the back burner? Both were true, but which truth could a pregnant, confused teenager handle?

I longed to tell her how each night I prayed to this unborn child from the empty crib that we had prematurely erected in the room next to ours as our dream awaited us. Do I tell her that I speak to this child and call her to hear my voice because I believe that my child is out there and cannot come through me, so she must come *to* me? Would I frighten her off if I told her that I believed destiny was at work in my life and that I must follow my inner voice? Or would she think, as did most who knew me, that I was too "cosmic"?

I longed to tell the truth, but I didn't know which truth to tell. This was a damned assignment, and I resented having to do it. Yet, I had to reach this girl through my words, and now that I had to write them down, they seemed shallow and tired, lacking truthfulness even while being true. I was so confused because I was so afraid. My baby was out there, and if I failed, I would miss her—and so I had to tell a truth of sorts. *Forgive me, Miss Birth Mother. I want desperately to bear my soul, but I must impersonate an adult and not be the terrified child who now begins to write.*

Dear Birth Mother,

Jason and I have lived a love story. Like everyone, we both dreamed of finding that special person to love and share life with, but we never dreamed that we would meet the way we did. Jason walked into my life as the classical piano teacher to my three children by a former marriage. I adored him. The kids adored him, too, because he understood them, was patient, and made them feel special. You might say that they fell in love with him first. As the years progressed, our eyes were opened to one another. We have always felt that God led us to each other, that everything in our two lives prepared us for the moment when our paths would cross.

Jason has a bachelor's degree in music. He is an outstanding artist and musician. He writes music, performs, and teaches classical piano. Before we met, Jason worked for eight years teaching music. After college, he traveled for four years and organized children's programs in Mexico. For the last twelve years he has concentrated on private lessons because he loves children and loves to work with them one on one. He has been a substitute father for dozens of kids, but his one dream is to raise a child of his own. When we married, we knew that I could not have any more children. It was heartbreaking for us both; however, since our love was strong, we determined to adopt a child. This has become our strength.

I graduated from college and taught German and English for twelve years while raising three kids. I think my three children are my best references as to what kind of mother I would make. I can say that I never shortchanged them. I viewed them from conception on as a sacred gift. People used to say that I did too much, but I have always felt they deserved the best of me. Christian, now nineteen, is at college. He is a handsome, wonderful young man; he is creative and plays classical and popular piano. He is also an outstanding athlete. Liam, now seventeen, will go to college next year. He's a great athlete, too, plays piano, and has the best sense of humor in the world (next to Jason). Daniella is fifteen and is a great girl; she is kind to animals and people and is sweet and funny. I am proud of them because they live clean lives and have good values. They attended Christian schools for many years. I have no regrets. I love them. Jason loves them, too; we are good parents. They will make incredible siblings for the baby and great role models, too. We cut no corners with them; we will cut no corners with our baby. We know what it takes to be good parents. We know it's a hard job.

Presently, I am a counselor and work directly with troubled kids who have no one. I am like a mother to three hundred fifty children. I get involved with my students, as Jason does with his.

We jog every morning at five thirty, and in our spare time we camp, play tennis, and simply have a lot of fun. Jason and I both paint, he in acrylic and I in watercolor. I write poetry. The bottom line is that we have a healthy lifestyle. Our home is a place of peace and joy. The one thing that is so important to us is to raise a child together. We feel blessed having found each other and want to give something back as our gift to each other and to the world.

We don't know what the right words are to say to a birth mother. Naturally, we want a baby with all our hearts. But there is much to say, and words are poor vehicles of expression where a decision so great for both of us is concerned. In the end, Jason and I have learned that there is only love. It is love that will allow you to release this child into a family's arms for safekeeping. It will require great courage and wisdom. It is love that will open the hearts of two people to make room for a new life to enter.

All our lives, our decisions, our successes, and our failures have led us to each other and this moment. We believe that God has prepared us for a child who needs the kind of love we have to offer: home, education, and commitment to music, art, and sports. Our time is given to family above all. Our priorities are healthy because we have lived enough to know what is important. At a deeper level, however, lie the real strengths we possess: an abiding love for each other and a desire to raise a child. Just as your decision to relinquish the child required great and thoughtful decision-making, our decision to adopt was the result of much soul-searching and prayer.

The child we receive, wherever he or she is at this moment, will be welcomed into our hearts—a gift from a loving birth mother to us. There will be happy brothers and sister, grandparents who desperately want a grandchild, aunts, uncles, and many cousins. Our home will be a safe place for a child to grow into a human being who has something to offer this world. He or she will be exposed to music and art, will have room to be creative, and will be supported if he or she wants to play sports, sing, and so on. We value education and will provide every opportunity possible. There will be good home-cooked meals, lively family conversations, and much, much laughter. You would have to spend time with us to really know how true this is!

But most of all, the child will receive what every human being needs and longs for: a safe and loving home in which to be cherished by parents who value him or her and be surrounded with love.

Sincerely,
Jason & Alaina O'Connell
P.S. Enclosed is a song Jason wrote for the baby.

Yes, there are many truths. Had I told the truth in my letter? Had I lied to the birth mother? Had I lied to myself? Was this truth *the* truth? I honestly did not know at the time.

The wait for February 14 was excruciating. I made a feeble attempt to keep my mind on my work and pretend that I was not paralyzed with terror. I think Jason felt the same, but we didn't speak of it. My principle fear was that the birth mother would find me too old or not like me and thus ruin Jason's chance for having the baby he wanted.

I had still not overcome the inadequacy I had felt during our dating period, when the five-year age difference was a major determining factor in whether I would be good enough to be Jason's wife. When he got afraid of our love, he would remind me of all the younger girls he had dated and that I was the oldest woman he had ever dated. His family and friends, of course, reiterated this. Why would any thirty-eight-year old man want to marry a forty-two-year-old woman with three teenage kids? It was a legitimate question, I suppose, but the way it was presented, the five years' difference was like twenty years. Naturally, this played into my fear of inadequacy, and when I looked in the mirror, I didn't see the blossoming woman who was there; I saw an old, has-been, used-up, worn-out hag who had no right to love this man-boy. This was my personal hell.

After Jason and I committed to each other, it never again seemed to be an issue for him; however, it remained an issue for me. The scars were deep, and they oozed like an infected wound. I thought they had only to do with Jason and me and our stormy courtship, but in truth, they had more to do with my father's rejection of me. I was the one who had ended his young life by my entrance into the world, and I always carried an unnamed shame for having existed at all. It had become a leitmotiv, a recurring thread, in the parenting classes I taught with a colleague: The father determines how the daughter feels about herself. He is the giver of the message of her desirability. I had not received a good message from my father, and with my mother now dead, I had no place of value in the family for him. My message was instead, "You are not good enough. You are not worthy to live." No one said these things to me; I said them to myself. But this knowledge was not in my conscious awareness at forty-two.

Now, on February 14, 1991, all I wanted to do was look young and acceptable to this young woman we were about to meet. I took off from work and primped for hours. The hair had to be perfect. The outfit had to be right—not too flashy, not too old, and not too young. All I wanted to be was me, but of course, "me" would not be good enough. Jason dressed as he always did, in jeans, a clean T-shirt, and tennis shoes. Jason was not the dress-up type. I had to fight him into a pair of real shoes on our wedding day. He was one of those people who truly did not care what people thought. I, on the other hand, always had my antennae out for the slightest nuance that I had displeased someone.

We drove to Jack Hartnell's office. This meeting was so important. By now, I was committed to this baby and scared that my marriage depended on us having it. We entered the office, where the secretary told us that Jack was delayed in court and would arrive a little later. He wanted to talk to us before introducing us to the birth mother. We were escorted to Jack's opulent office, where pictures of his children, including his adoptive child, hung on the walls. I liked him. He was a mensch.

My teeth started to chatter, and I felt my body flinching involuntarily. God, I was so scared. What would she be like? Would she like us? Would we like her? A pregnant woman is so unpredictable; I remember that much about myself during pregnancy. What if she didn't show up?

Jason was jumping out of his skin, so he decided to take a walk. Thirty seconds later, he returned with a platinum-haired pregnant woman who was wearing an awkward but wide smile on her face. Her face was cleanly scrubbed and radiated health. She was quite visibly pregnant; in fact, she looked ready to deliver. I, too, had gained a lot of weight during my pregnancies, so I understood. She wore open-toed shoes, and her ankles were swollen. Funny, the things one remembers during important times in one's life. I don't know whom I expected, but my heart stopped. Suddenly I was in another zone. I extended my hand to her. Her name was Alex.

Alex began to talk. She was bubbly and full of energy. I, who am usually quite articulate, was tongue-tied. Each word was so important! We tried to tell each other who we were—an impossible task. Jack's secretary had told Jason that Jack didn't permit the prospective birth mother and adoptive parents to meet for the first time without him, but Jason's charm prevailed.

We told Alex how much we wanted to be parents, and she told us that she wasn't ready to be a mom. She had a story. We had a story. I saw pain in this young woman's soul, and I wondered if she could see mine. Suddenly, after just three minutes, Alex exclaimed, "You are the parents of my baby!"

At that moment Jack walked in, and Alex announced that it was a done deal. Jack was surprised and happy. He wondered what had transpired in his absence. What *had* transpired? There was a kind of cosmic click—it felt right. I tried to imagine what Alex's child would look like. I imagined raising this child with the same love I had shown my other three children. I was drawn to her belly and visualized the tiny creature sleeping peacefully in her womb. Was this the child I had been talking to over the last few weeks? How would I know? I felt an indescribable need to touch Alex's stomach, to feel this child. I knew that my intuitive self would know whether this baby was the one.

Jack was talking on about the financial details, but I didn't hear anything except the beating of my heart, arrhythmic and racing. Suddenly he was asking us to say goodbye. We exchanged phone numbers with Alex. I wanted to hold this woman. I wanted to get down on my knees and thank her for her gift. I wanted to touch her. Spontaneously, we embraced in a promise and prayer, much the same way one might shake hands after a deal has been struck. For me, this deal had been decided in Heaven.

I got up the nerve to ask Alex if I could touch her stomach. She looked at me oddly but nodded. As I leaned down and placed my hand upon her belly, energy ran through my entire being. This was my baby. Yes, this was the baby I had been praying to. What a long journey this little one had taken to get to me. I couldn't help myself; I whispered to it. I felt its tiny spirit reach out and embrace me. But it wasn't just this child that I felt; I felt Alex's spirit, too, and this spirit was heavy and sad. I looked up into her eyes and saw the same kind of grief I had seen in my own when I had encountered unbearable loss. I couldn't stop the tears. She probably thought I was happy, but in truth, I was grieving for her. I was taking something that didn't belong to me, yet I knew that this child was meant to be with us. I couldn't reconcile the conflicting feelings I had.

I reached into my purse and retrieved the poem I had written, the one that had come to me in the night. Maybe she would understand it. It was not profound, but it spoke of a journey that we were about to make together.

§

Alex

We stand, two women – each with a gift
Yours a child – a soul to be entrusted
A child to complete our love, our family
And mine a haven worthy of that gift
And the freedom for you to fulfill yourself,
Your dreams, your destiny
We stand, two women – forever connected
By this tiny, sleeping soul within you
Sisters, mothers, friends.
February 1991

§

CHAPTER 6
Alex

The morning of February 14 was full of excitement and uncertainty. I had called Duncan earlier and told him of my impending meeting with the O'Connells. I had sent him their portfolio the week before so I could get his input on them being parents of our unborn child. Getting up and dressing for this meeting was a challenge. I was now reaching my seventh month, and time was going by fast.

Something about this couple attracted me. They seemed so close to what I wanted in a family, and now I had the chance to meet them, to see if they were as wonderful as their portfolio portrayed them to be. I wanted to make a good impression on them.

I arrived at Jack's office early and sat in the lobby, expecting the lawyer to greet me. Instead, a handsome, dark-haired man walked toward me and introduced himself as Jason O'Connell. My heart jumped. I hadn't realized they were already there. Jason said that Jack was detained and would be with us shortly.

As we walked into Jack's office, my heart was pounding in my throat. A tall, thin woman who looked to be in her early thirties was standing there. She seemed very pleasant but appeared to be as nervous as I was. Jason was friendly as he introduced me to his wife, Alaina. I could tell this was new to all of us, which made me feel a little more at ease. I took the first chair available to me and sat across from these two people who could be parents to my child. They sat down and held hands tightly.

Jason and Alaina looked like the perfect Washington couple. They were both tan, in great shape, and looked wonderful together as a couple. I didn't know how to start. What do I say? *So, you want my baby?*

I started with their religious background and asked how they would feel if the baby chose a different lifestyle that what they believed in. I asked about what kind of music Jason played. How long had he played? What had Alaina taught in school? What were their other children like? Everything they said about themselves was perfect. I kind of wished that they would adopt *me*. In the short time of our conversation, my heart knew that this was the right couple. My search was over.

They asked me why I was giving up my baby. I said, "Duncan and I are not ready to be parents." I knew that line so well, and it was the easiest one to give; however, I couldn't look at them when I said it. Looking people in the eyes and lying to them was too hard, so I had learned to look away. They didn't question me further. Looking at them now, bursting with hope and happiness, filled me with jealousy.

I wanted to be Alaina. I wanted the handsome husband, the beautiful house, and the great life, but it was not to be. Giving them this baby was a gift, and they were grateful. I sat in silence while they talked about how they met and fell in love. All I could think about was the love I felt for Duncan and our love story. Part of me was happy that I had finally found my baby's parents, but another part was sad because this baby was not mine anymore; I had made up my mind. My heart told me that they were the parents I had been searching for. I told them that I would give them my child.

We all stood up, had a group hug, and shed tears. Through my anguish and tears, all I could say was, "I'm trying to do the right thing for this baby." The baby's future now lay with the O'Connells.

At that moment, Jack walked into the room. Before he could say anything, we told him I had chosen the O'Connells to be my baby's parents. He was surprised that it had all happened so fast; I think we were all surprised. We made the final arrangements and decided when I would stop working. I stood on my feet for six to seven hours a day and was now going into my seventh month, so it was getting harder and harder for me to cut hair all day.

Jack asked if he could take a picture of the three of us. We gathered together with our arms around each other, smiling. I was trying so hard to smile the biggest smile I had, trying so hard to be happy. I didn't want to spoil their happiness. Alaina put her hands on my stomach and talked to the baby, and then an odd thing happened: the baby moved when she put her hand there. The baby had not moved in days, and I had been worried. I felt very territorial; I didn't want anyone to touch my baby yet. But she was only doing what came natural to her.

Before saying our goodbyes, we exchanged phone numbers and promised to keep in touch with each other over the next two months. Alaina gave me a poem about two women, a gesture I found sweet and touching. When I first read it, it didn't make much sense to me, but later, that poem would shape our relationship forever. I was feeling overwhelmed; I had to get out and escape all the happiness they were experiencing. Everyone was happy but me.

Oh, how I wanted to be sharing their happiness at that very moment. I had no idea how our lives were being shaped as I left the office that day. I didn't realize how I was connecting to this unknown woman who would be with me for the rest of my life and share a common love.

I called Duncan that night and told him about the events of the day. He agreed that their portfolio was wonderful. I told him that I had picked them to be our child's parents. He grew silent; maybe he realized then that our baby was no longer ours but now belonged to someone else. After we hung up, I lay on my bed and thought about everything that had happened. Now that I had found Jason and Alaina, I had to prepare to let my baby go; I had to disconnect. I felt sure that this baby was a boy, and I thought I could give a boy away much easier than a girl. I knew that sounded strange, but it was how I felt.

Now I had to face the next two months and somehow get through them without losing my mind. I had made my promise to the O'Connells and to this baby, and I had to keep it. I consoled myself by rereading their portfolio.

§

CHAPTER 7
Alaina

fter we left Jack's office, I immediately regretted having given Alex the poem. Was I being presumptuous? I was also afraid that she might have taken offense at my wanting to touch her stomach. As we were leaving and I had stood there looking into this young woman's eyes, my glance had fallen on her belly. I knew that within this stranger was the child I had been calling. I knew it. I wanted to touch this child, to acknowledge that I was here, that nothing could harm her. I reached out spontaneously, then thought better and asked Alex if I could touch her stomach. She nodded, but I felt her awkwardness. There was something about this woman! I touched her stomach gently and bent down and kissed her belly. *I love you, my little one*, I whispered to myself. I knew the child didn't belong to me. I knew how territorial I always felt when I carried life within me, but I was drawn like a magnet to the baby. "I love you." Naturally, after we left and I had a chance to review our talk, I realized that everything I had said was absolutely inane and that surely Alex would get home and change her mind. I shared nothing of this with Jason.

We walked silently to the parking lot and sat in the car for what seemed like forever without speaking. She had said yes, yet we didn't feel secure. There was no baby yet. One of our friends had supported a birth mother for seven months only to have her disappear a few days before the birth of the child. They had spent thirty thousand dollars and ended up with no baby, but we didn't have that kind of money. We were very vulnerable—and very scared.

Since Jack's office was near a mall, we decided to walk around before dinner. We found ourselves in the baby department buying two packages of undershirts. It was as if we were sleepwalking. *Yes*, she had said. "Yes." Yes, we will be parents in seven weeks. Maybe. But we were pretending as if it was all true.

We ate dinner at a local restaurant before starting our trip home. We spoke little; I'm sure Jason didn't know what to think. The enormity of the meeting was beginning to sink in. Instead of allowing ourselves to be happy, we became dreadfully afraid. I told myself that it would be wrong to bond with the child until we actually had it, but it was too late. Just putting my hands on Alex's belly had done it. I had fallen in love, hopelessly and forever in love. I knew this was the baby whose spirit I had spoken to. I knew in my core that destiny was playing out a script and we were simply learning the lines. I knew that my heart hurt for Alex. I had an advantage over her, for I had had children and knew what she was giving up. She didn't know yet, but she would soon. Could she then let it go?

I learned the term "guarded optimism" that night as we drove home and held each other tightly. I would be able to give the man I loved a child. He would be a father. So much depended on this to happen; at least, I felt that way. I had no idea what Jason was thinking, for he held me in silence. Later, I listened to his sleep-breathing; I knew that I would not sleep again for a long time. I knew that I would live in fear for the next two months, until the baby was asleep in the crib beside us.

Friends were excited about our good news but warned us not to get too invested. So, naturally, we went out and bought clothes and bottles and a mobile. We were setting ourselves up, because there are no certainties in life, and this adoption was definitely not certain. Nightly, I stood by the crib and prayed while Jason was working. I prayed to God to allow us to have this child. I prayed for the child to come to us. I wondered if Alex wasn't also standing next to her empty crib, praying that Duncan would change his mind and marry her. What was this young woman praying tonight? And whose prayer would God answer?

§

Jason ordered his first-ever glass of wine. It was quite an occasion, because that night we named our child—a real child—who had only been a dream until this moment. It was a Friday night, and we had made reservations at our favorite Italian restaurant in Seattle. We had signed the papers the preceding week, and already we were talking about names. This was to be a special child, and it had to be the perfect name. "Michelle" came up, and it reminded Jason of our Beatlemania days. We toasted our decision to become parents together and promptly announced it to our waiter and anyone else who would listen. *We were going to adopt.* No—*we were going to have a baby!*

Jason ordered his usual, angel-hair pasta with fresh tomatoes and basil, and I ordered the special, duck, because I always wanted whatever was special, no matter what it was. We bantered a few boys' names around but decided we didn't like any of them, so we were just going to have to have a girl. That was all there was to it.

"What about Sara?" I said. "Sara O'Connell sounds like an adorable, energetic, cute little girl with a twinkle in her eyes." "Yeah, Sara sounds like a girl I'd like to meet. Sara O'Connell." It was just that simple. It felt right, and there was no more discussion. Sara it was. Girl or boy, the baby was to be called Sara O'Connell. We raised our glasses in celebration.

"What's a Sara?" the boys asked when we returned home and announced our choice. "Never heard of it," Christian said. "Sounds like someone from Little House on the Prairie to me," he added cynically.

Naming Sara was one of those moments in life like all other decisions I had made—to marry, to get pregnant, to go back to college, to risk. It was spontaneous and from out of some clear part of myself. "Never spend too long on the big decisions," I always said. "Ponder the minutia, but make the grand decisions on impulse. That way you know it comes from the deeper, wiser part of yourself." Like the night we decided to adopt—just go for it. Don't wade around in pros and cons; just do what is right for you.

Sara O'Connell. Perfect. Boy, I hoped it was a girl. This kid would sure catch hell on the football team if it wasn't.

§

Lullaby to an Empty Crib

Hear me, my little one
From the dark home that cradles you tonight
Hear my song in your quiet sleep of eternity
Calling you back into my arms
For there is a space for you here with me
A place no one but you can fill
Since you cannot grow in my belly
You have been conceived in my heart
Hear me, my little one
I reach out to you with a promise of safety and love
I cradle the dream of you
As my spirit ascends into forever
To seek your tiny face
Do you recognize my voice from times
Forgotten but etched within us?
Return again as my child
Once my lover or sister or mother
Now I will mother you
Hear me, my little one
Mommy is calling you so gently
Come home
For I am ready for you
At last.

§

Dear Alex,

A couple of weeks ago, you were a "birth mother," a nameless person we dreamed would call and say that she had a baby for us. When Jack called us and set up a meeting, both Jason and I were anxious and happy to meet you, but we had no idea that you would be, too. Now that you have given us a promise of this great gift—and truly, this is the greatest gift we will ever receive—I want to talk to you from my heart. I want you to know that the woman who will be the mother of your baby, the woman who will hold the child to her own breast when he cries, will sit at soccer practice so he feels supported and loved. I want you to know the woman who will worry about each sore throat and pace the floors at night when he is sick, the woman who will nurture him to become a man, capable of sensitivity and affection and true masculinity.

I am speaking as if the baby is a boy only because you seem to feel strongly that it is a boy. However, the same goes for a girl. I adore girls, too. The prospect of helping a girl become a competent, confident young woman is something in which I would take particular pride. So, if I continue the letter saying "he," please know where I am coming from.

I know that motherhood takes a special kind of selflessness. It requires decisions based on love that provide time for the baby even when you are too tired and when there seems to be no time. I am thinking of your own mom, who obviously had a hard life trying to hold things together through hard work and devotion. Sometimes we women have to dig deep within the well of our beings to be strong and often are called upon to choose the well-being of our children over our own. The art of parenting is to be able to remain a whole, fulfilled human and a dedicated mother. I know what it takes to do this. It's not always easy; in fact, sometimes it's incredibly difficult. One must be an adult in the most profound sense. One must be a whole person in order to help another tiny person to become one, too.

My heart is tightly tied to you right now, Alex. I see that life has not been easy for you, yet you have survived. That is something I really admire in you. You have had many losses, but they have not vanquished you. I know how important it is to reach your highest potential as a woman and how difficult that can be when you have no one to fall back on. To be without parents at so young an age must be awful at times. You were called upon to be your own parent, to love and care for yourself, and to make decisions that are in your best interest. I don't think I would have been so strong.

There is a maternal part of me that wants to take care of you right now. There is a part of me that I carry through each day as I pray that the little one within you is safe and sound. I feel very protective of you both, and I am touched by those feelings. Although the baby is in your body and not mine, I carry him in my heart.

The kids are so excited yet a little jealous, I must admit. The grandparents are calling everyone and telling them about the impending arrival. There is no hint anywhere or from anyone that this child is adopted, only that the child's birth is a thing of great joy. I think of young Rose, my sister's adopted baby in Arizona, who will have a little playmate to grow up with and ultimately share a special camaraderie. We all feel so blessed.

I have been trying to put myself in your position, and I have a thought you may want to consider. I thought it might be a wonderful gift for you to put together an album of pictures and letters from you to the baby, which we could give to him when he asks about you. This would allow you a chance to express your great love for him and the reasons for your decision while offering him a segue to you later in life. It would be therapeutic for you and a wonderful gift for him. Please think about it. Children can deal with the truth; their fantasies can be painful. Forgive me if this suggestion is not what you wish. Please feel free to do things your own way. It is just that, in an effort to make the transition easy on all of us, I thought of it.

The most important changes in our lives usually begin with incredible pain, yet it is through pain that we become the selves we were meant to be. As for me, I consciously and willingly accept your sacred trust in me to care for your child, who will live his life in safety, love, and peace.

Love,
Alaina
March 1991

I believe there is a test God puts prospective adoptive parents through in lieu of pregnancy itself—a zone of insecurity where one's faith is put to the test, a *Feuerprobe* (test by fire). In the weeks before Alex was to deliver, our *Feuerprobe* was hot and punishing. We tried to go through our daily routines, but my insecurity was bordering on madness as I was torn between wanting to befriend this young woman and wanting to escape the possibility that all of this was for nothing, that she had the power to alter the course of our lives anytime she chose. I had feared working with a teenager, but Alex was no teen; she was a twenty-six-year-old woman. She was old enough to know what she was doing, what she was losing, what she could do to us. I was disoriented, obsessed with writing to her, with reaching out, partially out of a growing attachment to her, partially out of fear.

What was she thinking today? I obsessed as I numbly carried out my duties at work. Teens filed in and out of my office. I ministered to their needs, listened to their stories, but I was lost in my own. I was out of control, and I knew it. Yet I also knew that I had to remain centered and focused so as not to upset her. I would write a letter and then stand helplessly by the mailbox, wishing I could take back what I had written. I feared I had said too much or too little. I feared I might anger her. Was she getting pissed off at me? I tried to put myself in her shoes and didn't like the way they fit. Had I been in her shoes, I would have hated me. I couldn't leave it alone. I wanted to fix everything. I wanted to take her pain away. I wanted to take my own away. I wanted to have this baby, yet I didn't want to do it at her expense. There was no way that both of us could emerge from this happy; one woman would walk away empty. The guilt was overwhelming at times. Yet my spirit wanted this child, felt this child belonged to me from a distant destiny that I couldn't share with anyone.

I tried to hold up things at home. I knew Jason was dying with fear. This was his only chance to be a father—with me as his wife. If I failed with Alex, I would live eternally in fear that every fertile woman was a direct threat to us. Our nights were fraught with trepidation, and we tried to connect physically with the urgency one feels when trying to time insemination. It was forced and scripted. Who were we kidding? Afterward, as I listened to his quiet breathing, I would cry and pray. Often, I would get up and run my hands over the new baby sheets that we had already put on the crib, imagining a baby there, imagining our baby, imagining Jason's happiness, and imagining eternity. I would stand until my feet were numb and tears were streaming down my cheeks. The next day, I would arise and write another letter, another attempt at contact, at understanding, at this mystery we were caught up in, and at the fragility of being alive.

Alex and I were fusing our destinies. Did she know it? I knew. I didn't know how or why, but I knew. There were no accidents.

Dear Alex,

When Jason got off the phone with you yesterday, the feelings I had been having for the last few days were confirmed. Ever since Friday, I had had this horrible anxiety in my stomach about you. I am beginning to think that we are really connected and that your selection of us goes beyond the superficial, beyond the comprehensible. This is probably good because it means that there are profound reasons that you have selected us and that we are connected on a deep, unconscious level. Perhaps this is why I felt you so strongly on Friday. I got depressed, and I feel so many emotions right now—it's as if I am feeling my feelings *and* your feelings.

On the one hand, I am excited beyond words. We bought more clothes, bottles, supplies, and so on over the weekend. We want everything to be just right for the baby. Jason painted some more shirts; this baby will really have a designer wardrobe, even if the designer is his daddy. I stand in stores selecting things for the baby, yet there is not a baby in me. It's a strange feeling. I get scared a lot.

There is another side of me, just as potent, that is grieving for you. I know that this is a difficult time for you. Being in the Lamaze class must be a strain without Duncan—without someone. These important times in one's life are not meant to be experienced alone. Sure, we can do them alone, but it's hard. We can also raise children alone, but that's hard, too. Your mother knew that. I know that. You know that. I know that there must be times when you really need someone to hold you and console you. Duncan cannot be there. We are not there. My heart really feels this pain in some inexplicable way.

My offer to attend the Lamaze classes with you is still good. I do not wish to intrude on the delivery with Duncan being there, but if you need emotional support beforehand, I will do it. I offer this not out of selfish motives but out of real care for you, the woman. One of my worse traits is that when I need help the most, I usually reject it. This comes from never being able to trust anyone when I was growing up. I now believe, however, that we all need each other and were never meant to endure hardship alone.

The other thing I am feeling for you is that you do not have a mother now. I am a lot older than you, but there are still times when I wish I could just walk to the phone and call my mom and say, "I need you." But I can't, and neither can you. This is a great loss, no matter how old a woman is. Perhaps I can be that person for you. If I were to do this, you must believe that I really care for you, apart from the baby. That will be hard, because without the baby, we would have never even met. We are both going through something difficult. If you need me, call. We need each other.

I am happy that you told Jason how you are feeling, but your feelings scare me. You need to feel all the feelings—the pregnancy, the abortion, the death of your mom and *Oma*—so that you will be free to claim your life and get to the place you want to be. Your education is important. Without it, you're destined to a life of hard, hard work without great fulfillment as a woman. Our mothers did not have that education, so their lives were difficult and they both died too soon. You have chosen a different path; it's a lonely path, at first. Alex, this is not the end of the world for you. It is the beginning for you, for Jason and me, and for our—your—child.

When we signed our contract with Jack to support you, it went beyond financial support. Our promises to each other will last a lifetime. They will not be over when you give us the baby. You and I are irrevocably united for all time. Have faith in your decision and the wisdom of the fate that has put us together.

You are not alone.

Love,
Alaina
March 1991

§

CHAPTER 8
Alaina

*I*t had been two weeks since I had heard a word from Alex. Just after she had chosen us, we had talked often. She responded to my attempts to understand her, and I had begun to believe that all would go well. Adoption is so different from experiencing your own pregnancy. When you carry a child within you, your fears are whether the child will be healthy, whether you will be a good parent; but when someone else carries your child, you have no claim to any feelings at all. I lived with a dread and a rock-like weight in my belly where a child should have been. I was constantly attacked by the what-ifs that plagued my days and haunted my nights. What if she changed her mind now that we had fallen in love with this unborn child? She spoke often of the baby as a boy and relished the idea. What if it was a boy and she couldn't part with him? I knew in my heart that she still was holding out hope that Duncan would change his mind and commit to her, that perhaps when he saw the child, he would be overcome with paternal instincts and take Alex in the deal. Perhaps she in fact did not feel that way, but I imagined that I would feel that way were I in her shoes.

Days passed at the speed of cold honey. Every time the phone rang, Jason and I would pretend we didn't need to throw up in terror. What if? What if? My fears as a woman who could not give the man she loved a baby showed on my face as plainly as the glow a woman has when she is pregnant. I feared that if we lost this child, I would lose Jason, and I often lay awake and hated him for making me feel this way. He had said that I was enough, but when I saw the look on his face when we had been chosen, I knew that I would never be enough without a child, despite what he said daily to reassure me.

I reviewed the glib manner in which I had flaunted my three pregnancies, which were easily conceived. Fertility ran in our family. It had been my claim to fame as a young woman, while Johann's colleagues' wives, who were older before they began their families, struggled with infertility. I had been one of the lucky women who wished for a child, seduced her husband on the fourteenth day after her period, and got pregnant. Now karma had swung around to bite me hard as I, now the older woman, felt barren and inadequate. It preyed on the child within me, who had always known that she was not enough. Now Alex was the young, healthy, fertile girl, and I even feared that Jason would want her instead of me. Did all adoptive mothers feel this rivalry? I would never know, because I was too ashamed to ask or share my own vulnerabilities.

So much rode on this child. I knew Jason's mother, Elise, wanted a grandchild. I knew his brother wanted to marry and produce the "O'Connell Seed," as he would say with a hint of sarcasm. It always went straight for its intended target: my heart. Ouch! My brother-in-law would explain how "men would always want much younger women because nature arranged it that older men would win younger women, who could carry a fetus to term." Insensitive bastard! I would look in the mirror, and instead of seeing a beautiful, vibrant woman, I saw a milkless, barren woman who would lose everything if she lost this baby, who would suffer a psychological miscarriage she would never recover from. Jason consoled me, laughed at my folly, but I never believed him, not after I had seen his eyes when he thought he would at last become a father. My three children were no longer on his radar, and that fact made me want to slip into unconsciousness or unknowing rather than see what was happening to them or what it meant for our future. Jason was forgetting that my children were *my children* and that they were my life long before he walked into it.

The call came on a Wednesday afternoon in mid-March. Irene, our office secretary, took the call and buzzed my office phone. "It's Alex!" The mere mention of the name sent a chill through everyone in the office. Was it good news? Had something gone wrong? I said a silent prayer. *Oh, God, please don't let her change her mind. I'll do anything. Anything!* I was a notorious dealmaker and must have appeared quite foolish to God; I reprimanded myself and took a deep breath.

"Hi!" I said casually, as if nothing could possibly go wrong. What a fucking faker I had learned to be in the last month. "Well, I just got back from the ultrasound—and it's a girl." Her voice sounded sad, and that alarmed me. I had expected that had it been a boy, she would change her mind. A girl was safe, or so I thought. "That's absolutely wonderful, Alex. I am so happy. Really." She met my response with silence, and I faded from the reality of my office and daily concerns.

"I thought you wanted a boy?" I asked sheepishly.

"No, it really didn't matter, but I never thought about the prospect of giving up a baby girl," she said.

God, please don't do this to me. Please, I begged silently. And to her, "Alex, does this change anything?" I waited.

"No, it's fine. I just never thought I would have to give up a girl, that's all. I'm a little shaken up."

I wanted to be empathetic, but I felt selfish. I wanted that baby girl. She was our Sara, the one we had named from the beginning. She was the one I had been calling to every night in the darkness as I stood beside her little crib and prayed, *Please let Jason have this child. Please, God, I'll love her so much and keep her safe. I promise.* I knew God believed this promise because my three other children had been my religion, the only thing I truly believed in. Motherhood was sacred to me.

In that moment, however, I felt desperate. *Keep cool. Don't let her sense your desperation.* Then I hated myself for begrudging her her own child. I was a monster to have these feelings. *Hell. I am in hell. This must be what Hell is. This is it.*

"Well, thank you for telling me. Now I can buy clothes for a girl so that all will be ready when she arrives." What an utterly dumb and insensitive thing to say! "No, don't worry. I'm not going to change my mind. I'm just a little shocked." Her reassurance didn't help, though. The room was whirling out of control. I wanted a girl. "It's a girl" had been the sweetest words I had ever heard when the doctor had pulled an unwilling Daniella from my stubborn uterus seventeen years earlier. After two wild-ass and deviously intelligent sons, a girl had been like a delicate dream floating into my life. And now there was to be our little

Sara, the cute little girl we had invented over a glass of Merlot, the name that sprang of its own accord from my lips and felt so right. I had known all along, hadn't I? I had known all along.

The click of the receiver snapped me back into reality, and I ran into the outer office. "It's a girl!" Everyone gathered around and embraced my empty belly and congratulated me. I ran back to the phone and dialed Elise, Jason's mother. "It's a girl!" I cried, and she burst into tears of celebration because she, too, had secretly wanted a girl.

Daniella walked into my office at that moment, and I broke the news to her. "Oh, shit," she said calmly. It was the first time I realized that a little girl could pose a threat to my seventeen-year-old baby girl, the girl of my heart. "Oh, don't worry, Daniella, you'll always be my Bobitz." *Bobitz* was a term I had made up and used every time I put her to sleep when she was little. After tucking her in and kissing her sleepy face, I'd say, "The Momitz?" to which she would reply, "The Bobitz!" and drift off in the security of our relationship. We knew what this meant; loosely translated, these words meant that I would always be her mommy and she would always be my special baby. All of that was in jeopardy now, and I felt for her because I knew no words of assurance would help at this moment. Time alone would show her that she would always be my Bobitz and that Sara would be something—someone—else.

Liam sauntered in, and on hearing the news, gave the high-five sign to the air with a resounding "Yes!" He had been afraid that the baby would be a boy and threaten his position. I realized then that each of us was living his own personal hell through this ordeal: the kids for their own reasons, Jason for his, I for mine, and of course, Alex for hers. Yes, this is what Hell is like, no doubt about it.

At home later that night, I waited for Jason to return from work at ten o'clock. I usually heard his radio before I heard the car's motor, and this night was no exception. He lingered in the car for a few moments to savor an old Beatles tune, and then I heard the motor die. When he entered the door, I said directly, "It's a *Sara*!" "What?" he said, and I knew that he thought the baby had been born. "No, no. Not yet. I mean the baby is a *girl*! A little girl. Our little Sara O'Connell, the girl you always wanted to meet."

I saw that look in his black-brown eyes again, that longing, that powerful desire to love a child who was just within his reach. As he danced around the room and cried, I died a little inside. *I am not enough. I am not enough! And if Alex changes her mind, I will lose everything. God, don't do this to me, please.*

"It's a Sara," he said quietly through his tears, and he walked silently upstairs, leaving me alone at the bottom of the stairs, my bare feet acutely aware of the cold tile floor.

§

Alex's due date was drawing closer, and my anxiety and fear were unbearable. Jason tried to hold up his end of the charade by acting calm for me, and I was trying, too, but unsuccessfully. I felt afraid and out of control, as though I were in imminent danger. I tried to keep busy, so I relied on my old standby: cleaning out closets.

Like a madwoman on a mission, I straightened and rearranged my clothes and even tackled old boxes of papers from the past. Why did I think that by cleaning out my drawers, my life would get back in order? I was being reduced to my lowest common denominator: fear. I was used to fear, had grown up with it like an old friend. Fear was familiar. As I rummaged through some of my old writings, I found a poem I had written to my sister while I was in therapy. Words were my way of dealing with the past, and the smallness I felt now was reminiscent of our childhood, when I was always terrified.

§

I see you under that heavy table
Hidden by those pillared legs
Crouched so tightly
Dark, blank eyes covered by chubby fingers
Peer through lace to the stage.
Baby sister, who sees you
Amid snarling, screeching beasts
Our protectors
Arms flailing, threatening death.
There is stillness amid the horror

Created by your need to be safe
Stillness as you leave your body for
A safer place.
But what a price you paid for safety!
Numbness upon numbness
Safety at a great price
A worthless porcelain knickknack trembles
Through the china cabinet beside you
Tumbles and is broken
For a moment the drama halts
To assess the damage
One lost trinket tonight, the toll
Not counting, of course, the broken child
Clinging to the strong, sturdy legs
Of the dining room table
Baby sister
Who will protect you tonight
From the screeching monsters?
I would
But I am little, too.

§

I was remembering the past now, which wasn't good, so I tried to escape into denial. It was all too much. The kids were fighting me. Jason was unhappy with them and me. We were terrified of losing the fragile family we had created. Suddenly, the phone rang. I picked it up, still crouched under that dining room table of my childhood, still so very small and alone.

"Alaina?" Alex asked, and I heard a strength in her voice that frightened me.

"Yes, Alex, how are you? I haven't heard from you for so long." My words trailed off weakly. She had all the power now. Did she know it?

"I just wanted to ask you not to call me anymore. I need a few days to myself. Nothing has changed; I just want to be alone." She was resolute, and I was getting smaller and smaller. "That's all I wanted to say. So, I'll talk to you when I'm ready." She hung up, and I slid to the floor of the kitchen and cried. I knew that tone. I recognized it. It was the tone of a mother lion that wants to find a dark place to bear her cubs, that will fight to the death to protect them. God, how I understood her! Yet with that understanding came abject terror. I knew in my heart what she was thinking now: she didn't want to give her baby away. This was no teenager who wanted to give birth and go out and buy a prom dress. No, this was a woman in need, a woman who knew what she was losing. This was a dangerous woman to me—and yet, I understood her. I respected her need to find that cave, bear her baby, cut its cord with her teeth, and lick its tiny chest until she breathed life into it. I knew these primitive feelings. I had had them three times before, and knowing this, I knew that she was in Hell. And so was I.

That night I tried to explain to Jason that all women go a little crazy right before birth; it's as natural as rain and gravity. But I didn't tell him about the power I felt in her voice. Instead, I sat on my kitchen floor and remembered what it was like to give birth: the shift in my core identity, the awe, and the godlike power of creation. In that moment, I loved Alex—and I feared her. In that moment, I wanted to hold her, to comfort her, but she did not want me. I was the last person on Earth she wanted, but maybe I was the only one who could possibly understand. The bond that tied us two together was deepening. She didn't know it. I didn't know it. But that didn't negate the truth of it.

§

CHAPTER 9
Alaina

*T*he day Sara was born was much like the days of my other three deliveries; however, since I was not pregnant, I didn't recognize my labor pains. I clearly remember that in the weeks and days prior to Christian's, Liam's, and Daniella's births, I had gone into a weird zone understood only by other mothers-to-be. I felt a need to clean, to prepare the nest. I got a tremendous surge of energy to clean out closets. I felt antsy and fidgety and lost my patience with anyone unfortunate enough to be within a block's range of my voice. Things weren't right, and no one could right them. It never occurred to me that I was dancing an ancient ritual and that my behavior was normal, instinctual. With all three pregnancies, when my water burst, I stood in a puddle of life's sea, and the proverbial light went on. "Oh, that's the reason I've been so strange. It's time to have this baby." Ironically, I monitored every day down to the last millisecond with each pregnancy yet overlooked the obvious when delivery finally became imminent.

For me, an inner tension built that exploded in an unexplained energy to redo things in the house, and I was a terror if you got in my way. In each case, the explosion had ended with a rainstorm, which suddenly made me feel better—relieved, really—and then the water would break. At least there were a few mortals in those times that could conjure up some sympathy for a rotund, pregnant woman about to give birth. But now, awaiting the call telling us of Sara's birth, there was no sympathy forthcoming; I was just a bitch. I had spoken to Alex on Thursday, the eighteenth, and she had made it clear that she would call me "if and when" she wanted to talk to me. My anxiety increased as she pulled away, and we were helplessly going crazy.

"What does she mean, she'll call us? What the hell?" Jason asked me in a state of utter and dismal panic when I related our latest conversation to him. "Oh, Jason, she's just going crazy because she's getting close. But I am scared to death. She's probably feeling an overwhelming guilt about giving the baby away. Maybe she's realizing the enormity of what she's about to do and is chickening out. And probably the pressure and guilt are being laid on thick right now. All we can do is wait and pray. I hate this so much. A pregnant woman is capable of anything."

I had tried to sound composed on the phone. "Yes, Alex, I understand. I won't call again. I'm sorry for disturbing you." But when I put down the receiver, I felt a hopeless powerlessness and anger at her for cutting me out of the birth and maybe even from the baby itself. I was so busy identifying her symptoms that when I awoke on Saturday morning in a first-class funk, I didn't see that I, too, was showing all the signs of being about to give birth.

I dressed for our mutual run. We were both on edge over the situation, and now, even with each other. Jason was pushing me to exorcise the demons in my disposition, but the faster I sprinted, the more violent I became. "It's just not fucking fair. She can just cut us off now. Why is she doing this to us? Fucking shit! We did everything she wanted. We drove three hundred miles to buy her that Persian cat, complied with every demand, and now she has all the cards, all the power. Shit!" By now I was crying in the street, yelling and venting all the fears we both felt. Jason was numb; after all, he wasn't pregnant, I was.

Jason had scheduled a recital for the next day to deal with the imminent birth in his own way, and we were expecting a hundred and fifty people at our home for it. There was work to be done, and we busied ourselves with preparations: making programs, running to make copies, arranging rental chairs, and fighting with each other. I wanted to explode. I felt like something in me was going to go off and I would be left in thousands of angry little pieces. Jason didn't notice my obvious pregnant state and engaged me in battle, trying hard to fix something that was unfixable. Ultimately, we climbed into bed at nine o'clock, exhausted from preparations and desperately confused and scared. My eyes were swollen from crying the entire day, and in spite of all the work we had done, I felt the urge to spring into action and paint a room or clean out a closet.

That's when it began to rain, and that familiar relief I always felt washed over me. "Thank God; I must have been crazy from all the ionization in the air today before the rain." Jason dismissed my folk diagnosis. I am one of those people who pace the night during full moons and am sensitive to anyone and anything that is negative. He was about to engage me on the topic of whether ions in the air could affect my already despicable mood when the phone rang.

The first words I heard were, "Sara was born at 12:37 p.m. today!" I went numb and cold and hot and prickly all at once. Jason caught my eye and sensed the inevitable. "Oh, God, Alex. Oh, God! Is everything OK?" I asked gingerly and waited. I wanted to ask if she had changed her mind, but I could not bear to hear the answer. I waited . . . and waited. . . . The silence told the story, I feared.

"Yes, I had a quick labor, no stitches. Duncan didn't make the birth, and I had a chance to shower before he arrived. She is perfect!"

She is perfect, and you are going to keep her, I thought, and held my breath. And waited again.

"Yes, we've been playing with her all day, and . . ."

It was over. I knew it; my life was over, too. Our dreams, our life, our future. I was trying hard not to betray my misery or grief. My mind was spinning somewhere in the right corner of the bedroom ceiling, and Jason was boring black eyes into my heart. I knew this was going to break his heart. *This is one you can't fix, Alaina*, I thought. *You can't make this OK. You're out of control.* Perhaps only a few seconds had passed, but in the space I was in, images from my childhood passed before me.

> I am a tiny girl in a crib. I am eighteen months old, and my drunken grandfather has stumbled into my crib. His breath smells of rancid whiskey, and the stubbles of his whiskers feel like tiny razors on my soft innocence. Things become fuzzy and confusing after that. I do not know anything except that I cannot move and that my mommy is not there. "Mommy! Come now!"

I am a child in my home, and my parents are arguing bitterly about my father's drinking. It is two o'clock in the morning, and I am standing in the doorway of our tiny garage-like home. "I'm going to kill you, you son of a bitch!" my mother screams. I turn to my baby sisters, who are sleeping, and wish I were asleep, too.

I am returning home in a cab after a date where I was almost raped. I have no money to pay the cab driver.

I am out of control. I must control my world. I must control my body.

I am floating away from my pain and ultimate nightmares; my inner child is still afraid. I am drawn down from the corner of the room by something that sounds like Alex's voice.

"We're finished saying our goodbyes, Alaina. You can come and get her tomorrow morning." Her voice was utterly without emotion.

"What did you say?" I managed to croak out.

"I've breastfed her all day. She has her immunity from me now. We've taken pictures, and you can come at eleven o'clock tomorrow." She sounded so businesslike, and yet I knew it was all she could do to say the words.

I began to feel immense guilt about wanting to take this baby from this woman who had just delivered her and who probably felt all the things mothers do when they first lay eyes on the miracle of creation— her creation, not mine. I felt I had no right to this baby, yet I also felt that she was meant to be mine. Hadn't she answered my call? Hadn't this tiny creature heard my prayers and come to us? Hadn't Alex simply been the vehicle for Sara to find us again? Part of me believed that, but the rest of me thought that I was a criminal to want this woman's baby. I was confused and torn, and all the while, Jason's eyes told me that what I said would decide our fate, his fate. She had told me that she had breastfed Sara. How in the name of motherhood could a woman hold the child of her own body to her breast and then give her up? I didn't believe her words. I knew better. I had delivered. I had suckled a child. I knew the power of motherhood and creation.

"Alex, I don't know what to say. I can only say that I promise . . . I promise . . ." I couldn't hold back the tears or the agony in my words. "I promise to love and care for this baby. We will love her so much. We will never let harm come to her. I promise. I know this must be very hard for you, Alex. I know." My words trailed off. "God bless you, Alex. God bless you."

"I have to go now. Pick her up at eleven o'clock tomorrow." Click. The sound of the receiver told me that she was beyond speech and beyond reach. I turned to Jason. "Sara was born at 12:37 this afternoon. She's fine. We can pick her up tomorrow, Alex says." We were in each other's arms now, crying tears of joy and terror. It would never be over, the fear.

We couldn't wait until tomorrow. Tomorrow was three hours away, and that was too long. I called the hospital to see if we could come over that night to see Sara. There was a pause as we waited for her to ask Alex's permission. It was granted. We grabbed our shoes and Daniella, who was standing at the foot of the stairs, a little confused herself. She had her own cross to bear. What would this child do to Daniella's status as my little girl? She had to be pondering her future as we sped down the freeway to the local medical center. The rain was beating against our windshield. I realized as I watched the swishing of the wipers that I felt much better, physically. I had, after all, given birth today. I had raved and raged the way I always had on the days my children were born, and I felt that same relief at the first sound of rain on the window. Now I had delivered a baby girl; however, I could lay no permanent claim on this child, who at this very moment was suckling another woman's breast. I knew what Jason could not know, what Daniella could not know: that no woman could suckle a child and then hand her over to another. We drove silently to our future, to our baby, but with each mile closer to the hospital, I felt her slipping away from me.

"Sara, don't let go now. You've journeyed so far to be with us. Don't give up now, baby. We're coming. We love you. We will never be separated again. I promise you, my little angel." My words of supplication were heard only by me and Sara and God. But did God hear only my prayer tonight? What prayer was Alex saying at this very moment? And why should God listen to mine?

§

CHAPTER 10

Alex

*L*abor started at eleven o'clock Friday night. It was very faint at first; I was able to sleep until two. I called Duncan in Berkeley, waking him up. "This is it!" I was trying not to sound alarming. "Can you get here?"

"Are you OK?" he asked. Hearing how tired he sounded, I felt a little guilty for waking him up.

I tried to conceal the concern in my voice. "Duncan, please try to catch the next plane out of Oakland." I needed him to be strong—strong for us, strong for me.

"I think the next plane is out around seven in the morning." Hearing this made my heart sink. I really needed him now. I thought to myself that I didn't want to be alone in this. I'd been alone this whole pregnancy, in all the decision-making, and damn it, I didn't want to be alone in this. Anything but this!

I said, "Duncan, just please be ready to leave on the next plane out. Get here soon." As I put down the receiver, a contraction hit.

Wasn't this supposed to be the best time of one's life? Giving birth? Happiness, joy, and fulfillment? *Right*. All I felt was lonely, helpless, and utterly cheated.

At four in the morning, the contractions were forty-five minutes apart. I lay on my side and whispered to this little girl, "Soon, my little one, soon!" I thought about calling Alaina and Jason, but I needed this time with my baby. Selfish? Yes. For now, she was all mine. The pain, the ache, the life inside me was all mine, and no one could take it away. I did not want to share this with them. *I'm sorry*.

At six o'clock I called Cathy, my birth coach; she said she would be right over. The contractions were twenty-five or thirty minutes apart now and getting stronger. I called the hospital to let them know I would be arriving shortly.

Cathy arrived, and we started breathing exercises and walking. Cathy, a mother of three children herself, never said a word about me giving up the baby. She never questioned me and was always supportive in my decision to give the baby a better life. I would always be grateful to her.

A beautiful day greeted us as we arrived at the hospital. The sun was shining, and it felt warm upon my face. We checked in a little after nine o'clock. The contractions were now five or six minutes apart, and all I could think was, *Where is Duncan? Did he miss the plane?*

The nurse showed us to my room and asked me to change into one of those ugly hospital gowns. The doctor came in and checked me to see how much I was dilated. "Five centimeters," she cheerfully said. "It won't be long now, Ms. Porter. I say by three o'clock you will have your baby." For the first time since being in labor, I was feeling excited. My God, my baby was really coming! And soon! "I'll be back within the hour, so keep up the good work." The doctor disappeared as fast as she had come in.

Cathy was helping me breathe through each contraction, holding my hand and telling me how well I was doing. During each contraction, the pain was so overwhelming that I felt like I wanted to run as fast as I could away from it. Every time a contraction hit, my whole body would tense up against a wave of pain, causing it to hurt even more. I wasn't getting any time to rest between them. I began to feel dizzy and dehydrated, so I was hooked up to an I.V. I told Cathy that I couldn't go on much longer, but she kept on saying that it would soon be over.

Twelve thirty. All of a sudden, I felt like I had to go to the bathroom. The nurse ran in and called the doctor. My room, which had been so silent just minutes before, was suddenly a madhouse, with nurses running everywhere. The doctor came in, and all she would say was, *"Alex, whatever you do, do not push!"* I thought, *Are you kidding me? My whole body is screaming to push this baby out, and you don't want me to push?* My heart started to beat harder. *I am going to give birth.* I had waited so long for this, and the time had come.

At the next contraction, the doctor said to push down as hard as I could. As it hit me, I pushed like I had never pushed before. Cathy yelled, "I see her head!" "OK, Alex, when the next one hits, **push hard!**" the doctor ordered, but before she could finish, I pushed so hard my baby's head came into the world. "OK, Alex, only once more!" I pushed, and my beautiful daughter came into this world, all fresh and pink. I cried with joy, "Please let me hold her!"

The doctor laid her on my stomach, and I wrapped my arms around her. With a trembling voice I had never heard from myself before, all I could say was, "Hello, beautiful one, I'm your mommy." At that moment, and even with Cathy there, there was no one in the room except my baby and me. I didn't care anymore whether Duncan showed up or not. All that mattered was that I had given birth. I felt powerful as a human being. I had done something remarkable, something billions of women have done before me, and that day I joined their ranks by giving the most precious gift anyone could give: life.

Cathy said she wanted to make some phone calls and left the room. The baby wasn't crying; instead, she hummed the whole time I held her. A hospital staff member came in and asked me what her name was to be. "Faith Maria Porter."

Faith Maria Porter. I kept saying her name over and over. The nurse took her and weighed her and cleaned her up, wrapped her in a pink blanket, and gave her back to me. The doctor had come in, and I turned to her and said, "I'm giving my baby up for adoption." I don't know why I said it; it just came out of nowhere. Maybe my soul was saying, "Don't get too close. You made a promise, and you must keep it!" I noticed that the whole room fell silent. No one said a word. No one looked at me.

All of a sudden, I felt the pain—*a pain coming from my very soul*. Only once before had I felt this pain: when I saw my mother's lifeless body in front of me. Now I was feeling it once again. There was heaviness upon my heart, upon my chest, a deep, physical pain inside me.

Suddenly, Duncan came running into the room with his mother behind him. "Am I late? Is everything OK?" When he saw that I was holding our baby, he bent down and kissed me and kept saying how sorry he was for not being there for the birth. I handed Faith to him, this beautiful baby we had created together. All the love that I felt for this man and his child poured out as the tears ran down my face. We were all together, and I was not alone anymore. We took pictures, and I let Duncan's mother hold the baby. She left shortly after with tears in her eyes. I never did ask her how she felt about the baby, and she never said.

Cathy returned, and I told her I wanted to breastfeed my baby. As soon as I put her to my breast, she latched on, and I felt whole. The nurse moved the baby and me to a private room. As soon as we were settled, the nurse let me give Faith her first bath. The whole time, I could not keep my eyes off her. Soon all my friends came to see her. They brought gifts of teddy bears and balloons, and everyone was happy for Duncan and me. They stayed until the nurse told them that visiting hours were over. After they all said goodbye, Duncan, the baby, and I were all alone, and we talked.

"I have to call Alaina and Jason to tell them about the baby. I know they will be angry because I didn't call them when she was born. I hope they'll understand that I needed this time with Faith and you . . . and time to say goodbye."

I called Alaina around nine that night. She picked up the phone, and I said, "Guess what? Our baby was born at 12:37 this afternoon." At first there was silence, then she asked if everything was OK. I tried to sound happy, but I was talking to the woman I would be giving my baby to tomorrow, the baby I worked so hard to bring into this world and whom I loved so much. Now I was supposed to just hand her over to someone that I had just met a few months earlier. Alaina wanted to come and see the baby immediately, but I wanted to wait until the next day. I wanted to say, "No, you can never see my baby! Not now, not ever! She's mine." But I had made a promise to Faith that she would have the best life I could give her, and that life was with Jason and Alaina. So I said, "Why don't you just come tomorrow; it's so late now. You can see her tomorrow." But she wanted to see the baby then, not later. They had waited so long.

After I hung up the phone, the nurse called and said Jason had called the nurses' station and asked to see the baby now but they needed my permission. I wanted to say no again, but I knew in my heart that they had a right to see her. I didn't want to hurt them. The one thing I knew was that I could not bear to see them that night. I couldn't face them, watch them with my daughter in their arms and being so happy, falling in love with her as I had just done a few hours earlier. I put Faith in the nursery so they could be with her and have their time.

At two o'clock in the morning, I knew that they had gone and went to the nursery. I stood there, tears running down my face. How could I go through with this? How could I give this beautiful baby away? I loved her so much. My body ached for her. My heart was dying. I asked the nurse to bring Faith back to my room so I could hold her, be with her, so she would know that I loved her.

Morning came, and I was alone with Duncan and the baby again. We didn't talk much to each other because we both knew what was going to happen. I paced the room like a wild animal, carrying the baby with me, not letting anyone near her. A woman walked into the room and handed me some papers to sign. The papers would release Faith to Alaina and Jason so they could take her home. I knew then that this was the point that I had to either sign or change my mind and walk out with my child in my arms. I handed Duncan the baby and took the pen. My hand shook with each stroke. My heart screamed, "No! No! No!" On the outside, there was only silence and tears.

Leaving the hospital after giving birth with nothing in your arms is the most painful, horrible feeling one can experience. Before leaving Faith, I bent down and kissed her little forehead and whispered, "I made a promise to you that I would give you the best, and I am keeping my promise."

With that promise in my heart, I turned to Duncan and handed the baby to him so that he could say goodbye. I promised to carry with me the smell of her, how she looked at me for the first time. Everything would go with me. No one could take that from me, no one.

We left, and my soul died a little that day. I carried the flowers and balloons my friends had given me in my arms as I left the hospital. Tears blurred my vision. I could hardly take it. It took all my strength to not turn around and run back to get my baby Faith. Duncan was crying too. We didn't say a word to each other; we were each in our own eternal hell.

Alaina had sent me some flowers and a card before I left the maternity ward. I read the card, but the words meant nothing to me right now, and as I reached the car in the main parking lot to get in and leave, the card fell out of my hand. I turned to see that it had fallen to the ground, but I didn't reach for it. Everything was gone now, and this card meant nothing to me. I only felt hopelessness and sadness. My baby was back there, and I was leaving her. This was the right thing to do, right? My God, I was dying.

We drove away in silence, and my breasts began to ache. I had breastfed my baby, and I knew she was hungry again. But my arms were empty. My breasts would ache for hours, as would my heart.

We arrived home. I fell into bed and cried and cried. I didn't want to eat or sleep or breathe. Duncan could only hold me. I deserved this pain. I had lied, cheated, kept secrets, and so I deserved this hell. That night, I had to call Alaina and Jason and see how Faith was. I dialed their phone number, and Alaina's older daughter picked up the line. I said, "Please, may I speak to Alaina?" She said that they were asleep, but I pleaded, "Please tell her I need to speak to her."

Alaina came to the phone, and my trembling voice said, " She is beautiful, isn't she?" "Yes, she is," Alaina said. She asked if Duncan was with me, and I said yes. She tried to comfort me, but all I could do at that point was try to hold on to my sanity. I wanted to say to her, "I have changed my mind and want my baby back!" But I only said, "Love her for me." Now the table was turned. They had the power and the baby and the happiness. They had everything.

That night, I was awakened by a dream that jolted me from my swollen-eyed sleep. I dreamed that I was walking in a crowded store, carrying a pink baby carrier. I walked to the corner of this madhouse and set the carrier all alone in the corner; I looked down at it one last time and walked away. All these people were staring at me and pointing their fingers and screaming, "You're deserting your baby!" All I could do was run, cry, and scream. I tried to reach the baby, but everyone crowded around her, and I couldn't get her back. My demons had begun.

The next day was hell, and dreams haunted my nights. The third morning, a nurse came to visit me. I told her my breasts hurt, and she told me to bind myself tightly so the milk wouldn't come in. That day, Duncan left to go back to school, and I was left alone once again. All my family sent flowers to me, which I found very weird; it felt like a funeral. I had nothing to celebrate. I just let the flowers die.

I called my therapist on Monday to make an appointment to talk to her and have her help me get myself together. That first week, I was a zombie; I cried a lot and walked around, not going anywhere. I received a birth announcement in the mail from Alaina and Jason. It read *SARA ELISE O'CONNELL*. They had changed her name. I started to cry. "Goddamn it! They changed her name!" It was right there on the announcement. I don't remember them ever telling me that they were going to call her something else.

I went to my therapist's office a lot that first month, and she helped me try to get my life back together. I would walk down the street, and people who knew me would ask about the baby. They would invite me to bring the baby over or ask me who was watching her. I would always lie. Lying was my friend; I couldn't tell the truth to most of these strangers: *Oh, I gave my baby up for adoption.* I always had an excuse—she was with her father or a friend. I would promise to bring her the next time. But, of course, the next time never came.

I called Alaina and Jason often, wanting to know about the baby and how she was doing. They always kept it short by saying everything was wonderful or they were too busy to talk. I started getting angry that they didn't want to tell me anything. I really was losing my baby. They got what they wanted, so why bother with me anymore?

A month went by. I called Alaina and Jason and asked if I could come and see the baby, but every time they were always busy. Finally, during one of these conversations, I threatened to take the baby back. I said, "If you take the baby from me, then I'll take the baby away from you!" This scared them, and they called Jack Hartnell, who made an appointment with the therapist so we all could meet and work something out between us.

The morning of our meeting, I was scared; I knew that I was going to see Alaina and Jason, but would they bring the baby? I knew in my heart that Sara had a good home, but I needed to see her. I felt they were pushing me out of her life, and all I wanted was just to know if she was real.

As I approached the building, I saw their car, and in the back was a baby seat. My heart jumped. As I walked in, they came in, too, and sat across from me. I sat down, and the tension was heavy. I pulled out a picture of Duncan and showed it to them, then the therapist appeared and took us back to her office. We all sat down, and I started by explaining that all I wanted was to see Sara once in a while.

I could tell that they were not happy being there, and I didn't want to hurt them. But damn it, *I* was hurting. The therapist said that we all wanted what was best for the baby. Alaina and Jason said they had not tried to keep Sara away from me, but I didn't feel that way. Alaina said that we could work the whole thing out by agreeing on things together. She wrote down my conditions:

1. I wanted pictures and notes once a month.
2. I wanted a call once a month, the timing to be determined by both parties.
3. I wanted to visit the baby and Alaina and Jason once a month.
4. The visit would be with at least one of the parents present and would last one hour.

We agreed to adoption information honesty; this would affirm that if Sara ever wanted to know or see me when she was mature enough, they would assist her in finding me. Sara would determine whether or not a reunion occurred.

We all signed the paper, and I agreed to sign my rights away to Sara before I got to see her. I got up and thanked them—thanked them for the right to see my own flesh and blood. I knew that my attitude was not fair to Jason and Alaina, but this was all I could do to see my baby.

That meeting was a big turning point for me. I felt better now. I wasn't going to lose my baby completely. I was going to be able to see her every month for one year, and that was all I needed. Just to see her one more time! Thank you, God!

§

CHAPTER 11
Alaina

I remember the parking lot, all wet and shiny from the rain, as Jason, Daniella, and I approached the hospital. We were all trembling as we ascended the elevator to the third floor, the maternity ward. It had been seventeen years since my last trip to a maternity ward. The door of the elevator opened. As I stepped out, I saw that there was a dark hue to the ward. It was eleven thirty at night, and the new mothers and their babies were silent.

We approached the head nurse and explained that we were here to see our baby, who had been born that day at 12:37 p.m. The nurse was a young woman of about thirty, sturdy and stern. The nurse looked at me—I will never forget her eyes, as though we were intruders, interlopers, thieves arriving to steal an infant from the arms of her mother. I was too paralyzed with fear to feel emotional. I was sure that Alex had changed her mind in the interim, that Sara lay safely within her arms at this very moment, and that we would never even be able to see her.

The nurse led us to a tiny, dimly lit room. There, in the center of the room, lay a bassinet, and in that bassinet lay a tiny girl, wrapped in pink. She was lying on her right side, facing away from us. Jason's feet did not move, could not move. Daniella's blank face mirrored the emotional paralysis Jason and I both felt. I walked over to Sara. My first glimpse of our baby was of her upturned little nose. It was a perfect ski jump. Her hands were folded to her chin. My heart melted. I was in love. I instinctively reached for her as I had all of my children. It was so natural. I lifted her, and her face turned toward me as her eyes opened. Large, dark blue eyes scanned the distance in front of her little face. An incredible recognition poured over me, and I like to think over her, too. She moved her face back and forth, trying to discern her captor. I wanted to hold her, but I knew that this was not my moment. I lifted her up into Jason's arms. "Here's your baby, honey! Here's your little Sara."

There is a moment after a woman gives birth when she is willing to share her creation. I had felt it before. During pregnancy, the father, no matter how bonded to the unborn child, can never know the relationship a woman has with her own body and her creative abilities. After birth, when the cord is severed and the child becomes a citizen of a larger universe, there is a moment when the mother hands her child to the world, in a sense. It's a kind of, "Here is the child of my creation. Here is my gift to you." It was in this spirit that I handed my tiny daughter to my husband. I wanted it to be like the real thing—because it *was* the real thing. This was not an adopted child. This was my gift, my baby to the man I loved so dearly. I had chosen to become a mother again after raising three children almost to completion. I had been willing to start again because I loved this man so much. Before this moment, I had thought that I had done this act for him, but here in the twilight, I knew that it had been as much for me as for him. I wanted this baby with all my heart. This was a strange, unreal bond of eternity trying to right itself. Sara was my child, my baby.

Jason held his baby daughter for the first time and could only say, "Is . . . is she normal? I mean, is she all right?" I opened the blanket and showed him. "Yes, honey, this is exactly what she is supposed to look like. She is perfect. She is beautiful. God, she is so tiny." Daniella was also in awe. "I want to hold her, I want to hold her." But I knew this was Jason's time. "Can we feed her?" Jason asked the nurse. "Well, she just finished breastfeeding." "What do you mean? I mean, who was breastfeeding her?"

"Her mother, of course!" the nurse quipped curtly. Jason stood up. "She can't do that! We're her parents. We're adopting her. She can't do that!"

"Yes, she can, Mr. O'Connell. Faith is her baby. She has not been released to you yet."

"Faith? This is Sara. What do you mean, 'Faith'?" I knew I had to calm Jason. He was about to lose his composure.

"Her birth certificate reads Faith Maria Porter." The nurse was rude and cruel. Didn't she realize how insensitive she was being? Didn't she realize that Alex didn't want Sara?

"Jason," I stopped him. "Please calm down. We'll straighten this all out," I lied. "She is still Sara's mother until she signs the papers. We have to stay cool."

The nurse left us alone for a while, and we composed ourselves. We tried to feed Sara, but she had, indeed, eaten and was not hungry. She was, however, very curious and gazed at us with uncertain eyes. We were in the hospital with our baby and with absolutely no security that when we returned tomorrow she would be there waiting. We were in the Twilight Zone if there ever was one. We didn't want to bond with this tiny creature lest we be totally and forever devastated. Hell, adoption is definitely not for the weak or cowardly. It takes great courage to ride this rollercoaster. Our experience could be summed up in three words: powerlessness, terror, and hell. No, indeed, this is not for the weak of spirit. You have to want a child more than anything to take this E-ticket ride.

Eventually, we put Sara back into her cocoon-like wrapping and left her with the nurse who had treated us as if we were kidnappers. We would return at eleven o'clock in the morning, but Jason wouldn't be able to accompany me. We had a hundred and fifty people arriving at nine o'clock for a piano recital: all of Jason's students, their proud parents, grandparents, and assorted friends. He had to be there. It was almost midnight and too late to cancel. The show must go on, so Daniella and Jason's mom and I would return in the morning to fetch her—if there was a tomorrow.

As we left, the nurse said matter-of-factly, "You cannot have this child until the mother signs the papers. And you must bring an infant car seat." "OK, thank you," Jason said, and we walked into the elevator and pressed the ground floor button. It might as well have been the "Purgatory" button, because that is where we were going to spend the night. We both knew that.

As we fell into bed at two o'clock, we held each other in a way that we had not done before. We were clinging to life, to our future. We had nothing solid to stand on but our own courage and the fleeting bird of hope whose wings we had grabbed as she attempted to escape our grasp. This was the test of our love, of our commitment, of our dream.

I got no sleep that night, and neither did Jason. We spoke not a word to each other. We didn't have to. Finally, we uttered these simple words: "Goodnight, Jason." "Goodnight, Alaina." "Goodnight, Sara." It had been love at first sight. We were hopelessly and eternally in love with Sara. There was no turning back. We were living now without a safety net.

§

High on the rope
Balancing hope and despair
Risk and loss
I can't do it, I fear
But I am here
With you
No net to catch my fall
Just you and me and the high wire
We call destiny
Without a net
Is what I wanted
Before I knew the costs
And what I'd pay again for you
Without regret
Don't look down or
Back, you say
So forward I step
With a net
Everything to lose
Everything to gain.

§

Morning came as no surprise on April 21, 1991. I was waiting for it. I had not slept a wink in anticipation of returning to the hospital and bringing Sara home; that is, if she was still there waiting for us. I called the hospital as soon as I felt I could and asked what time I could pick her up. The nurse reported that Sara would be ready at eleven o'clock and that Alex wished to spend a little more time with her before she left. I asked if

I could speak to Alex, but the nurse said that she didn't wish to speak to me, only that I could come at eleven.

Nausea intruded on fear, and trepidation on misery. I wanted to scream, to run, and to escape, to rescue. I wanted to die. What was happening at that very moment in the hospital? Was Alex cradling her child? My darkest fears were a reality now. I didn't want to tell Jason that news. I knew that he was hanging on by half a thread, that one word from me would push him over the edge of the abyss. On top of that, we had all the people for the recital arriving soon. We could not afford to panic or falter.

I showered, dressed, and tried to make something of my swollen face. Jason busied himself with preparations for the recital—adjusting the microphones, testing the sound equipment—and passed me silently several times before it was time for Daniella and me to pick up Elise and begin our journey to Sara. I wanted to comfort him, but I needed comfort. I tried to feel hopeful, but there was no hope in me. At the same time, I felt for Alex, lying there in a new nightgown, watching new mothers receive gifts and flowers for the most joyous moment of their lives. How could she possibly withstand the guilt and pressure? I know I couldn't have. But then, I would have never given a baby away. But I had been married, loved, and supported, and she was all alone. I wanted to help her, to comfort her, and I wanted her baby, my baby. I was torn between two emotions: compassion and selfishness. Now I felt guilt. I was a thief. It was as if I had planned a kidnapping and was about to perpetrate this heinous crime against an innocent young woman—and yet, I prepared for the crime with numb stoicism.

Daniella and I pulled away from the house, and the last look I had of Jason was him standing in the driveway. We were truly two lost souls, powerless and desperate. His look said, "Bring home my baby!" That is exactly what I wanted to do more than anything in the world, but what was happening in the hospital? Was Duncan holding his child and realizing that he couldn't go through with it? Was he realizing that he truly loved Alex? Was he asking her at this very moment to marry him? I knew that was her secret desire. Yet, Alex had always said that she wanted him to want her without the baby. How well I understood that; I wanted Jason to want me without Sara, to want me just for me. In that respect,

Alex and I shared a common need. Our car disappeared from Jason's view as we headed for Elise's house.

Elise was visibly fearful when she got into the car. It's funny how you don't have to say a word at times like this; everyone knows what's going on. Everyone plays his role. Everyone endures. We were all cued up for the scene to come.

As with my previous births, all of which were precipitated by rain, the storm gave way to a beautiful, sunny day, and today was no exception. The sun glistened on the damp pavement where it had rained the night before. We entered the hospital lobby like prisoners awaiting sentencing . . . three criminals about to hear their punishment. I stepped to an in-house phone and called the maternity ward. We were early. We were informed that we needed a car seat to take the baby home in. I had forgotten that. We were told that Alex was feeding the baby and would be leaving at ten thirty. It was only nine thirty.

"May I come up and say goodbye to Alex?" I asked politely. After an interminable pause, the nurse came back with the answer, harsh and direct: "The mother does not wish to see you. Come back at eleven." I stumbled back to Elise and reported the news. I didn't want to end things this way. I wanted to give her something, but I didn't know where anything was in this part of the city, where to go, what to buy. Besides, it was nine thirty on Sunday morning, and no store would be open. I saw some small vases of flowers in the hospital gift shop and looked them over to see if something was presentable enough to send to Alex's room. I settled on a small bouquet of roses, slightly wilted, but they were the best thing there. I paid the twenty dollars and scribbled a few words to her.

Dear Alex,

We will always be together.
Sara will be safe in our keeping.
I will always love you.

Love,
Alaina

My words fell abysmally short of my feelings, but my heart could not muster anything else. What could I say? What does one say at a time like this? Alex had cut me off. She had cut us out of the delivery, and now she was probably figuring out a way to cut us off from Sara. I couldn't even blame her. *God, forgive me for wanting this child at another's expense.* I didn't think God was listening.

"Let's go buy a car seat." I gestured to the door, and Elise and Daniella obeyed, grateful that someone, anyone, had found an escape from the tension. We drove south for a few miles only to find ourselves deeper into a residential area. We turned around and drove north for a while. We finally found a shopping center and saw a Sears. "They always have car seats at Sears. Let's go there," Elise offered.

We parked and entered—right into the infant department. Momentarily, our fears subsided as we looked around for a safe and decent car seat for Sara. After we decided on one, Elise threw in a few other things: a couple of receiving blankets, a rattle, a Gerry carrier. She was obviously thrilled and excited. We stood at the counter, and Elise took out a hundred-dollar bill to pay. I motioned in protest, but she countered, "No, let me. George and I want to do this for our granddaughter." The sound of those words felt like a heavy weight on me. I wanted everyone to be happy, but in order for us to be happy, a young woman had to be unhappy. This was the E-ticket. I felt like the little child that I was, wanting to please everyone yet knowing deep inside that I was not enough. I was filled with shame.

"We have to get back to the hospital right away," I said. The saleswoman asked, "Oh, did someone just have a baby?"

"Yes, I did. Yesterday!" I added proudly.

"Wow, you sure look great!" We all started to laugh out loud. It was therapeutic and contagious, and a giddiness overtook the seriousness of the event.

"Yes, this was my easiest pregnancy. A great labor!" I quipped, and we laughed again. Something in me didn't want to reveal the secret. I wanted this young woman to think I had actually delivered my baby myself. I hadn't wanted to share this moment with another, but I finally confessed, "Well, actually, I adopted a baby, and we're off to pick her up now."

"Oh, how wonderful. How wonderful." I learned then and there that people are a little in awe of people who adopt. Often, they can't comprehend how one could love and accept another person's child. But then, to me, Sara was not another person's baby. She was mine, returned to me after lifetimes of searching. I felt ownership. I felt pride. For a few moments, we had transcended the fears we had brought into the store.

On the ride back to the hospital, though, as the clock recorded ten forty-five, we all went a little rigid. We parked. The sun was bright now, and the pavement had dried completely. As we approached the entrance to the lobby, my eye caught sight of a tiny card lying in the gutter, floating actually, down toward the drain-off. Had I been there thirty seconds later or earlier, I would have missed it. I stopped. My heart stopped. I bent over and picked it up. The words were blurred but visible:

Dear Alex,

> We will always be together.
> Sara will be safe in our keeping.
> I will always love you.

Love,
Alaina

Alex had been here. Now she was gone. But the real question was, was Sara with her? Had she thrown this meager offering into the gutter as a way of saying goodbye? I could not breathe, but I managed to slip the card into my coat pocket. "It's the card I wrote her, Mom."

"Oh, my god. What does it mean?" Elise couldn't conceal her panic.

"I don't know, but I do know that Alex is gone. Come on." I took her arm on one side and Daniella's on the other. We pressed the elevator button for the third floor and ascended to our fate, silent, motionless, and numb. What was to be had been decided. We were not in control.

The door opened, and my eyes were flooded with the bustle of morning rounds. Babies were crying, mothers were shuffling down the hall trying not to tear their episiotomies, nurses were walking to and fro with layettes and formula. We approached the nurses' station cautiously, and I tried to croak out the words I needed to say.

"My name is Alaina O'Connell, and I am here to pick up my adopted child, Sara." There! I had said it. It was just a matter of time now. I tried to hold on.

That day, the nurses were kinder to us. They saw our joy, or maybe they realized that we were the ones who wanted this baby. We were not the villains, after all.

"Come this way. Sara is ready!"

I don't think I have ever heard or will ever hear such beautiful words: "Sara is ready!" Alex had made her choice, and in doing so, she had chosen for us. This twenty-seven-year-old woman-girl, who had just given birth, had decided the fate of an entire family.

Elise was tearing up, and Daniella was glued to me in anticipation. I unpacked a nighty I had bought to take Sara home in and began to unfold it. We found her exactly where she had been the night before, but this time she was awake, and I noticed she was dressed in a new little outfit, not the hospital gown of the night before. I knew it was from Alex and realized that it was her gift to Sara, so I stuffed my Dior nighty back into the carrying case. *Let her have this,* I said to myself.

"Hi, my dolly girl. Mommy is here and is taking you home. And look who's here, too. Sister and Grandma." Sara responded to my words immediately. I noticed her heel all bandaged from her PDQ test and the blood stains on her tiny foot. As I lifted her into my arms, a familiar sensation of wonder greeted my senses. *This is bliss,* I thought, but I also thought of the grief in Alex's heart as she drove somewhere in the city, empty and alone. Hell.

Elise opened her arms to cradle Sara as I signed the papers that would release her to us. I noticed Alex's signature and made a mental note that it was shakier and more erratic than the handwriting I had seen in her letters. No wonder. She must have had a hard time signing those papers. God, I will never know just how hard—and yet, she had done it. She had breastfed her daughter for one whole day and still had given her up, a feat I was to learn rarely happens. It attested to her resolve for her life, I guess, or to her confusion, or to fate itself. I would never know.

Papers signed, we made our way to the elevator, where I noticed two couples arriving to retrieve their adopted children—fellow E-ticket riders. There was an instant of recognition as we passed. We headed for the exit, but just before we left, I said, "Hold Sara, Daniella. I want to let Jason know all is well."

I ran to the phone and dialed. Actually, I had to dial several times, because my fingers were shaking so much. I knew that he would be in the midst of the second recital at this point and would probably not hear the ringer. Normally, we turned the ringer off during recitals so that the phone wouldn't disturb a performance. But this time, it did ring. I fingered the tiny card in my hand as I waited for either Jason's voice or the tape to come on.

You have reached 206-555-3457. We're not here right now, but if you leave your name and number, we'll call you right back.

My message was short: "We're coming home, Daddy! We're coming home."

§

CHAPTER 12

Alaina

Elise, Daniella, and I left the hospital with Sara. I sat in the back seat as Elise drove; I didn't use the car seat. I held Sara in my arms, simply looking in awe at her tiny face, large blue eyes, and roaming gaze. I smelled her head and wondered if Alex had done the same thing; it was so natural to want to take in all that innocence. Daniella kept looking back at Sara from the front seat. I saw in the rearview mirror that Elise was smiling. What a journey we were making. We couldn't go directly to my house because Jason still had over a hundred people there for his recital. We went instead to Elise's house, where George, a new grandpa, was waiting.

We entered the house. I placed Sara on the couch and unwrapped her so that everyone could admire this treasure. It was like opening a Christmas present; all eyes were upon her. It had been seventeen years since I had changed a diaper, but it was as if it had been yesterday. My hands just knew what to do. I was a mother, born to be a mother, born to be this baby's mother. Yet, lingering in my mind was the knowledge that Alex was out there alone in the world, and my heart cried. I said nothing to anyone; it was a knowingness I was sharing with Alex.

Finally, Jason called to say that the last of the guests had left and it was safe to bring Sara home. Daniella and I packed her in the car and drove ever so carefully home. Jason was waiting in the yard, pale and trembling, when we pulled into the driveway. He wanted his baby. He wanted to hold her. He wanted to feed her. He was so in love. I stood back to watch this man I loved so much and wondered if he knew what was happening, this bonding, this eternal, forever love that no power on Earth can undo.

I could see Daniella's maternal instincts emerging, as well. Gone was any trace of threat in her eyes. We were all like children admiring an exquisite prize, won at a great price.

By the time bedtime rolled around, the stress of the last weeks had begun to show. Although we had had the crib prepared for two months, Sara's tiny body was not to touch those sheets for weeks. Jason took off his shirt and lay flat on his back next to me. He placed Sara on top of his strong, muscular chest. Sara lay, stomach down, on top of him. His hands rested gently on her tiny back. And there we fell asleep.

Some hours later, I heard a sucking noise. Sara had rooted around until she had found Jason's nipple and was suckling it. This proved unsatisfactory for her, and we soon got up to prepare a bottle. I felt jealous that she had chosen Jason's nipple to suckle, because the instinct to breastfeed was present in me. Sara drank greedily from her bottle and fell back to sleep. I lay next to Jason for hours watching the two of them, watching him hold his tiny princess. At some point, as the moon shone through our window, I saw her wide eyes gazing at me, and for an instant, I felt an amazing recognition; it was the closest I had ever felt to God.

§

Do you know who you are, my little one
As you gaze searchingly into my eyes?
And do you recognize the voice
That called you from the slumber of another's cradle?
Did your ears tune to listen
As I sang the song to you
No one ever sang to me?
It was I, my sweet child
Who lured you from the depths of eternity
Back into my arms again,
So long separated
So sweet this reunion
And recognition.
Do you know
That you are a child of God
And I am to be both your teacher and student

On this, our newest journey together?
Do you recognize my touch? For I recognize your spirit
As your breath passes my cheek just now.
Welcome to my arms, dear daughter
We are home at last
And you are safe in my heart
To hear the song
No one ever sang to me.

§

A strange and warm peace descended upon me then, and a prayer of thanks went to God. But even in this state of grace, there was a section of my heart reserved for suffering, Alex's and mine. As I watched Jason's and Sara's breathing rise and fall on his chest, I knew that this glorious, frightening, blissful, excruciating journey had just begun.

§

Sometimes I stood off from myself and watched myself with little Sara. How different a mother I was now compared to when I raised the other three. I was awake to every minute experience she had, aware of my own joy and appreciation of her innocence, cognizant of the continuum of life, its passages. I would spend one day with the big kids and find myself talking to opinionated young adults filled with anger, themselves, passion, and humor. The next day I would spend with a baby and see how it all came to be: all the years of caring, work, frustration, and joy. There is sadness, too. They learn to walk, and the first step they take is away; so is every step after that, if we are doing our job right. I wanted that, yet there was the pain of letting go.

Kids do make you crazy. When they are little, you're happy if you survive the day and can't wait until they go to bed. Yet the minute you tuck them in, you feel lonely and want them back. Who can figure out this mystery? When they are grown, you want them back—until they're back. Why? Because they don't like you so much, or if they do, their code of honor forbids them from showing it too often.

Now I watched Sara and was taking the time to really *see*. Twenty years before, I had so much to do. Oh yes, all those important tasks like scrubbing the floors every day, watching the wax build up, and thinking it would glaze over the fears and unfinished business of the past. It didn't help. So much to do! Cook three meals a day, wash all those diapers, entertain all those acquaintances who seemed so important for Johann's career and who dropped me like I was a leper after the divorce. For them I rushed through my children's lives and stressed myself out. What a waste.

Now I let the wash go. I let the housework go. I washed the floors once a month. And I saw my child grow. Never again would I sell my time to strangers. Never again would I justify my priorities to women who called themselves feminists but knew nothing of the feminine. I was a complete woman. I had earned the right to talk about this. I had a man, I knew how to love—finally. I had raised three healthy, angry kids who turned into strong people. I had a profession. I had a baby. I had chosen my own path. I had thought about the consequences and paid the price. I had wrinkles. I sagged in all the appropriate places. I dreamed. I pushed myself. I was alive. There were parts of me that would never be healed, but by God, I at least knew what they were. I suppose that was worth something. I also had feelings that many women would never feel, because I had taken some chances and won a few rounds with life.

Now I looked back at who I must have been at twenty-six, when I first became a mother. I had wanted Christian so much. God knows I almost killed him the first year, trying to do everything right. I fed him too much, I clothed him too warmly; I doted on him. Somehow, the poor kid survived me. I would look into his beautiful peaches-and-cream face and get chills. That I could produce something so wonderful, so miraculous, was magical to me.

As I looked back, I saw that having that child was the one thing I truly felt proud of. There had been precious little else that had been noteworthy in my life. Having come from the family I did, I had always carried the feeling that I was not as good as anyone else. I always felt separate. But this baby, my son, made me feel like someone. That was probably why I set about the task, initiated by me alone, to have two more in rapid succession. There I was, not yet defined myself as a person—*empty* of any sense of self—trying to be the perfect mother to three children, three babies. I lived in a sea of diapers and earaches, visits to the pediatrician's office, food shopping, and everything else that goes with having children.

Now I tried to picture myself back then and find Alaina, but she eluded me. She had become a *mother*, and this metamorphosis had pushed out the buds of the person. I remembered going crazy every once in a while when the responsibility got to be too much. I remembered calling my mom, only to hear, "You made your bed, now lie in it." She was always overly empathic, my mother. Take a minute to enjoy these wonderful babies? No time! There were dinner parties to prepare for Johann's colleagues, babies to feed, bruises to bandage. But the gaping wound inside me lay open and unattended and unnoticed, by me or anyone else.

Now I could say, "Fuck the housework!" That was freedom. But, of course, that would have been impossible if I hadn't been married to Jason, who wanted to do half the work, be a partner, and not just have a slave. However, I was angry with myself for blooming so late in life. I was twenty before I had my first independent thought, thirty before I questioned the order of things. I was thirty-five before I got mad or felt mad. And I was forty before I decided to do something about it. I was slow, one might say. Now I was angry that I was unconscious for so long. I wish I could have forgiven myself for taking this long to start, but I was sure I wasn't alone.

So, at forty-five years old, I had walked into a hospital, took an elevator to the third floor with my seventeen-year-old daughter and mother-in-law, and entered a nursery, where I was handed this perfect and wondrous child. All the pain of a lifetime had faded as I saw her tiny features and large, bright eyes scanning my face. "Yes, I am your mother. And though I will be older than some of the kids' moms when you're in school someday, I will be totally yours. I will have time for you. I will not put housework, dinner parties, and other assorted inanities in front of you. You will be the most important thing. I will put down the vacuum, buy disposable diapers, cook fewer meals, and be more to you. This is what I have learned. I will be aware of how I feel. When I am angry, I will say it instead of harboring the unspoken rage for months on end, only to explode for 'no reason.' I will hug you more than I criticize you. And I will love you more by loving your father best. I will show you how to be a woman, not a martyr. I feel like I am ready to be a mother because there is someone inside of me to give to you. I feel sad for my other children, who were suckled by a lost child. She is gone now—no, she is within me, but she is stronger now."

I jokingly referred to my marriage of eighteen years with Johann as my "first lifetime," because it produced and I raised three children to young adulthood, brought a new PhD graduate to national renown, and grew me up, so to speak, from a fragile, scattered mother and reluctant faculty wife to a competent teacher, experienced mother, and the bud of a complete human being. Then, in 1989, I reincarnated into a new marriage with a musician, and things began to go a little crazy—at least to my unconscious mind. Jason questioned my routines, my "givens." "Why do we have to eat three meals a day?" "Why does a meal mean 'meat'?" "Why do you have to do this now?" Why? Why? Why? Of course, as he was asking all these questions, I was busy at work and trying to change him into my first husband.

It never occurred to me when we courted that I would have to alter my life; I just thought I was exchanging men, from a traditional European who flourished with precise timelines for dinner, vacation, and sex to a Bohemian who had rarely known a boss. Jason made his own rules, went for days without food if he wasn't hungry, and had only a single yogurt in the refrigerator. Food was a problem because, for me, food meant love. It was the aromatic fragrances emanating from my mother's kitchen that translated into affection for me as a child, because my mother could not touch in comfort. One of my methods of bestowing affection, then, had always been to prepare food. Just to watch my children devour a meal was bliss. I felt like a good mother. Suddenly, Jason was asking me to skip a meal here and there or eat a bowl of cereal instead of preparing anything. I felt that one of my techniques for validation had been removed. How could I be lovable if I couldn't provide these love services?

But in no area was I more threatened than in the sacrosanct ground of motherhood. Motherhood was not next to godliness, motherhood *was* godliness. I had defined myself by this title and had no greater hubris than in my role as mother, earth woman, savior of the children, and feeder of the hungry—nurturer. Johann had enjoyed my taking this responsibility. It freed him up to write and get ahead professionally. Our roles were defined clearly, and we each respected the other's territory.

But Jason was not your typical man. In some ways, he was more feminine than I was. I both liked this and hated it. He cared little for convention, timelines, or roles. In fact, he always wanted to be Mr. Mom. I used to say that Jason had the body of a man but the soul of a woman. This profound need to protect and nurture was what attracted me to him, first through his music and then through his relationship with me. Johann had changed an actual diaper only once with our three kids, so I assumed that Jason would be the same way. I thought that bringing our new baby home from the hospital would be a nostalgic experience, one that I could simply pick up from where I had left off seventeen years before. I was in for a rude awakening, as my mother used to say.

When Daniella and I had brought Sara home from the hospital and unloaded all six pounds and fifteen ounces of our precious cargo, I had no idea what was in store. Jason came running to meet us, swooped Sara into his arms, and disappeared into the house, where I found him atop our bed with Sara. He examined her millimeter by millimeter as a jeweler might a precious gem. I told him we needed to change her diapers, and he wanted to do it. I recalled, amusingly, that Johann asked me once where I kept the diapers. Daniella, our third child, was one year old at the time. So this was new, Jason wanting to change Sara's diaper. It was nice, but a strange jealousy began to move in me. My other three babies had been mine. They knew it, I knew it, and no one questioned it. I would have to share this baby, though, and a part of me didn't like the idea at all. The thought crossed my mind that Jason had promised that it would be easier for me this time around, that things would be different, but I hadn't yet realized how much.

Sara began to fuss a little, and I checked my watch to see if she might be hungry. Jason jumped up. "I'll feed her." "No, honey, I'll feed her, no problem," I quickly interjected. "No, I want to. Please! This is my first baby." His eyes were determined. At that moment, I was torn between wanting to allow him this pleasure and wanting to open my blouse to offer a breast so that he would be excluded from the whole process. But my breasts were empty this time, and I was going to have to share this tiny creature with a new kind of man, one who wanted to be totally involved.

He returned with the bottle, and Sara's large eyes roamed the face of this pivotal figure in her life: Daddy. I rejoiced for her good fortune and waited my turn. I began to feel a deep pain within me, a nameless, monstrous pain that emerged from nowhere. Seeing the love and nurturing Sara was receiving from her father was making me feel something I didn't want to feel. There was a great hole in my soul that was now beginning to make itself felt—the emptiness of not having had a father who adored me or wanted me. I stood by and watched how it was supposed to be. It hurt, and yet it was healing. In a sense, I could be a baby again and be loved by my daddy. Jason had no idea at the time that my own need for a father was awakening and that, in addition to his roles as friend, husband, and lover, he would now be a father to two new daughters, for there was a part of me that wanted to be his little girl, to be cherished, adored, valued above all things. But a rivalry was forming in my mind. Jason wanted to do so many tasks involving the baby, and my time-worn identity as "mother" was in grave jeopardy.

I had only six weeks off from work, and time was flying by. Soon I would be back at work, missing all the bonding and fun and love, and so I began a non-post partum father envy, a where-do-I-fit-in, adoptive-mother depression. I doubt if there is such a category for this in the DSM IV, but I had it anyway. Jason and I began to argue. I must admit, I was probably the most at fault, because I was the one who was the most threatened. I obviously knew how to care for a child, but Jason's comments made me feel inadequate: "She doesn't like that!" "She won't eat that, Alaina; she likes her fresh applesauce mashed up more." "Don't feed her now; she's not hungry!"

I began to cry a lot. My whole identity was at stake here. Jason was enjoying parenthood and had no clue of the effect he was having on me. "I am the mother, Jason! Let me make some decisions." "What are you talking about? Of course you're the mother." But he didn't get it. I would be sitting at work, knowing they were together, and I would feel so isolated, so left out. "You already have three children! Let me have this, please."

Why are situations so complicated with humans? I saw a triangle, an intra-dynamic rivalry, shaping up. First, I was jealous of Jason because he got to play mommy and I was cut out of the loop all day long. Then, I was jealous of Sara. She, after all, was getting all this father love that

I longed for more than I cared to admit. I wanted Jason to hold me all night, comfort my every fear, and feed me. I was reverting to my own infancy, and the father emptiness I felt—had never before allowed myself to feel—was attacking me. And then there were the other three children, all teens, who were also jealous and threatened about everything that was happening. The house became a battlefield. Each of us was fighting for some territory, a piece of the pie, and a piece of the love. One could almost taste the feeling of scarcity.

Once I sat down and wrote out the conversations I experienced over a couple of days:

Married Again with Children: The Blended Family

Jason: Alaina, do you know that those boys slept until ten o'clock this morning and then just lay around for two hours?

Christian: Mom, did you know that Jason was upstairs with the baby all day long and didn't even talk to us except for the screaming at six in the morning? He is only nice to Sara.

Liam: All Jason does is criticize us. He doesn't love us now that he has Sara, the real kid. I told you this would happen, Mom.

Jason: Those kids are in the fridge all day. Don't they realize what it costs and that we are under no obligation to feed them?

Christian: Why does Jason begrudge us every bite of food we eat? Isn't this our home?

Jason: When I was eighteen, I was on my own. No one gave me a cent. These kids have it too good. They don't appreciate anything I do for them.

Liam: I know it's hard on you, Mom. I can see that you want us all to be happy. But Jason is not happy when we're here. He doesn't need us anymore.

Christian: Jason doesn't respect that we're men now. I am not a little kid who doesn't question his unreasonable ultimatums. If he would treat me like a man, we would get along better.

Jason: I am the man here. Don't put me in the same category with those boys. I am the man!

Liam: Maybe Jason is upset because we're taller than he is now.

Daniella: You don't listen to me. You have Sara now. You don't care about me anymore.

Jason: Alaina, Liam is upset that I want the biggest piece of chocolate cake. I get the biggest piece because I am the man.

Liam: Mom, Jason won't let me have the piece of cake I want. I always get this piece. You promised me the middle piece. That's the way we do it.

Jason: I notice, Alaina, that you made meatloaf again. You always make the boys' favorites, but you go out of your way to avoid making the kind of food I like.

Daniella: We haven't had meat in such a long time. Do we always have to eat that health food crap that Jason likes?

Liam: I'm hungry, and you don't cook anymore.

Jason: You haven't made macaroni in six months. The last time you made it, you put spicy cheese in it. I think that is a passive-aggressive act!

Christian: When do we eat? There's never anything to eat in this house.

Jason: I'm afraid that you will choose the kids over me.

Boys: You only care for Jason. But we are your flesh and blood. Don't we count anymore? Jason wants us out of the way so you, he, and Sara can be the perfect little family.

Daniella: Don't call Sara "the Bobitz." That's my nickname when I was a baby. I love her, but I'm jealous of her sometimes, too. She needs to get her own nickname.

Jason: Alaina, you have really changed. You are not loving anymore.

Christian: Mom, I can't live like this. I'm moving out, and you won't see me again.

Liam: Mom, Jason doesn't want us.

Jason: Alaina, you're angry again. You are always angry.

Jason: I can't have sex if the kids are in the house.

Liam: I just wanted to be his real son.

Christian: Jason got to play tennis after the gym today, and then he took three naps during the day. What did you do today, Mom? I mean after teaching all day. He's using you.

Liam: Jason is jealous because you love us. He doesn't realize that you love him more than us. He doesn't know how you used to be with us.

Jason: I never took anything from anyone. I am a man.

Daniella: Mama, I'm sick. Make me something.

Sara: Waa! Waaa! Waa! Ga ga.

Liam: You made Daniella Cream of Rice when she was sick. Now you're too tired to make me anything.

Jason: Oh, I see that you made meatloaf tonight.

Alaina: *I AM GOING FUCKING CRAZY.*

August 1991

I felt for my older children and the predicament that my choices had created for them. They knew I was not the mother who had raised them. They knew that I was trying to please Jason, but in doing so, I was confusing and angering them. They were trying to grow up amid all this change and with this new mother, and they didn't much like it or me. I didn't blame them. Every time I submitted to Jason's rules, I felt I was betraying them. Blended families are not for sissies.

The man I had built a pedestal for had feet of clay. His petulant and infantile insistence on being the man made me wonder if I had married a man at all or if I had married an adolescent who was trying to work out his own issues at the expense of my children. I remember so well one evening when, shortly after Sara was born, Liam told Jason with tears in his turquoise eyes, "Now you don't need me to be your boy, do you, Jason?" Jason barely let those words in as he cradled his baby girl, and something in the pit of my stomach told me that Liam was right. The fairytale I had conjured as my second marriage had major flaws, but now I had a new baby and another job to do: be Sara's mother.

Each of us was struggling with the new rules and roles. I was so caught up in needing Jason's love that I failed to see my own flesh and blood crying out for normalcy. I wondered how many men and women had gone through this when they tried to create a new family out of the remnants of old ones. Sometimes the writing is on the wall, so you just look out the window. I don't think my older children would describe it that nicely. I was failing them on many levels, but I was too blind to see it, too confused to ask for help, and too busy to notice that all my values and beliefs were being scrambled.

Last but certainly not least was Alex, who called every couple of days, always describing herself as Sara's mother. There were no guidelines for any of this. Maybe adoptive mothers who have never given birth themselves didn't grapple with these issues. Who could find sympathy for a woman who had it all?

I felt alone, like the first fish that crawled out of the depths of the ocean and onto dry land. It was evolution, progress, but it was damned hard. I was having to live on dry land, but there was no signpost that read "You're on track today!" or "No, you're off a little; just veer to the left." I was lost. I only knew that Sara had three mothers: Alex, Jason, and me, and I wanted to be the only mother. Something had to give, and it looked as if it would have to be me. I began talking to myself.

Just because you did it differently before doesn't mean it has to be that way this time. This is a new time. It's OK to share Sara. You are her mother. Let Jason have her, too. She can only benefit from all that acceptance. Alex is also her mother, and someday Sara may need her. Let go! Open your heart, Alaina! What's to fear? There's enough love to go around. Stretch! Grow! Expand! Learn! Get ahold of yourself, Alaina!

As life would have it, those wise words from my inner voice, my higher self, the unwounded child within, were interrupted by Alex's voice on the phone. "I've decided not to sign the final papers releasing Sara unless you agree to let me visit her once a month for the first year of her life. If you're nice to me, I'll be nice to you and won't take back my baby. So when can I come over? Remember, I am the mother!"

No, Alex, I am the mother. No, Jason, I am the mother! No! Where exactly did I fit in? And where in the hell was the instruction book? Now I had a new enemy: the phone. Now the phone could strip me of my role as mother, and the long wait was about to begin.

§

Every time the phone rings
Potential loss looms
Will she change her mind
Today?
As I rock my daughter to sleep
I wonder
If she will be in my arms tomorrow
Dependent on whim and folly
How great this love
How great the loss
Could be
Every time the phone rings
I cringe
No one deserves this much
Power
Please, Alex
Don't call today.

§

The instant I put down the receiver, I dialed our adoption attorney. "What does this mean, Jack? Can she do this? We agreed to all her terms. We agreed to support her therapy for another month, to give her rent for another month. Can she keep doing this? I'm so scared!"

Jack Hartnell was the incarnation of serenity, a man whose higher purpose was to connect children with loving families. He was empathetic and kind to birth mothers. He was a master counselor. He was a man of God. His voice was calm and did not betray concern, even if he felt it.

"Listen, you're ahead already. She breastfed Sara for twenty-four hours and still gave her up. No one on Earth would have laid odds on that. She just needs assurance that you're not going to drop her. She's afraid, too. Why don't you all meet with the therapist and talk it out?"

My heart opened a little with his words. We set the appointment, and a more rational part of me understood that for birth mothers, their fifteen minutes of fame end when the baby is handed over. Alex had probably never been so cared for in her whole life as she had been during the last few months. We had supported her financially, called her, sent flowers, bought her a Persian kitten, wrote letters, and put our destiny in her hands. It had to be hard for her knowing that all of that would come to an end when the adoption was legally finalized. I could understand it, but, nevertheless, I resented her power and the tenuous line we had to walk.

What-ifs were stepping all over each other in my mind. *What if she sees Sara and wants her back? What if she is milking us dry financially and then will reclaim Sara with no regard for us? What if Sara is taken? Could Jason and I survive the loss? What if I say the wrong thing in the session? What if . . . what if . . . ?*

It was too scary, in fact, to think about, and little by little, as the day for the session neared, Jason and I would catch ourselves looking at Sara in fear. "What if she's taken away? Could anyone be that cruel?" Yet one had only to pick up the newspaper to know such things were happening more frequently and that judges were finding for the birth mothers, as if the one who gave the child up should have more rights than the people who chose her. And never, it seemed, did a judge consider what it would be like for a child who had bonded with her parents to be ripped from their arms, what irreparable damage would be done. I, who could not bear to leave my cats at the vet overnight lest they suffer trauma, and I, who never trusted a babysitter with the first three kids, was haunted by specters of my baby Sara lying afraid in a strange crib, crying for her mommy and daddy. Every inner demon button I possessed was being pressed. Memories of my own fears as a small child were encroaching on my dreams now, memories I had hidden from myself. Too much was happening, and it was happening too fast. I couldn't assimilate it all. I was going to have to resolve some things, but I honestly didn't know where to start.

The day of the therapy session arrived. I dressed for the meeting in a dazed panic. Jason passed by me several times, eyes filled with rage and territorial armor. He was a patriarchal time bomb, and I had to be strong and try to tap into whatever counseling skills I had left. After all, I did feel an incredible bond to Alex in spite of her behavior and demands. I knew she was on a rollercoaster herself.

Sometimes I lay awake wondering how empty and dark Alex's nights must be, belly still stretched from life yet no life sucking at her breast, no life to cradle in her arms, no one to hold her as she grappled with her decisions. Had she merely gone numb to survive her choice, or was she writhing in spiritual hell, riddled with guilt and longing to undo what she had done?

When the day came, I tried to dress nonthreateningly. We left Sara with Jason's mom so as not to show Alex how adorable she was. We were afraid—no, we were terrified. We arrived an hour early, awaiting the appointment in a parking lot across the street.

Alex caught my eye first. I had not seen her since she was nine months pregnant, and no woman should be judged then. She had suffered from toxemia and had gained a lot of weight. So had I with my pregnancies. Today, she was different. I watched her saunter across the street, mini-skirted, platinum hair, stylish and short low-cut halter top, and mesh hosiery. Wow! This was definitely not the woman whom I had met in Jack Hartnell's office three months earlier. This girl was *back*! I suddenly felt old and threatened; not only was she going to take Sara back, but she was going to take Jason with her. Demons!

We followed her into the office, the décor of which was too corny to be believed. Apparently this adoption therapist wanted the birth mothers to feel comfortable, so her office was packed with stuffed toys and cute little dolls, which seemed to me would have the opposite effect by reminding them of babies and thus their loss. I had to move a teddy bear to sit down. Everything had this "country home" feeling to it. I wanted to throw up. The therapist herself, though nice enough, was obviously one of those eternal aunt-types who would never marry but would play aunt to all her friends' children. *What could she possibly know about this?* I thought. I couldn't even begin to describe the look I saw on Jason's face. We held hands, our knuckles white with fear.

After some small talk, Alex gave a run-down of what she wanted: She wanted to visit Sara once a month to see how she was doing. She wanted to bring Duncan, the birth father, along. She wanted to be able to call us whenever she wanted, but she didn't want us to disturb her—ever. Mainly, she didn't want to feel as if we had just used her to get a baby; she wanted to feel that she was a person, too, and of value to us.

We were being manipulated. We sat there and acquiesced to everything. What choice did we have? None. Zilch. Nada. *Nichts.* The therapist frantically wrote out all of Alex's wishes, and we signed them. We had made no requests. We did want assurances that she was going to keep her end of the promise, but we were not to get them. I was very angry, but I was also hearing her real message. I didn't hear that she wanted Sara back, but I did hear that she wanted to be valued and wanted, not just discarded. These were the same things I wanted myself.

I watched Alex from across the room; her long legs were crossed high on the mesh tights, her animated eyes looking very much like my baby's eyes, who was sleeping at her grandma's house. I saw a little girl who needed love, who needed to know that she was loved for herself and not just for what she had produced. It was clear that she did not really want to lose her new family, and it was to this little girl I spoke. "Alex, have I ever made a promise to you that I didn't keep?"

"No, you've always done what you said," she responded.

"Then I promise you now that you can visit Sara for the first year of her life and that we will honor all of your requests. You are Sara's birth mother. To hurt you would be to hurt Sara. We will not do that." I meant every word; I really did. As angry as I was, the mother in me felt Alex in my heart. I saw through the mesh nylons and the false bravado; this girl was in pain. Although I ranted and raved all the way home, I knew that I would keep that promise. Her gift to us had been too great to renege on. It was almost May 15, and that meant that she would be visiting us the next week.

That night, with Sara one month old, Jason agreed to let her try her own crib. I stood for a long time, looking at her tiny countenance. My prayer was to God, the host of angels, and the Devil himself if he was listening. *Please, God, do not take our baby from me. And please, for the love of all that's holy, don't take Jason's baby from him. He would die. Sara is home.*

She has traveled so far to be with us. We are her parents. We love her. She is not a whim, a doll. Please, God, I'd give my life for her right this minute. Take me now, but don't take her from Jason. I ask in the name of the God of my childhood, the God of the universe. Amen.

It would be almost a full year before I knew if God had heard my prayer.

§

We had planned an ecumenical baptismal service at Union Lake for Sara. Even in the midst of the looming disaster of Alex changing her mind, we went ahead with it and found an incredibly beautiful and quiet spot.

Right away we had a problem of what to say and who would say it. Those who were going to be present represented many different religions. We all—Jason and I; my other three children; Jason's parents, sister, and brother-in-law; my best friend and her husband—represented Christianity, Judaism, New Age, you name it. Jason's brother would do the ceremony. We solved the problem when I decided to write a dedication, and after I read it, everyone would get a chance to speak as his or her heart dictated.

The day of the service, the wind was blowing, and my papers were flapping in it. Jason held Sara. My son Liam gathered some water from the lake. My words were simple and from the heart.

> Some people don't believe in miracles, but I do. When everyone around us said that it was not possible to find you, I knew in my heart that you were already out there and that if we could only open ourselves, you would find us. And you did. Today we celebrate the miracle that is you, Sara. You have come into our lives, bringing joy and hope to everyone. You have traveled far to find a home with us, and we are grateful for you. We couldn't love you more if you had come from our own bodies; in fact, our bond transcends mortal ties, for we have chosen each other to learn and grow together.

Sara, our family is diverse. We come from many walks of life and from many beliefs. We will not limit you with the rules and conformities of any given system, for to do so would be to build walls, and you are free. Today we dedicate you to God, the same God who created this beautiful Earth, the same God who created the love in us all that brought us together as a family.

Today we say thank you to God for blessing us with you, and we promise that your life will be one of peace and joy. We promise to allow you to grow unhampered by fear and limits—to be your best self. When you fall, we will be there to pick you up. When you falter, we will steady your steps. Our love will always be there, unconditional and strong. You have only to reach out to find our hands. Sara, your life will be special, because you are the union of two whose spiritual love created the space for you to enter. It is our prayer that you will find ways in your own life to return this love to the world.

Today we dedicate our lives to you and renew our commitment to each other and your brothers and sister. Today we thank our Heavenly Father for you. And today we baptize you in the name of God, in the name of all that is beautiful and pure on Earth and in the human soul. Sara, you are proof that miracles are possible.

Sara Elise O'Connell, while you waited in the darkness, your tiny knees curled to your chin, the Earth and all her creatures listened for your small voice. While you waited in the darkness, safe from chaos and harm, the entire vast firmament came out to light your path. While you waited in the darkness as in a dream, God was preparing a home for you. For you are a child of God, and everything that is beautiful and true can be seen in your eyes. Look through those eyes at the world and know that your life has great meaning.

Today, we, your parents, celebrate your life and the profound gift that you are. We thank the God of All for the honor of being your parents and acknowledge the sacred charge that has been given us to raise you as a loving, caring human being, to teach you to live in love and not in fear, to guide you to yourself, and to allow you to live your destiny for good.

Our Mother Earth is your sanctuary, the creatures of the Earth are your friends, and all humanity are your brothers and sisters. May you walk a path of peace for mankind, and may you grow in wisdom at the feet of your parents. You have been placed in our care, and *we welcome you!*

Because God is Love, we baptize you in His name and in the name of all that is God in those present. Amen.

We all walked back up the path to where food and drink were waiting. Silently, I finished my prayer in my heart. *And most of all, thank you, Alex.* Somewhere deep within me, I sensed that something else miraculous was happening between Alex and me and that prayer was only the conscious beginning.

§

CHAPTER 13

Alex

I called Cathy and asked her if she would come with me to see Sara for the first time since her birth. It had been a month and a half since I had last seen and held my daughter in the hospital. Now I wanted to look upon her beautiful face again.

I called Jason and Alaina to set a time and date. At first they didn't want me to see the baby because they were scared that I would change my mind. I was angry and scared that they were going to change their minds and not let me come over. I was so scared.

I kept calling to make a time, but they would always have something going on. I felt that they wanted me to sign my rights away before I saw the baby. All I wanted was to see my baby. Hell, I didn't know what my rights were, anyway, so I agreed.

I had to go to the Social Services Department in Seattle, sit in a windowless room with some god-awful woman, and sign three pages that said I did not want my baby and would not attempt to get her back. I hated every moment I was there. I felt like trash. All of this was a nightmare. I wanted my baby. At one point, I wasn't going to sign anything, but I kept telling myself that I had to keep my promise to my baby. I wanted her, but I had signed my rights away, and now she was no longer legally my child. Signing my rights away had been so hard.

After Jason and Alaina heard that I had signed the papers, we finally scheduled a time and day for my first visit, since I was no longer a threat to them. All I ever wanted was just to see my baby.

The day of my first visit came soon, and Cathy being at my side made it easier. Since Cathy had been at the birth, she knew how I felt about everything and understood what I was going through. She had always been supportive, and I needed her, especially, on that day. I was shaking from head to toe by the time we reached Alaina and Jason's house. I had had Sara with me for such a short time after her birth, and I felt like I was going to see her for the first time all over again.

We rang the bell, and Alaina let us in. I had not seen her and Jason for almost two months, and it felt strange to be in their house to visit my own flesh and blood. We were all smiles, and Jason went to get the baby, who was sleeping upstairs. I sat next to Alaina. My heart was pounding so fast that I felt like it was going to jump out of my chest.

As Jason descended the stairs with little Sara in his hands, I looked at him and the baby, and then I grabbed Alaina's hand. We shared something that I couldn't explain. Maybe she saw my pain and understood what I was feeling, or maybe it was something only two women in this unusual position could share. Tears were running down my face.

As Jason handed me the baby, I felt the way I did when the doctor put her on my tummy—as though I were holding her for the first time. I was overwhelmed by this love I had for my child. I loved her so much, and yet she was no longer mine. When I was carrying her inside of me, I kept telling myself not to get too close because I had promised her to someone else. Now all I wanted to do was hold her close and look at her beautiful face. For a second, it was only Sara and me in the room. It was weird calling her Sara, because in the beginning she was Faith Maria. Now Sara was her name, and that was the name she would hear for the rest of her life.

After I regained my composure, the visit was wonderful. I told them about Sara's birth and how hard it had been for me afterward, how I would never want to feel that pain again. We took pictures, and I started to feel comfortable and good about everything. I saw how much they loved Sara and that she was in good hands. I was so grateful that they had let me see her.

When we said our goodbyes, I didn't feel like I was losing her again; instead, I felt an overwhelming peace engulf me. I couldn't explain the feeling; it was something I hadn't felt in a long time. When I left, I felt good. I felt real happiness in my soul. My journey toward healing began that day, although I had a long, long road ahead of me. I said goodbye to

Sara and kissed her on the forehead before handing her back to Jason. My emptiness was not as painful now because I had gotten to hold her again. My love for her was great enough to stand it until I would see her again.

Two days later, I opened my mailbox and found a letter from Alaina. As I read it, I realized that I was not the only one who had felt what I had during the visit. Something was going on between Alaina and me, apart from Sara. I felt an energetic chill run through my body, as I had the day she first put her hand on my swollen stomach in Jack Hartnell's office. It was the same current I felt run through our hands when I first saw Sara again.

Dear Alex,

If it is humanly possible for a human being to know what another human being is feeling, then surely I know what went through your heart, body, and spirit when you first saw Sara last Friday. I felt the tears well up in my eyes as they did in yours. We were somehow connected, and the great rush of emotion—of joy, of loss, of overwhelm— we shared together, for we were one in that instant. I have felt that intensity only a few times in my life: at the birth of my three children, at my mother's death, when I first saw Sara in the hospital, and now with you. Surely we are united for all eternity through this experience.

I heard that you have signed the papers consenting to the adoption. I thank you for that. I thank you, too, for not aborting Sara eleven months ago. She is a wonderful example of why life should be honored. She was meant to live and be someone great, and you have given her that chance. Jason and I will be forever grateful to you.

The last months have not been easy for any of us. For me, it has been like living on a precipice, never knowing the direction my life would take, yet knowing that whichever way it turned out, it would be forever altered. For someone like me, who hates to be out of control, it has been the ultimate nightmare, yet Sara has made it worth the agonizing fear.

After I heard the news that you had signed the papers, I calmly went about my business at work, knowing that within me churned so many feelings of relief, happiness, and joy that if I had allowed them to surface, I would not have been able to work. When I got home that evening and was rocking Sara to sleep, I became overwhelmed with my love for her, this great treasure that I held in my arms. I know she senses this love on the only level we as humans really function: the reality of the heart. Funny how the only things in life that are real are invisible.

I promise you that I will be a good mother to Sara and that she will benefit from my living and learning. She couldn't have a father who adores her more, and hopefully I can be the kind of role model she will need to become a good woman. I will make mistakes, but hopefully not the ones of the past. There is a calm peacefulness in my soul for her. I have nothing to prove. I simply want to watch her grow and will walk beside her on this journey.

You have made a profound choice, one that will forever alter your life. May your life be worthy of this great decision. You owe it to Sara to make the most of your life, to transcend the past, and to carve for yourself a healthy, fulfilling future. I will always remember the moment when you held my hand to your heart. It is your soul that I felt, not the beating. We are now one, loving Sara, helping her reach her best self. Sara deserves the best of each of us. Our strength as women will show her the way.

Love,
Alaina

I put the letter in a drawer. I felt many things in that moment, but the letter helped to make the monthly visits easier.

§

My journey always began in King County. The drive from Ballard to

Seattle was tedious, depending on traffic. It was always hell, but knowing that I was coming to see my baby was all worth it. The drive would give me time to think about our pending visit. Would Sara know I was her mommy? How would I feel when I first saw her? How would she act toward me, a perfect stranger? I would daydream as I drove, thinking that she would be happy to see me. The reconnection between her and me would connect us as mother and daughter once again. But that never happened. I was a stranger to her, and she was a stranger to me.

My visits were never longer than an hour. Sometimes they were shorter than thirty minutes. I was always nervous. On one of my visits, I came early and no one was at home, so I sat on the front doorstep and waited. I then saw Jason with Sara in his arms walking down the street. He stopped at all the trees and flowers and showed her the beauty of them all. I just sat there and watched and thought how wonderful he was. Sara looked so safe in his arms and so happy. I saw the beauty in him.

Jason was the only one to greet me at these visits. Alaina was always at work, and that way, Sara was never with a babysitter. Jason had her in the morning, and Alaina had her at night. He always held Sara; she was his top priority. On one of my visits, Jason put her into my arms. She was very unhappy to be there, so I gave her back to him. I must admit it hurt because my arms longed to hold her. He always told me about the things she was doing, what kinds of food she ate, what wonderful adventures she was having. I saw how much he loved her and how much she loved him. This made the pain I felt in my heart not so bad, because I knew she was safe and happy. Those visits were so good for me, and every time I left, I knew that I had given Sara the best that life could offer. Jason was the best father. I kind of even fell in love with him myself.

I never knew how hard it must have been on Alaina and Jason with me coming over to see Sara. I never wanted to cause anyone pain; All I wanted was to keep my promise to Sara. I wanted to make sure that everything was alright and that I had done the right thing by giving her to the right people. I never knew the grief I was causing, yet Jason was always nice to me, and just seeing the relationship he had with Sara made me see what a father-and-daughter relationship was all about. Never having had a father, I hadn't realized how important a father was to a child.

Between my monthly visits with Jason, Alaina would send me photos of Sara along with little notes saying how grateful they were to have Sara in their lives. Those notes made me feel so good, knowing that I had given them so much joy and happiness. They also had given me my life back just to know that Sara had a wonderful life. Because of those visits, my life was better, and I had become a better person.

My life was getting back on track. In March of 1992 I decided to move to San Francisco because I wanted to be near my beloved Duncan and start a new life for myself. I began going out again, seeing my friends at nightclubs, going to the movie theater, and getting my body back, which I had lost more than a year before. I started to live again.

I told Alaina and Jason about my moving to San Francisco and that it was because of their letting me see Sara and how happy she was that my own life could move ahead. It was the whole key to going on with my life. I had kept my promise to my baby, and I had done the right thing for everybody. Alaina and Jason were Sara's parents, and I wanted a new life for myself. I knew that I would get letters and pictures from them and always know how my little girl was doing. Open adoption was wonderful! That was, until the day I got the letter.

§

CHAPTER 14
Alaina

*J*n March of 1992, the adoption was finalized in a court of law. The long months of agony were over. Sara was ours. Hearing the judge's words were sweetness to us, but nothing could erase the year that had preceded it. Jason and I both felt as if we had barely survived a long battle with fear. Scars, hidden but present, would stay with us forever.

When Alex announced that she was moving to San Francisco even before the first year was up, we began thinking about how to relate to her in the future. Up until this time, we were honoring a promise we had made in the therapist's office. Now we had to decide what to do from here. This was no problem for our friends, who already thought we were crazy for agreeing to such terms in the first place; however, they weren't in our shoes, had never adopted, and didn't have a clue what we had experienced. It's so easy to give instructions from afar.

The previous year had not been complicated only by the adoption; my other children were upset with us. We were having major problems blending two families. They were trying to grow up, and our problems were in their way. I was torn in half between my big children and Jason. Everyone seemed to want me to choose. I was high-functioning at work, but at home, despite Sara, my inner world was falling apart.

Sometimes I got so furious with Jason that I would scream, "OK, let's just give Sara back. Let's just quit!" I never meant those words, but he would never forget them or believe that I didn't mean them. Had anyone tried to take her, I would have laid down my life, but in anger, I wanted to hurt Jason, and Sara was his Achilles heel. I didn't think he realized how much love I had had for him to begin a family again after I had already raised one.

I didn't feel appreciated. He felt in over his head with my three children. This was not a *Father Knows Best* life. He wanted to be the man of the house, but my sons no longer respected him or his unfair rules. Even though he called himself a feminist, he was quite authoritarian and dug in with my boys. After Sara arrived, he totally washed his hands of the other children. A deep chasm was forming between us, even though it would be many years before I was engulfed by it. We were losing our ability to heal one another. We felt alone. It was the hardest period of our lives to that point. Our dream of the perfect blended family fell away, and we were left with broken hearts, many broken at our own hands. Sara was the only light, our redemption.

My relationship with Alex was complicated. I knew that her love for Sara was real, so I struggled constantly with the feeling that I had stolen her baby from her, that because of her suffering my life was enriched, that my joy was earned at another's expense. Nights would find me lost in her world, her losses. I knew what loss was about. I knew she was alone. I knew Duncan didn't have what it took to be there for her. Who had ever been there for her? She was a grown-up child who needed love, just like me. My kinship with her was uncanny; however, I finally got the courage to write the letter to sever ties. Jason and I felt that it would be less confusing for Sara to have one set of parents. But doubts lingered within me.

Dear Duncan and Alex,

Jason and I have emerged from some serious soul searching and have come to a decision that affects us all. I am not good at soul-searching decisions in person, so I am writing you both before your visit so you'll have time to absorb my words.

Over the last year, we have really come to care about you both. In many ways, I have adopted you, Alex. It seems that you have lost so much in your short life, and I feel deeply akin to you. I admire your indomitable spirit and optimism. Duncan, you are like my own sons in so many ways that it is often difficult for me to differentiate. Although your visits have caused some ambivalence for obvious reasons, we have all shared one common thread: Sara.

She has brought us together, and she will remain the link between us for the rest of our lives. But it is in her best interest that we have come to the very difficult decision that after your next visit, our relationship should be severed until the time when Sara herself wishes to meet you.

Now that I have written the words, let me say that we have agonized over this and consulted several psychologists, and we are convinced that it's best for Sara—not necessarily for you or us, but for her. Sara needs one set of parents right now. She needs one identity, one mom and one dad. Any other arrangement would be confusing to a small child. Her development, both physical and emotional, must take precedence over our individual feelings at this moment. She will always know that she is adopted, and I believe that she will be able to deal with this truth. However, to see her biological parents, even if they stand on the periphery of her life, would deny her the one thing she has a right to: a normal identity and sense of self.

Jason and I need to get down to the very serious business of raising this little human being. She takes constant care and attention, stability, and centeredness. She needs the four of us to do the best thing for her. Please know that it is very difficult to say goodbye.

We all have given Sara a great gift. When the time comes, she will see that she was not abandoned, but that four adults who loved her enough to put her life and happiness first made conscious decisions. We all must protect Sara.

We are looking forward to seeing you. Sara is becoming quite a little flirt. You'll see. Let me close with my greatest gratitude for this wonderful, precious child who is loved so much. Her life will have meaning and purpose, for we profoundly treasure her. I wrote these next words one night last May while rocking Sara to sleep. I think they have more meaning today as I write you.

§

The moment has come to let go
To release these tiny hands and entrust them
To us
The moment has come to do
What you have asked us to do:
Be Sara's parents
For Sara is already on her path
She is home.

§

I love you both,
Alaina

I put my pen down and then took it up again. Then I wrote what I really wanted to say, what was really in my heart. These are the words I didn't send.

§

I may sound together
Mature, open, centered
As if I know what the "right"
Thing to do is.
The truth is
I don't know anything for sure
Only that I want Sara all to myself
Can you understand that?
I want to say the right things
I want you to stop hurting
But forever I must live knowing what you
Have lost.
Do you?

§

CHAPTER 15
Alex

J knew that I wanted to go and start a whole new life for myself, and that life lay in San Francisco. I had been offered a position in my company to manage a salon in the East Bay. What a great city to start all over again! A whole new set of rules. It would be perfect for me. I knew that I had given all I could give to Sara, and it was time for me to move on with my own life. This chapter had to be closed.

In the beginning of March, just before moving, I received a letter from Jason and Alaina. They thought it would be best for everyone that Duncan and I no longer have contact with them or Sara after our next visit. As I read on, my heart began to pound. They wanted to be Sara's only parents and didn't want any interference from me. Did they not know that I was leaving to start my life over? I thought we had had an understanding that after the adoption papers were signed, open adoption meant being open with letters, that I would still be in contact with them if even just in letters and pictures. That's all I wanted and nothing more.

Alaina promised me before Sara was born that she would stay in contact with me for the rest of our lives. And now this! I felt so betrayed. I had trusted her. I believed what she had told me. Was she just telling me those things before the baby's birth so I would give them the baby? What happened to all the trust? I started to cry, because now I was losing Sara forever. Now I knew that my last visit with Sara would really be the last, or at least the last until she came to find me when she was older. That was, if she ever wanted to find me.

There are no guarantees in adoption, but still I felt hurt, angry, and betrayed. I understood why they wanted Duncan and me out of the picture; they wanted to raise Sara to have a normal life with only two parents rather than four. I really did understand and respect that. I, too, only wanted the best for her, and that was what they were giving her, right? I had done my job; now they wanted to do theirs. Hell, I was leaving anyway. This was a good thing, right? The best for everyone. That was what my head kept saying, but my heart was saying something else.

Maybe we should have talked about what to expect after Sara's birth, what contact I would have, and so on. Now I had nothing. My rights were gone, and so was she. Maybe I was being selfish and had asked too much. I knew that one day I would have to let go, and tomorrow was that day.

Jason and Alaina were perfect parents for her, but I wondered if they would ever tell her about me. Would I become the family secret? Would she ever know how much I loved her? Would she know that I had chosen a better life for her than the one I had to offer? Would Sara understand any of this? Would she even know I existed?

Many people loved her and wanted the best for her. I wanted the best for her most of all. I knew what I had to do, and that was to let go—this time for good. No more calls and no more visits. I called Alaina and told her that I understood what she and Jason wanted. After Duncan's and my last visit, I would no longer interfere with their lives. I had to do what was best for Sara, and that meant I had to go on with my life.

The night before our last visit was to take place, I made a book and filled it with pictures and letters, telling Sara the story of me, trying to explain how I felt about her, trying to fit a whole lifetime into a story and a small book. I filled it with as much love as I could, hoping and praying that she would one day read it and come to understand a little of me. I did not want her to think that I had abandoned her or that I didn't want her in my life. I loved her with all my heart. Coming to see her once a month, calling to see how she was doing, was all that had ever mattered to me. I hoped when she read my letters that it would matter to her, also.

Duncan picked me up the next morning, and we drove in silence to Seattle. This was the first time he and I were going together to see the baby. We said hardly anything to each other during the drive. God, what *do* we say, knowing this might be the last time we see our baby together? Duncan was a quiet man. He always kept to himself. He had to return to school soon, and I was going to be with him shortly. It seemed that he, too, had been fighting his own demons as we drove to our destination. I knew that I was fighting mine. My heart ached for him at that moment. My thoughts kept going back to the beginning. If I had only gotten an abortion or not gotten pregnant on purpose, all this pain would not be in our hearts. Well, in my heart, but not in his. My selfishness had won out, and now I had lost everything, maybe even Duncan.

As we approached the house, my heart started to beat loudly. This was it. Never again would I hold my baby. Never again would I smell her, touch her, or kiss her. I was never going to see this house or my beautiful daughter again. I kept thinking that I had to be strong, to fight the tears back.

Duncan and I held hands as we approached the house, and his hands were so cold. I wondered if his heart was pounding hard, too. Alaina and Jason greeted us at the door with smiling faces and hugs. I had brought my camera so I could take this last hour with me forever. We sat on the couch opposite Alaina and Jason, and they placed Sara on Duncan's lap. I could tell that this made Jason uneasy. There was a lot of tension in the air, as this was the first time we had all been together.

Jason was probably feeling threatened because of Duncan and Alaina because of me, but we were there only for our daughter during these precious few minutes. I wanted to hold her so tight, but I knew that if I did, I wouldn't let go this time.

Sara was almost a year old now. When I looked at her face, I could see that she looked like Duncan. She had his nose and forehead, but her eyes and smile were all mine. Her hair was blond, and her eyes were blue. She was a happy baby and was always smiling. I was proud to have given birth to this beautiful child. She was just starting to walk a little, and she crawled everywhere. She was so beautiful and sweet. We took our pictures and made some small talk, and before I knew it, it was time for us to leave.

I got up and walked over to Alaina. I was only going to hug her and try to leave everything that had happened this year behind, but as soon as I put my arms around her, my heart broke and I started to sob. I was back in the hospital, leaving my baby for the first time once again. All my sadness and emptiness filled me, and I cried so hard that my whole body shook. I held on to Alaina for what seemed like an hour. As I held her, I put my hands on her face, looked deeply into her eyes, into her very soul, and pleaded, "Please, Alaina, tell her about me and don't let her think that I didn't love her. Let her know that I wanted her with all my heart. Let her know she was loved by me, *please!*"

Then something happened as I looked into this woman's face. She put her arms around me and wiped my tears from my face. She held me like she would her own child and promised she would tell Sara about me. She didn't have to comfort me, and yet she was doing so. As Alaina held me, I felt safe and protected in her arms, as if I were in my own mother's arms. As I looked into her face, I realized that I had found the mother I had been searching for. I saw the face my daughter would see every morning when she awoke, the woman who would dry her tears and be there when she had a nightmare. This was the woman who would be called Mommy. I saw that my promise to Sara was being fulfilled.

I felt a connection with Alaina for the first time in that I had known this woman before. Maybe not in this lifetime, but in another. I felt total love for her, and total trust. At that moment, my heart felt like it was going to be OK. I was going to be able to move on now. It was time to let go.

As we walked out the door toward my car, I gave Sara one last kiss on the forehead, just as I had done in the hospital eleven months earlier. I turned back one more time and said, "I love you," not only to Sara but to Alaina, too. I considered myself lucky to have shared a little part of my daughter's life. As we drove away, I looked back one more time. My search was over. I had not only found a home for my daughter but a love for Alaina, my kindred spirit. I felt that we two women had the same love for one child. I was able to keep my promise in my heart forever. Suddenly, I understood the meaning of the poem Alaina had given me the first day in the attorney's office. It was all about us, her and me, and the road we were taking together.

§

CHAPTER 16

Alaina

*T*hat last visit with Alex was one of the most profound experiences of my life. We were finally, all four of us, in one room, searching for something nonthreatening to say. I was feeling Alex from across the room. It was as if her spirit had entered my body and I could read her mind, see all the losses of her life, all the disappointments, all the tears. I saw her mother, and I saw mine, cold in their graves. We were orphans, Alex and I. Later, I would not remember anything that was said or any of the motions we went through to survive the meeting.

When the hour was up, we all stood at once. Sara was happily crawling, unaware that a major event in her life was underway. I hugged Duncan, then I turned to Alex, and the world just went black. Giant tears began to jump from her eyes and landed on me from several feet away. Hers was an inconsolable grief, one too big to contain, too deep to comprehend. All I knew was that she was in my arms and our hearts were fusing into an uncertain destiny. She held my face, and her eyes bored into my soul with powerful resolution. I was crying openly now, too, and I would have promised this child the world had she asked it of me. It was a mystical experience, but in that embrace, another promise was made. It was not yet fully formed, but nevertheless, it had been conceived. I would never betray this young woman, who had been betrayed by everyone in her life. She and I became one spirit on that afternoon.

As Alex and Duncan drove away, I fell into Jason's chest for comfort. "Don't worry. It's over, Alaina. We never have to be afraid again." I couldn't articulate what I was feeling because I didn't know. What I did know was that Alex Porter and I had not said goodbye. One chapter in our lives was over, but another was on the horizon.

I walked into the house and went upstairs to write down my thoughts, but before I could do it, some papers fell out of the book Alex had left. I read them. They were a letter to Sara.

Sara,

I sit here and think about how to start to tell you who I am and to tell you why I gave you to Jason and Alaina. I first want to say that you were wanted. I wanted a baby in my life. I was so happy when I found out that I was expecting. I was very much in love with your father, and out of that love we shared, you were conceived.

As the months went by, things started to happen that were out of my control. In December, I fell into money troubles, and all that I had saved for you and me went to bills and rent. I turned to my family for help, but they couldn't help me out. Duncan's family also could not help, and I didn't know where to turn. I was very scared and very, very alone. I went to many people for advice and help, but it all came down to what was best for you. I looked into adoption and wanted to know how it worked.

The old way of adoption was where you gave away the baby and never knew where the baby went or who the parents were. But open adoption is different. I was able to look for the right parents for you, to interview them, to talk to them, to see if my beliefs were the same as theirs. I looked for a long time. I went through twenty couples, but none of them fit what I wanted for you until Jason and Alaina. At our very first meeting, I knew right away that they were right for you; my heart told me. I know that sounds funny, but it felt right. They looked like they could give you so much love and wanted to be parents so badly. After that meeting, I knew who would raise you.

After you were born, I was so happy because I was able to be with you for one day and one night. I felt so much love in my heart for you. Duncan was there with me when you were born—well, he arrived just after your birth. We held you and could not keep our eyes off you. On April 21, I knew that I had to let go of you. That day was the hardest and saddest day I have ever felt. I felt my heart break, but I also felt that I was doing the best thing for you.

As the months went by, I was able to come and see you for an hour every month. I saw how wonderful your parents were to you, how much they loved you. I was so impressed. I wished that they were my parents. I also saw how happy you were. My heart told me that I did the right thing. Your parents kept all their promises and sent pictures of you to me all the time. Your mother, Alaina, is very important to me. She is a wonderful woman. She was able to share you with me in letters and pictures. I am grateful to her and your father.

I want you to know that when you grow up and are able to understand all of this, I would like to meet you— that is, if you want. I know how hard this must be for you, but I just want you to know that I will always love you. I know that you will grow up to be a wonderful woman and that great things will come your way.

For myself, I will go on with my life and hope that one day you and I can sit and talk and maybe get to know one another. I made a book of pictures for you so you can see what Duncan and I look like.

I write this letter to you so that you will have some idea of why I did what I did. I gave you to Alaina and Jason not because I didn't want you but because I loved you, and I'll always love you. Your father, Duncan, is a man whom I loved with all my heart. He was very scared and unsure about everything, and he didn't know how to handle the situation. He went through a lot of sadness, too. I don't know what will become of us, but I don't think that we will stay together. Our lives are so different and are going in different directions.

I wish I could have shared in your growing years, but Alaina and Jason are the best parents to give to you what you need. I feel all things happen for a reason, and you, Alaina, and Jason were meant to be a family. I hope when you grow up that I can be in your life, even if it's a very small part.

I also hope that your mother and I can keep in contact as the years go by. Your mother is a great woman. She has been very understanding and caring. If it weren't for her, I wouldn't be able to write this letter to you.

Thank you, Alaina. Thank you for understanding and caring. I will close this letter knowing that you will be reading this one day and know a little about me.

Sara, your adoption papers are open to you. I wish you a life full of happiness and joy and much love. I will love you from a distance. I will care for you from afar, but you will be in my heart, no matter where you are.

Always,
Alex Porter
October 1992

My hands dropped the letter back into the book. I wondered how Sara would respond someday when she read Alex's words. I wondered if she would someday understand fully the journey her birth mother had taken so long ago. I picked up my pen again and said my goodbye.

§

Today we said goodbye, Alex
You came to say farewell to our baby
The baby you bore but I have raised
For one year
Today we said goodbye because Sara
Needs one mother

I had it all clear in my mind
It is the right thing to do for her
Our small talk was polite and appropriate
We said the right things
But when we stood to say our farewells
I knew
Holding you in my arms I realized that I had
Adopted more than one daughter a year ago
Your heaving sobs of anguish transcended all the
Right things we convince ourselves of as we attempt to live
I felt the same pain rise up within my own heart
And again I felt the bond we share, we two
"You must keep me alive for Sara! It's just you and I, right?"
You and I, mothers of one small child
I know you love her; that makes it harder
I did not want to let you go
I stroked your hand, saying, "I'm sorry! I'm sorry!"
Why can't we both have her?
But you chose to give her up, and I chose to love her
It was what we agreed
Right?
But why do I still feel as if I have stolen her?
Will that feeling ever fade?
Today Sara walked over to me, arms outstretched
And said, "Mama!"
Mama
I am her Mama
So are you
Will you ever really know what you have given up?
I do
And so I weep

§

And that's exactly what I did.

§

The next week brought about a shift in my life, a shift that would resonate for many years. The album that Alex and Duncan had put together for Sara as a parting gift became a thing of great importance. Jason was enraged that they had presented it to us. He hated that they had photos inside that called them Sara's daddy and mommy. He hated the photos that depicted a pregnant Alex with Duncan's arms encircling her and the words "Our little family" written underneath in Alex's recognizable script.

"I want you to get rid of this," he announced with a determination I had never seen in him. "Jason, we can't do that. This is a gift for Sara." He walked away, but a feeling took form within me that told me he would never allow it in our house. I sought out Daniella and asked her to hide the album in her room, somewhere that Jason couldn't find it. I didn't want to collude with my teenage daughter against Jason, but an inner knowing felt something bad was going to happen.

The next day, when we returned from work, or "school," as I called it, since I was a counselor at an elite high school, I asked Daniella where she had hidden it. We went to the spot, and it was gone. *Gone.* We searched everywhere, but there was no trace of it. We did find a letter that Duncan had written to Sara, but I didn't open it because it was addressed to her. Then we began in earnest to look for the album. Nothing.

I waited in panic mode for Jason to get home from work that night. I had a sick feeling in my gut. I knew how possessive he was about Sara and how upset he had been that Alex and Duncan had come for their last visit. When I heard his car pull into the carport, I ran downstairs and confronted him at the front door.

"Where is Sara's album, Jason?" My voice was shaking with anger. "It's gone," he replied calmly, and the look in his eyes told me not to go further.

"Jason, that was not yours. That was Sara's. You have no right to touch something of hers."

"I have every right. I am her father. They are not her parents."

"I know, but it was a gift entrusted to us for when she grows up. Where is it?" My tears were not sadness but outrage. By this time, Daniella was standing beside me.

"I destroyed it. Every page. Sara will never see another man calling himself daddy."

"You destroyed it? You took something that was hers alone and destroyed it? Who would do that?" The fight raged on, and ultimately, he stormed up the stairs to get away from me.

"Daniella, hide that letter from Duncan somewhere Jason will never find it. It belongs to Sara."

I walked up the stairs, a new sensation filling my awareness. I felt that Jason's act was one of betrayal. Human, yes. Forgivable, maybe. But something changed in me that night. I wondered what else he was capable of doing if he could do this to his daughter, invade her sacred space with this destruction. I knew she was everything to him, but I also saw that there was no empathy for anyone else. In that knowing grew something dark in my heart, something that would never trust him or look at him in the same way again. He had bullied my children. He had washed his hands of them when he got his own baby. I was losing respect for him and falling out of love with the man I had staked my life on. Now he had done something to my baby for his own selfish reasons. Now the game had changed.

That night, I knew I would betray his wishes to keep Sara for us alone. I knew I was capable of deception, too. However, my deception would not be to deprive Sara of something but to ensure that she would never lose something. That something was Alex.

§

CHAPTER 17
Alex

I left southern Washington and began my new life in San Francisco. Everything there was different: the people, the music, the food. Everybody seemed to have a cause. It invigorated me. This new world was open and new and fit me like a glove. I was ready for a challenge, not realizing that a great one was already just ahead of me.

I drove to Duncan's place. The plan was for me to live there until I got a place of my own. I was going to be with the man I loved, to start over, and to try to make things right. I was so happy. I had put this man through so much, but he still loved me.

After leaving Alaina and Jason's home, I knew that I would not hear from them until Sara was at least eighteen years old. I came to peace with that after I left them in Seattle. I knew that Sara was home. Now I needed to find a new home for myself. Duncan's town was a world of hundreds of different kinds of people from all over the planet in one place.

Duncan and I got along great at the beginning. I found a wonderful place to live in his university town, sparked up friendships with my coworkers, and was very happy with my decision to move. My new job was good, as I was learning all the new styles in the hair world and teaching them to others. Three weeks after my arrival, Duncan graduated.

Everything changed from then on. Our relationship took a hundred-and-eighty-degree turn. He was more distant. At first I thought I was being silly and assumed that we were just getting used to being together once again, but he soon confirmed my worst fears. He started talking about our lives going on different paths. In my heart of hearts, I had known that this was going to happen one day, but I didn't want to face the truth. And so I felt I had nothing to lose if I told him my deepest secret about Sara and how she was conceived.

Hoping to God it wouldn't backfire on me, I thought he would understand and see how much I really did love him. I took a deep breath and just said it: "I got pregnant on purpose to have a child to love when you went back to school in early August of 1991 and so I wouldn't be alone. I wanted to keep a little part of you with me. I didn't intend to trap you in any way. I didn't even tell you of the impending birth until you found out from a friend of yours. I planned to keep the baby and do it all on my own, but then all hell broke loose, and I lost her instead. The irony in all this now is that I'm losing you anyway!"

I had never seen so much hate and anger in a man's eyes. "I paid for my sins, Duncan," I pleaded. "I lost Sara, but I don't want to lose you. My thinking back then, even though it sounds crazy, was that I wanted you in my life so badly that I thought if I had your baby, I could keep a small part of you with me." Tears started running down my face, and I was shaking. He turned his back to me. I reached for his hand, but he pulled away.

"We were drifting apart back then, and I was so in love with you. I'm still in love with you. I know now what pressure that situation puts on a small child, but my mindset was only to have someone to love and not to be left alone again." My pleading fell on deaf ears. He turned to me then, and for the rest of my life I will never forget the look on his face as he said, "You have to go!" I had now lost everything.

I ran from his house, from his life, forever. He was never going to forgive me. I drove back to my house in a fog. I walked to the top of a nearby hill and started to scream. I screamed and cried forever. I let everything out—all my hopelessness; the loss of my baby, my mommy, and my love. I started thrashing about like a wild woman, grabbing at the dirt, rocks, anything I could get my hands on. Throwing it all in the air and onto the ground, I fell down and started to beat the shit out of my own hands, trying to get the pain out that I had kept deep inside of me.

After I gained a little control of myself, I realized I was full of dirt and grass, but damn, I felt better! I sat there hoping no one had seen me, but then, I really didn't give a shit anymore. I looked up into the sky and said, "God, help me!" I sat and did a lot of soul searching. I realized I had to get some help, to make things right. I walked away from that hill with a new purpose.

I needed to face all my life's deceptions. I needed to not lie about anything anymore, to be truthful to myself, and to learn how to deal with all of my losses. I needed someone to talk to. I went through the newspaper that day and found Anna. I called. She was concerned after I told her what I had done with my life, and I made an appointment the very next day. Needless to say, I had a lot of work ahead of me.

Anna was a counselor in her forties who was a single mother and raising two children on her own. I held nothing back from this woman; I let it all out. I kind of felt sorry for her because, after listening to me, she must have needed help herself. Anna helped me deal with all my sorrows and pain instead of keeping them locked up inside me. She brought them up to the surface and showed me how to deal with them, how to mourn the death of my beloved mother, the loss of Sara and now Duncan. She showed me that lying to Duncan and to myself was self-destructive.

Anna helped me work through many of my insecurities and showed me that I didn't have to be together all the time. She was wonderful. She listened and didn't criticize. She helped me understand more about myself and to value my self-worth. I went to her for a year, and I was able to find someone whom I had lost a very long time ago: *me.*

Because of Anna, I emerged a stronger person. I had a new lease on life. I was not afraid to be alone and go find adventure. She gave me back my self-respect. I was able to heal my demons, which I had hidden from the world. Now I had to hide no more. The lost little girl was gone, and a new woman came into her own.

I started my life over without Duncan and Sara and took a new direction. I concentrated on my career. I realized, through therapy, that because of all my unresolved problems, I would not have been as good a mother to Sara as I could have been. Maybe all of the things that I had to go through to get to where I was had made me a better woman than if I had never lost. I now could face and handle my demons. Because I was strong enough to find help, I was strong enough to learn and grow from those experiences. I was able to come to peace with myself and Duncan and little Sara.

Duncan and I spoke after a few months had passed, and we were able to come to an understanding. We would never again have the love that we had once shared, which had been true in the heart but filled with so many lies. We were even able to remain friends. I would always love Duncan, and we would always share Sara. I now could face the world, since I had nothing to hide from anyone or myself.

In July of 1992 I received a letter from Alaina. I was shocked and bewildered. The understanding we last had was that I would no longer have any communication with them until Sara herself decided to get in touch with me, and I thought that wouldn't be until she reached the age of eighteen. Before I opened the letter, I thought that maybe Sara was sick or hurt and that they needed something from me, like information about my medical history.

To my surprise, it was about Sara and what she was doing at fifteen months. I couldn't believe it. I was so sure I wouldn't hear anything more about her. Alaina wrote that it would be our secret between us. I was going on with my life, and now this wonderful woman was giving me this most wonderful gift. I was surprised and happy. Alaina was keeping all her promises to me. She didn't have to do this, but she went ahead and made sure I knew how Sara was doing. She wrote to me about what Sara was saying and included pictures of her. Now I would know about Sara through letters and pictures that Alaina would send. I started to cry. How could I ever thank her? Now I could keep my promise to Sara.

I could write to Alaina and send everything to her through her work. I wrote and expressed my total gratitude to her and this wonderful secret we shared. I would express my love for Sara, and Alaina would keep my letters for her when she grew up so that one day she would come to know that I loved her.

Thank you, dear woman, from the bottom of my heart.

§

Chapter 18
Alaina

§

I saw you stumbling over to me just now
Bold steps, wobbly, yet determined
My heart locked eyes with you
And I stood humbled
What a wonderful little girl you are
Sara O'Connell
One year old and already the
Earth is safe beneath your feet
Already your voice rises in song
For no reason
Your feet dance at the slightest
Prompting
I look at your trusting face and weep
How I want to protect you
Cradle you from harm's way
How I long to explain what you mean to me
Will you one day compare yourself
To your brothers and sister?
Will you feel less than blood
Because we chose you?
If only you knew the depth of love
Within every embrace
You have awakened the true mother in me

The wise mother
The patient mother
That my youth and emptiness could
Not fully give to the others
I see the strength of that in you now
Wobbly gait and contagious giggle
In your eyes lies
My destiny
In my arms lies
Your home.

§

Sara's first birthday came and went. Her charm captured everyone's heart. She was lucky; Jason cared for her during the day, and he gave five-star service. At three o'clock he would drop off a happy baby to my office, and Sara would stay with me for my last hour of work. That way, she was always with a parent—and Sara had many parents, for she was adopted by many of my childless friends, too. Since she loved people, she made them feel good. When she began to crawl, she would crawl out of the office and visit other offices. She was a kind of mascot, yet I knew that such luxury could not last forever. The people did have a school to run. By the following fall, Sara would need a babysitter for that hour.

Jason and I were still struggling over her; I changed slowly. However, in time I learned that children could actually be shared. Sara was a first-class Daddy's Girl, and her first word was Dada, not Mama. Though Jason may not have seen it from my outside behavior, major changes about love were occurring within me. Love, ownership, territory; I was realizing that there was enough love to go around. But with that realization emerged recurring thoughts of Alex. With every new word Sara learned, I thought that Alex would have loved to experience it, too. I would have.

It was a real conflict. Jason was happy that at last we were Sara's only parents, but I was still feeling that the bond between Alex and me was important and that it meant I needed to share Sara with her. I didn't own Sara, and I never wanted her to feel that she had been abandoned. Sara connected me to this woman; I owed her. Intellectually, I could justify keeping her all to myself, but my inner voice argued with my head continuously. There was also the change that had occurred in my heart when Jason had destroyed the album that Alex and Duncan made for Sara. A small crack, an opening, had illuminated Jason's inability to share what he felt was his. This, I saw, was what my older children had experienced with him when he disowned any need for them in his life after Sara arrived. My hero had feet of clay. I hoped that this was his only weakness. I was made of clay, too, but I had a deep trust in destiny and especially in promises made.

One morning, I woke up, took an envelope, placed pictures of Sara in it, and sent them to Alex. It was an impulsive act, and I didn't tell Jason. It was one of many secrets I would start keeping from him. *Why anger him?* I rationalized. He wouldn't understand my promise to Alex on that last day. I was riddled with guilt, but nevertheless, I sent the pictures with a conspiratorial note that this was to be just between her and me. It was so clearly right in my soul. I was expanding my capacity to feel another's agony, but at the same time, I was putting Jason's trust in me at risk.

It was easy for me to keep secrets. Living in an alcoholic family, secrets were normal; everyone had them. It was a way of life. I didn't want to lie, but lying was not unfamiliar to me. I had lied to Johann during our marriage, and now I was lying to Jason. This was a topic we had discussed, and we had agreed to total honesty. Now I was breaking my word, and I felt like shit. I didn't know how long I could lie to him, but the die was cast—I had begun a deception. I didn't want to hurt Jason; I loved him. I just wanted Alex to know Sara. Jason wouldn't find out for years. I knew it was wrong, but it was also right. So much grey.

A few weeks after I'd sent Alex the photos, I received her response, and our secret world began.

My dearest Alaina,

Thank you so, so much. I am so happy to see Sara and how happy and healthy she is. If I could only express to you how these pictures make me feel. They mean the world to me. Thank you for sharing them with me. Thank you for sharing a little part of her with me. Thank you for being so warm and understanding. I love you for this. I will always be grateful to you.

She is so beautiful. I can see both Duncan and me in her, but also you. She is becoming a little girl so fast! What an adventure she must be having. You all look so happy, and my heart is happy, also. Thank you for this wonderful gift we share—me and you as one with this child—because my love to her is through you. You make me proud.

When she is older and is ready to know me, let her know that I love her with all my heart and soul. I will be with her in spirit. I not only carried her for nine months, but I will carry her with me all my life. Thank you, Alaina O'Connell, for this gift. I will always be grateful to you.

Love always,
Alex

§

CHAPTER 19
Alex

$\mathcal{I}$n February of 1993, I found myself dating a young man named Doug, who was a year older than I was. This was the most serious relationship I had had in three years, since Duncan and had I broken up. I did date other men after Duncan, but this one was a whirlwind relationship. We had a lot in common; he had grown up without his father in his life and had lost his mother a year earlier.

For the first time since Duncan, I was really serious about someone. At the beginning of our relationship, we spent almost every day together. Doug's only transportation was a motorcycle, and we took trips on it up and down the coast of California. He was a kind man, and since he was a little older than me, he seemed to have his life in order. At one point in our relationship, I thought that this was the man I would like to marry. I felt protected and safe with him. We had a summer romance, and it all seemed perfect.

Doug had light brown hair and blue eyes and was of the Jewish faith. We talked a lot about our past, and he knew all about my abortion, Sara, and my relationship with Duncan. He never made any judgment about my past, and I was grateful for that. I didn't hide anything from him. I didn't want to be dishonest with him or myself, and I was committed to the truth. We even started talking about moving in together after Christmas.

In January, Doug lost his license to drive for six months because of tickets he had received for traffic violations over the past year. Then something happened; his mood began to change, something I hadn't seen in him before, and he started to drink and get depressed. This seemed to be a breaking point for us, and communication became very difficult. I had never lived with anyone who drank out of depression, and I didn't know how to handle it. At first, I tried to ignore it. Then I had to look at our relationship and question what I wanted from him and from us. We started to fight. Soon he was unhappy at work and with everything in his life. We had been seeing each other for only nine months.

We decided to let the relationship cool for a while and not see each other so we could clear our heads. I couldn't fix his life for him; he needed to do it for himself. If I learned anything in therapy, it was that I couldn't change a person into something he wasn't. He must change for himself.

During our separation, I planned a trip to Germany for the summer. My brother was there, and he had invited me to stay with him and his family for a few months. Having been born in Germany, I had dreamed of this was a trip for most of my life. In February I turned twenty-nine years old. I knew I wasn't getting any younger, so if I didn't make the trip this summer, I was never going to make it.

Alaina and I continued to talk to each other over the next several months. She and I had a wonderful relationship through letters and phone calls. She even let me talk to Sara over the phone once, when Sara was three years old. I wrote Alaina every three or four months. I wrote about my new relationship and to tell her that I was planning a trip to Germany. I had grown to love this woman. I trusted her with my deepest secrets. She was no longer a threat to me nor I to her. We grew to trust each other.

Dear Alaina and Sara,

I am glad all of you are OK. When I heard about the earthquake in Seattle, I was so worried because I knew that you live near the epicenter where it hit. I hope Jason wasn't upset when I called; I just wanted to make sure all was OK.

I have great news! I am going back to discover my roots in Germany for four weeks in May. I feel I must go and discover who I am and where I came from. Since most of my family has passed on, I need to find the others and discover who I am and where I come from. I will be in Germany from the middle of May until the middle of June. I am looking forward to it; I've been talking about doing this for years, and now it's my chance. My twenty-ninth year on this Earth is upon me, and I am feeling a lot older. I am beginning to hate birthdays.

Thank you for the pictures. They are great. I will get together with Duncan and show them to him. Sara is growing up so fast; she is beautiful. I can see most of myself in her now. She has my fine hair. Her eyes and nose look like Duncan's side of the family, but her smile is mine. Her temper is from my mother, and my mother's temper was not very small!

I have been thinking about starting a family for myself when I get back from Germany, but I always wonder if it will be the right time, if I will have enough money, and so on. I know I will be a good mother, and I want a child, but is the time right? I see the pictures of Sara, and I see what I am missing. Hopefully, I will decide when I get back from Europe. Who knows? Maybe Sara will have a brother or sister next year.

Well, that's all for now. I love you both very much, and thank you again for the photos.

Love always,
Alex

In the beginning of March, it seemed that Doug and I were going to get back on track. He had stopped drinking, and his work situation was better. We even started talking about our future. I met his family when his father and stepmother invited us for dinner. They were pleasant and were happy for us. I cared about Doug and wanted things to work out.

At the end of February, I saw my doctor because I was experiencing sharp pains in my chest. She suggested that I go on a lower dose of birth control pills. On March 9, I missed my period and was a little concerned. I called the doctor while I was at work, and she suggested that I keep taking the pills as usual. Her thought was that my cycle was just adjusting itself.

She didn't sound concerned, but she advised me to take a pregnancy test just in case, if I wanted to. . . .

At lunch, I got a test to take home after work. I didn't feel worried or say anything to anyone because I didn't think it was going to turn out to be important. I thought that I was just adjusting to my new prescription. I went home, took the test, and waited the three minutes. The whole time I kept saying to myself, "I have nothing to worry about. I've been careful."

Then the stick turned blue.

Oh, God. Oh God! I couldn't believe it. First my heart started to beat a hundred miles an hour, then I started to shake, and finally the tears came. I was crying not out of sadness but out of joy. How could this have happened? I didn't remember missing any of my pills. My mind went blank. I couldn't stay in my apartment a moment longer. I needed air, and I felt like I had to run—so that is exactly what I did. I started running. I didn't know where I was going, but I just needed to move. I was so overwhelmed that I was crying while I was running. God had given me a second chance at motherhood. But why now? I started to pray a prayer of thanks, then I calmed down and assessed what was happening.

God, what was I going to tell Doug? We were doing so well, and I was planning to go to Germany that summer. How was he going to take this? How was I going to tell him? I slowly walked back home. I thought that maybe I wouldn't tell him until I had had a chance to think everything through. *I won't tell anyone,* I thought. But then, I would be doing the same thing I did when I was pregnant with Sara, and I didn't want to repeat history. I had made a promise to be honest and truthful with Doug. No lies! I wanted to be totally upfront about how I felt, but how was he going to take this?

Doug came over that night, and I made dinner. I was sitting across from him, my heart pounding hard, my hands clammy. I kept chickening out every time I started to tell him. Whenever I would begin to bring it up, he would start talking about something that had happened at work. In mid-sentence, I just blurted it out. I don't remember the words that came out, but his reaction was unforgettable. At first, he didn't say a word, and my heart began to sink. He looked up at me and said, point blank, "I'm not ready to be a father, and I do not want to be responsible for a child at this time in my life. *You are getting an abortion.*"

I sat there and was transported back to my past. I was again sitting across from Duncan and getting the same reaction. There was to be no happiness for me, no joy, only emptiness. Doug already knew about how everything had affected me in the past. How could he possibly ask this of me, knowing that it would devastate me completely?

My mouth opened and I said, "NO! NO! NO!" I was not a lost little girl anymore. I was tougher and older. I was going to stand up for myself, so with all the courage I could muster, I said, "FUCK YOU! I will have this baby with or without you!" He got up, stared at me, and left, very, very angry.

After he slammed the door behind him, I sat at the table for what seemed like hours. I kept thinking, *God, how did I get myself into this mess again?* Then something came over me that I can't explain. It was strength, and it came from deep inside of me. This was my child. This was my body, and this was my choice! This time it was different. I did not deceive or hurt anyone to get this baby. I was not going to kill or give this baby away for anything. My heart was strong and so were my convictions, yet Doug's rejection of his baby, which also meant a rejection of me, hurt.

I cried a lot that night, but in the morning, I felt my inner strength return with a vengeance. I needed a friendly ear, so I called Anna, my therapist, and made an appointment to see her that day. I needed help to prepare me for what lay ahead. I was clear about what I wanted in my life, and no one, but *no one*, was going to dictate what it was going to be like. I was taking charge. I knew that I had a battle on my hands, and I was ready to fight.

Every day Doug would come over to my house and ask, "When are you going to have an abortion?" or "You need to choose between me and this baby." For two months, he yelled and threatened me, trying to make me get rid of the baby. But I held steady, and with Anna's support, I held on tight to my baby and my commitment. I tried to explain to him for hours and hours on end how much I wanted this baby. I finally came to see this man for who he really was and realized that I had no more respect for him. If he were a real man, he would step up and take responsibility. All he really was, was a coward.

At the end of August, Doug said he could never love a child he didn't want. That did it for me. My love and respect for him were gone. I knew that I would be traveling this pregnancy alone, and I asked him to leave. He left my life, and I hoped never to have to see him again.

With Anna's help and advice, I planned for my baby's and my future. On November 6, 1994, at 11:39 p.m., I gave birth to a seven-pound, seven-ounce baby girl. I named her Hope.

§

CHAPTER 20
Alaina

Dear Alaina,

I am happy to say that I am going to be a mother once again. The baby is due in late November or early December. My heart is filled with joy. Give Sara a big kiss and hug for me. I will keep you informed. I love you both.

Always,
Alex

§

Dearest Alaina

The baby is due November 13. I get to hear the heartbeat next month. The only sad thing is that I am going to be a single mother. The man I loved decided he wasn't ready to be a father, so he left. Now I face an uncertain road, but I have lots of faith and hope in myself.

I love you and Sara. Say a prayer for my baby and me.

Love,
Alex

*T*he words on Alex's card hit me like a bolt. My protective nature wanted to call her, warn her, and defend her against the road that lay ahead. Many times I had wished that someone who cared about me would have rescued me, but no one did. Of course, I felt and celebrated Alex's joy at the prospect of a baby. I knew what that was about. I knew why she needed the baby. I knew that more than anyone in the world, for in that moment, I knew that I cared more than probably anyone else about this young woman, who was all alone in the world. After all, she was my daughter now, born on the third of February, just like Daniella. Connections . . . all the unending connections.

My mom had always had a lot of things to say, but calm, quiet wisdom was not her forte. How could it be? She wore her own wounds so flagrantly. No one had helped her, either. We fought and raged against each other, loved each other, but failed to help each other. Maybe I could help Alex. But actually, how could I help anyone? My life was far from tranquil or ordered. Daniella had retreated into herself since her brothers had gone to college. The boys were still angry with me for all the wrongs they held me responsible for. Jason and I were still loving and battling through our demons together, trying to mesh the hearts of two wounded people, but rarely were we both acting from our adult selves.

Nevertheless, I did bring the harvest of life's lessons to my professional life, and I think that my own suffering had made me sensitive to my students and to Alex. I put on my counselor's hat and wrote her.

Dear Alex,

I was both happy and sad for you when I received your card. In fact, I sat at my desk at work and cried. You certainly do not deserve another abandonment. This time should be one of peace and calm and not of insecurity. It will be difficult being a single mother, and my heart aches for you, even though the child will bring you joy. I wish I had something profound to say.

As a counselor, if you were my client, I would want you to look at your choices in men and why you pick ones who leave. Maybe if you did that, you would heal the part of you that is hurt so that the next man you allow in your life will be worthy of you. I feel excruciating pain for your position, partly because I am no stranger to pain and mistakes, and partly because I feel like the mother that you no longer have but really need right now. If your own mother were alive, I am sure she would be grieving, too, and telling you to take better care of yourself.

You have a heart like mine, and people like us, especially *women* like us, because we're open, get hurt. The alternative, I guess, would be to close off and be safe, but then we'd miss the joy, too. Maybe there is someplace in the middle where we can keep ourselves sensitive and open but be more particular about who we let into those vulnerable areas of ourselves.

I pray that you have people around you who will be able to help you and support you in the years to come and that you'll find a man who will openly accept and love your child and you. You and the child deserve that *absolutely*. No one else deserves the two of you.

I want you to know that every morning on the way to work I stop by the Catholic church and say a prayer for you and the baby, that you'll both be well, protected, and safe from harm or pain of any kind. My thoughts continue with you all the day through, praying that you will be strong and protected.

I do love you, Alex. You are like a daughter to me, a daughter who has suffered too much and whom I feel helpless to help other than to simply pray for.

Please know that you can always write to me and that I will be your friend. When I told Jason of your situation, he also was truly sad about your friend leaving you. He said that if you ever change your mind about keeping the baby, even later, he would take it and love it as he has Sara. I know that you will keep this child; I know why, and I support you totally. I hope he or she brings you all that the rest of the world has failed to give you. If you ever need me, though, let me know. You just never know.

Love,
Alaina

I slipped the letter into one of my self-made cards and quickly sent it. What I really wanted to do was shake that bastard of a boyfriend and scream, "Don't you dare hurt that girl! Don't you dare abandon her and your own child and leave her alone! Can't you see the goodness in her? The need?"

I knew there was nothing I could do. I was an observer. I had made my decisions and had paid dearly for them when they were wrong. If A, then B. Nature is absolute and indifferent. I placed the card into the mailbox and with it sent a prayer: *God, please don't put her through this again.* Many times I had prayed for myself; now I was praying for Alex. It was out of my hands. Though we sent letters and exchanged pictures, Alex and I were each on our own separate paths—paths that were now splitting in two different directions. I knew, however, that they would one day intersect again.

I got her reply soon after.

Dear Alaina,

Your letter brings me great comfort. I am so grateful for your prayers. Please try not to worry, because I have a lot of faith and hope in myself.

I am seeing a counselor every Monday. She has been helping me with my fears, sorrows, and my understanding of myself. She has been preparing me for what lies ahead with parenthood: what to expect, how to be strong. We have talked about you, Sara, and the new baby. If I decide to give the baby up, you and Jason would be my only choice to raise the child.

I know that the road is going to be long and hard, but I'm going to give everything I can to this child. I made a commitment to be a good mother and to be strong for this baby and myself. We say that we cannot bear our troubles, but we can bear them.

I heard the baby's heartbeat for the first time, and it was strong and loud. It made my day! I will find out the baby's sex in a few weeks and will keep you updated.

Sara is so big and beautiful. I feel this child is also a girl, which is great, but if is a boy, that would be just as wonderful. Love to Sara and Jason.

Always,
Alex

§

CHAPTER 21

Alex

*L*abor started at eleven o'clock in the morning, while I was attending my roommate's son's forty-day blessing. I was feeling a little twinge but tried to ignore it. At the church after the blessing, I asked the priest for a blessing for my unborn child. He smiled and placed his hand on my large stomach and said, "Dear Lord, bless this child with health and strength." I left with a smile on my face. At twelve in the afternoon, I knew that this was the day Hope would come into the world. The pain started slowly at first but was consistent. I was jubilant. I called everybody: my family; friends; and most importantly, my coach, James.

James was a friend whom I had met two years earlier and who had become my best friend. I asked him if he would be my birth coach, and he had agreed. He was wonderful. I will always love him for all of his help. "Please don't go anywhere, because Hope is on her way," I said when I called. James asked if I was sure. *Yes*, I was sure!

He came over around five in the afternoon. He had his stopwatch and the paperwork we needed. We waited until nine o'clock that evening before we headed to the hospital. By that time, the contractions were six minutes apart. I had forgotten how painful it was, but this time I had planned on asking for drugs. We arrived at the hospital, but after I was checked over, we were sent back home because I wasn't ready. We walked around for an hour, and I took a shower at 10:39 p.m. We went back, and this time they said I could stay. I was so ready. They took us into the delivery room and got me all ready. Boy, I wanted drugs! But by the time they were going to give me an epidural, I had to push.

Hope made her entrance into the world at 11:39 p.m. on November 6. Her birth, like Sara's, was very fast and painful and all natural. I was amazed about how powerful birth truly is.

Hope's howl was music to my ears. I whispered to her, "Hi, baby. This is your mommy!" James cut the cord, and Hope was free from my body. The first thing she did was suck her thumb.

My baby was here, and she was all mine. No one was going to take her away. I was her mommy and would be for the rest of her life. The nurse put her into my arms, and I cried and smiled at the same time. This time there was no sadness, not one unhappy thought, just great joy. I looked up at James and thanked him for being there for me. I had a little girl, a perfect, beautiful, pink little girl!

James wanted to hold her, so he took her while they finished fixing me. After he placed Hope back into my arms, we went to our new room. I never let her out of my hands. I held her and talked to her and kissed her a million times. Poor James. He wanted to hold her, too.

She took to the breast right away. The amazing thing about Hope was that she looked just like Sara at birth. They had the same noses; one really wouldn't have been able to tell them apart.

When we left the hospital, I was so scared. *What the hell am I going to do now?* I had never had a baby to take care of before. I didn't know how to change her diaper, feed her, or know which cry meant what. Boy, I had a lot to learn.

Oh, God, breastfeeding hurts! When I put Hope on my breast for the first two weeks, I wanted to cry from the pain, but like everything, it got better. I was getting better at understanding this tiny creature, who was so helpless and little in every way. I learned how much she should sleep and eat, and I changed her diapers twenty times a day. It was hard to do this all alone, but it was worth every minute. She would look at me and know my voice, my warmth, and my breast. When she was mad or cold or wet, she would let me know.

When Hope was twelve days old, my two sisters came to visit me by surprise. They had flown overnight, made their way to my home, and rang the doorbell. I opened the door, and there they stood. All was forgiven for the time when they had refused to help me when Sara was born. They stayed for four days and helped me a lot.

I felt that God had put another me on this Earth—Hope was a mirror image of me. She had fine, blond hair and light blue eyes. Her personality was one of total excitement, just like mine.

When Hope was six months old, I moved to Arizona to be near my oldest sister's family. It was the best move I could have made. My sister and brother-in-law fell madly in love with Hope and treated her as their own. She got everything she wanted, but most importantly, she got love and family. I thanked God for her every day.

When she was two and a half years old, she weighed twenty-nine pounds and was quite tall for her age. When people first met her, they would think she was three and say how well she spoke. She loved to dance and sing to Barney tapes and be read to. She did not like to be ignored. She was a daredevil and would climb everything. She was shy when she first met other people, until she got to know them. She was so sweet and loving and loved to be hugged.

Everyone knew Hope. When I walked to town or the bank or the hardware store, everyone asked about her if she wasn't with me. She loved dresses and called every one of them her "Cinderella dress." She hated to brush her teeth and fought me with hugs. Hope loved to hear the story of her birth and wanted to see all the pictures of her in my tummy. When James called, he would always tell her the same story.

I had told Hope about Sara and why, after Sara's birth, I couldn't keep her. I wasn't sure how much she understood, but when she would see a picture of Sara, she would know who she was. I hoped that one day Sara and Hope would know each other and come to love each other as sisters.

I believe that if I had not given up Sara for adoption, I wouldn't have had Hope. I would have given my life for Hope, as I knew Alaina and Jason would have given theirs for Sara. I thanked God for Hope every day, and I promised to be the best mother to her I could be. I promised, and I keep my promises.

§

CHAPTER 22
Alaina

uddle time was a ritual at our house, a quiet window of opportunity when Sara and I would whisper in the darkness while Jason prepared for bed. After his preparations were done, I would lose my four-year-old daughter to her father's magical storytelling; I was no competition for the parade of funny characters who emerged from his imagination each night to send Sara into dreamland. I was no competition at all; rather, I was the "cuddling" parent, the one who leaped into the "big" bed with Sara for a few moments of sharing. Often we would "Say God"—Sara's expression for our prayer time—during which we would beseech the Higher Power for protection and guidance and the Guardian Angel to watch over Sara as she slept. Sara looked forward to these moments, and I needed them as much as she did; maybe more. It was our special time.

But I was not prepared for her question on this night, a question I had dreaded for four and a half years, ever since Sara's adoption. I spoke often of the time when she would ask the difficult questions that I wished she would never have to face. Adoption is a rollercoaster, and when a child's future questions about her adoption are compared to the actual decision to adopt—and the fear, after being selected, that the pregnant girl will change her mind, and all the other traumas that adoptive parents face—those questions seem far away and insignificant. Yet, I had always dreaded the moment when Sara would have to be told that she was adopted. I did not want her to ever, ever feel that anyone had given her up, no matter how reasonable the rationale. I wanted Sara, who was the center of our life together, to always live in the safety and serenity of our love. Who could have given this beautiful child away?

Thoughts like these are part of the ambivalence adoptive parents live with. Had her birth mother not chosen to give her up for adoption, we would not have had little Sara in our lives. The eternal vacillation between resentment and gratitude had become part of our lives, but still, the moment our child could conceptualize adoption remained a fear zone for us. We were Mama and Daddy. We were the faces into which she first smiled and whose hands she first had reached for from her crib. We were Sara's reality, her world.

As life encroached on us with scenes of mothers giving birth on TV, Sara became enchanted with the birth process. She often asked, even at three years old, to play the birth scene with me. She would crawl up inside my large T-shirt to simulate a pregnant mommy. I'd grunt and groan to approximate labor, and she would pop out and begin to cry like a newborn, at which point I would show great surprise and joy. She would giggle with delight and run off happily to play.

After this routine became a regular ritual of ours, I realized that of course this wasn't the way it actually happened. If we were going to introduce Sara to the idea that she was adopted, I had to begin acting out a different scenario. I resisted it passionately, yet it was a task I had to do. The sooner the child naturally accepted the idea, the less traumatic it would be, I reasoned, but the instinct in my gut to protect her was strong. Neither Jason nor I wanted Sara to feel abandoned, and that was the fear and our resistance behind broaching the topic of adoption. It was, however, inevitable—and imminent.

It took time before I had the courage to say, "Well, Sara, you didn't come out of Mommy's tummy. Daddy and I went to the hospital to get you. Let me show you how it happened." Sara seemed satisfied with our occasional ritual of "coming to get her from the hospital" and delighted in the fun of it. I didn't find this unusual at all, since my other three kids, then twenty-four, twenty-three, and twenty-one, still asked me to relate their births to them. They took exceptional pleasure in the details: how they cried, how one son peed in my face on the delivery table, how one always barfed on his dad as he kissed him goodbye in the morning. These are the stories of our lives that ground us to history and connectedness. Sara wanted history, too, but history for an adopted child is fraught with the choices of others and an uprooted destiny.

At school one day, Becky, one of Sara's teachers, had gotten pregnant and was having the inevitable discussion of where babies come from. It became a hot topic over several months as Becky's expanding belly sparked the children's interest. Becky and her belly caused great excitement in the "ducklings." Her situation was the impetus to light the fire of curiosity about the topic in Sara's little head. Sara's logic was beautiful as we lay snuggling close to each other, counting the neon stars pasted above the bed. "Mommy." Sara's voice was serious. "Babies grow in their mommy's tummy, right?" Since I think it's inane to engage in an anatomy lesson about the difference between a tummy and a womb in spite of the feminist purists, I replied simply, "Yes, they do."

"But I didn't grow in your tummy 'cause you and Daddy came to the hospital to get me, right?" I felt a sense of vertigo as my hold on the clarity of the moment swept into the present. *This is it!* I thought. *This is the moment I have feared. I'm going to blow it! I'm not ready. Poor baby; she's been thinking about this. She's thought it through and has questions. Damn, I am not ready!* The phony stars above us, which normally began to fade after a few seconds, were exceptionally bright even though the lights had been out for a while. The darkness was palpable. Sara's voice was sweet but earnest. She deserved an honest answer.

"Yes, that's right, sweetie, you didn't grow in Mommy's tummy." I said it. The rule most therapists would apply in this situation is that less is better; don't tell them more than they ask. Don't give them more than they can handle, and don't get too detailed. I secretly hoped that my brief answer would end it; I prayed it would. There was a long silence; I could feel Sara thinking about something, thinking big thoughts for a four-year-old.

"Then whose tummy did I grow in, Mommy?" I was thankful for the darkness at that moment, because I didn't want my little child to see the flow of tears from my eyes just then while I tried to compose myself. How could she understand? This was certainly not the time to discuss details about Alex, the reasons, the situation, and the fact that Alex now had another child who was Sara's half-sister, whom Alex had decided to keep. I couldn't explain those things, and silently I screamed at Alex for giving up Sara and leaving me with the hard questions. Future questions swarmed in my head at a dizzying speed, questions with no easy answers, for we lived in a world where all the roles had changed, where all the rules had changed, and in which we had to learn as we go. The "natural" things like parenting were complex and uncertain.

"You were in someone else's tummy." That was all I said, simply that. A simple fact. Someone else's tummy. No adornment. No elaboration. Again, silence from beside me. Again, pain from within me. My pain was great, and I hoped that Sara was sorting out this puzzle in a way she could cope with.

The stars were gone now, and I could hear Jason's footsteps on the stairs. I knew he would soon rescue me from this hell, this real moment in our lives. "Mommy, I think all babies need a mommy, and I needed a special mommy, and so you came and got me, right?" "That's absolutely right, Sara Doll." It jumped out of me.

"And so we'll love each other for ever and ever, right?"

"Right, my baby, you're so right. For ever and ever."

"Sara, it's time for your story." Jason appeared innocently in the room, smelling of aftershave and toothpaste.

"OK, Daddy." Sara reached over and planted her nightly kiss on my lips and leaped from the big bed into her daddy's arms. I heard the story through my quiet sobs—another silly, funny adventure that Jason took Sara on each night. At least for now she had been satisfied . . . at least until the next question.

That was the night I decided to begin telling Sara the story of her birth, at least my version of it. Every night, I lay down with her and ended the day with "our story," which went something like this:

> Well, once upon a time (all stories must start that way or kids won't listen, I've learned), Mommy and Daddy fell in love and got married. We loved each other so much that we wanted to have a family. Now, Mommy already had Christian, Liam, and Daniella, but she couldn't have any more babies. Her baby maker was broken. So Mommy and Daddy prayed every night to God to send us a little girl to love. Every night, Mommy would stand over your little crib and call to you in Heaven and ask you to find us.
>
> One night, we got a call on the phone. It was very dark outside and raining. It was a doctor, who said that he had a perfect little girl. He asked if we wanted her. We said, "Oh, yes! We've been waiting for so long." So the

doctor said that we could come and see you. So Mommy and Daddy and Sister got into the car and drove a very long way to a hospital. We were very happy and nervous.

We went up the elevator that led to a little room. There, in the middle of the room, was a little baby, all wrapped in a pink blanket. I went over to her and looked at her. It was you. I touched your little turned-up nose and picked you up and said to Daddy, "Here's your girl! Here's the one you've been waiting for."

Daddy was so happy. We unwrapped you and counted your fingers and toes: one, two, three, four, five, six, seven, eight, nine, ten fingers. Perfect! One, two, three, four, five, six, seven, eight, nine, ten toes. Perfect! The nurse said, "Now, who wants to feed this little girl?" and I said, "I do!" And your daddy said, "I do!" And your sister said, "I do!" But you said "Mama," so I fed you. (Actually, Jason got to feed her first.)

We were all so happy. You looked at Mommy with your big blue eyes, and I recognized you as the little girl I had been calling to. You were the one who had been calling to me, too. And I was happy.

This storytelling became our ritual every night from then on. It was our secret story, the story that grounded Sara to a heritage she could see and feel and remember. If I ever missed a word or phrase in the sequence, she would stop me and make me start over. I guess everyone needs a story. The thing is, I really *did* call for her every night beside that empty crib. The thing is, I really *do* believe that we were meant to be together from the beginning of time and that we will always be together. The thing is, I don't believe in accidents, I believe in magic—and when Sara announced to me after our story time that she had, indeed, heard my voice from "out there" and had "decided to come to be with me and her daddy," it was one magical night.

It was about that time that Sara began telling me her own version of our story, how she was an angel who had heard my prayer and decided that I would make a good mommy, that she had been looking for me for a long, long time, and now she had found me. "Now we are home again," she would say dreamily, and the spirit within me would know that this was no story, that it was as real as the sunrise, as real as hope itself.

Dear Alaina,

The last conversation we had was very emotional for me, as I know it was for you. I want to thank you for your truthfulness and honesty. Telling Sara must have been the hardest thing for you, but you're doing the right thing. Now that I am a mommy and love the ground that Hope walks on, I can understand how you feel. Also, being Sara's birth mother, I feel a little guilty. I feel I have caused you some pain. I don't want you or your family to ever feel hurt or pain because of me. Sara is a very smart little girl, and she has the best family she could ever want or need. As her birth mother, I know this, because my heart is at peace, and hers will be, too. Thank you again for your trust in telling me this very important decision.

You know, we should write a book so other birth mothers and adopting parents could read our story and know that adoption does work and can have a happy ending. It all comes down to lots of love and understanding, how two women with different lives came together to create a safe, happy life for one little girl. What great women we are. You go, girl!

Well, my little one needs me, so I will sign off for now. Always remember that I love you, and be strong. You're doing the right thing.

Love,
Hope and Alex
P.S. I got Sara's picture. She is so grown up. She is truly beautiful. Thank you again.

§

Dear Alex,

Just a quick note to say hello and send off a few pictures of the cutest baby in the world. I appreciated your last card and picture. You look very pretty.

I am saving everything you send for Sara. Someday they will mean a great deal to her. Rest assured that I will never forget you. I think about you often when I see Sara. I wonder what of you she is exhibiting that I am unaware of.

Sara is talking a blue streak right now. She repeats everything, even things she is not supposed to. The other day she said, "Oh, shit!" I said, "We don't say those bad words." Of course, she had heard it from me. The next day she said, "Oh, shit! Bad word!" So you see, she is quite a character.

All dogs are called "Sammy." She loves her three cats, but they don't always love her because she pulls their tails and then says, "Be nice!" What a kid! She dances all the time. She loves the Beatles and insists that Jason, Daniella, or I dance with her to every song on the tapes. She makes up songs, too. Here's her latest:

"I love you. I love you much. I love you more. Daddy, my daddy. Happy dinner."

There is so much to tell you about her that it would fill a book. She is the happiest, friendliest child I have ever seen. Everyone is her friend. When she goes into the bank, she immediately walks to the president's desk, climbs up on his lap, and begins to use his phone. "Hello, Baty," she says. Then she walks over to some group of old men, and before long, she is dancing and singing for them. Jason paints a lot during the day, and she always stands in front of his work and says, "Oh, Daddy, wow! Nice painting!" She's great for the ego. If anything ever happened to her, Jason and I would die. We love her so much.

Well, that's the update. Hope that things with you are well. I truly do, Alex. You deserve it. Take care. I love you.

Love,
Alaina

§

I am 54 years old
I have three grown children
Yet I visit an elementary school every day
I'm sometimes mistaken for a grandmother
But I'm not
What am I?
I am in two life passages at once:
Menopause and Chuck E. Cheese's birthday parties
I hate both
But if I had to choose one
I'd choose menopause
What am I?
I'm called Mother, Mom. And Mommy
I wake up with stiff joints
And notice the skin on my face is veering south
The parents of my daughter's friends went to high school
With my two sons
What am I?
I am heard to say, and often:
"I'm too old for this shit!"
Or "This is the best decision of my life;
I have been reborn."
The funny thing is
I mean them both
With all my heart
What am I?
My friends say that I'm courageous
But I say I simply follow my heart

My friends say I'm crazy
And yet they envy me
Secretly
What am I?
When men start over,
Society says: "Wow! What a man!"
And never think to question him.
When a woman dares it,
She's thought of as too old for such nonsense
I say to hell with them
What am I?
I am 54 years old
Almost 55
I have learned to stop and experience
What is in front of me,
No longer in a hurry, no longer
Running toward or away from
And every night I tell a bedtime story
About angels and destiny, and treasures
Of the heart.
What am I?
I am an adoptive mother.

§

"I am definitely going through something." That was a code between Jason and me that one of us was struggling with one of our inner demons. It could be the "abandonment" demon or the "you can't trust anyone" demon. Regardless of what was lurking about in one of our heads, it usually announced the onset of a problem between us, which then usually resulted in some soul searching. We both struggled with so many issues, as I suppose all couples do. But with us, they were complicated by the fact that both of us were extremely sensitive and could read each other like a book. Jason could walk into a room and sense if I was struggling or afraid of something. He knew that I struggled with getting older; that I was scared of dying young, as my mother did; that I mourned the fact that I didn't have a perfect relationship with my father. Once in a while, I would be attacked by one of these specters, then go immediately to "catastrophic mode" and step into what I lovingly called the "black hole of depression."

It was hard to find a woman who was exactly in my shoes. Either my friends had no kids or their kids were grown and gone, or some other configuration of lifestyle. There was no one who still, at the age of fifty-four, couldn't travel at will or go out with the girls regularly. I was still in the mother mode, which meant that I had to be home at night, taking responsibility for Sara. I knew they didn't understand and probably thought I was weird, but the truth was that I really was in two stages of life. I, too, had kids who were out of the house, but I couldn't be free like my friends who were in that category. I was also still in the mothering category, something I chose but something that was a 24/7 deal, as the kids said.

The biggest demon for me was honesty. Jason desperately needed me to be honest because his first wife left him for someone else. As a couple, we had decided to be honest. This had held true for most things in our lives. I didn't know if he had secrets, but there was something in me that had to have a secret of some kind. It didn't have to be a big, monumental secret; it just had to be something that I kept for myself. I knew intellectually that it was not necessary to do this anymore, that it was a holdover from my childhood, when I needed to protect parts of myself to survive. But now I was fifty-four, and keeping a little secret here or there was a habit for me. It was like a security blanket, and it drove Jason crazy. Consequently, he didn't believe anything I said—at least, I felt that way. I tried to explain to him that my keeping secrets wasn't serious, but deep down, I knew that part of my spiritual evolution was to rid myself of the habit.

Keeping my correspondence with Alex a secret from Jason was a real spiritual dilemma. I was plagued with guilt when I did things like that, but I had found from my life experience that the truth is the lesser of two evils, which brought me to downright lying.

Lying. We all do it, yet we teach our children never to. The Ten Commandments says "Thou shalt not bear false witness," yet I wondered if God thought that one through, because the older I got, the better case I was making for fudging a little. Lying can help one avoid an embarrassment, spare oneself grief, and spare another's feelings. Now, in marriage, I definitely felt that total honesty had its downside. Of course, Jason and I did vow honesty in the beginning of our marriage, but many times, an argument or hurt began with sharing honest feelings. How often had my honesty in reporting something my three older children had said wounded Jason? How often had his honesty been ill-timed or unsolicited? Who said that women wanted the whole truth about their weight, their age, or anything, for that matter? No, honesty was not all it was cracked up to be.

Take, for example, the brief and pleasureless affair that I had had at the end of my first marriage. It had been the worst year of my life. I was tormented by guilt from this sin, which took place more on paper than in bed. I thought that without a full and open disclosure of the truth, what was left of our dying marriage would be doomed. So I told Johann the truth—big, big mistake! That moment of naïveté bought me one and a half years of bitter rebuke and fighting and destroyed a twenty-year marriage, my children's trust in the safety of our home, their belief in their mother, and their view of reality.

During the early months of meeting and corresponding with Alex, I could not be totally honest. How could I? I would write a supportive letter, a letter revealing my higher self, but between the lines I swallowed hard on the fears, resentments, and insecurities I was feeling. I felt I couldn't tell it all. I wouldn't have had Sara if I had told the truth. Even Alex, I was sure, had to lie to me, and to herself, to survive. She once confided to me that she lied to the passersby on her daily walk when they inquired about her plans before Sara was born, and that after the birth, she lied about where Sara was. I didn't condemn her. On the contrary, I could imagine the incredulous stares of strangers who could not have comprehended why a twenty-seven-year-old woman would give up her baby. I pictured Alex trying to avoid people who might recognize her, dodging well-wishers and curious eyes. She lied again and again. "Sara is sleeping at home with friends" was infinitely easier to say than "I gave up my baby for adoption. Have a nice day!" because the next question would be "Why?" And that question would be hard to answer for anyone, no matter how convinced she was of her reasons.

Maybe it was Alex's honesty with herself and who she was at the time that allowed her to make her choice in the first place. Alex was, after all, an "out there" person, much like I was. But just as my apparent openness was a deflection of my own closet of secret pain, I believed this of her, as well. I couldn't speak with certainty of what her life had been like, but what I did know helped me to understand her: Her father, a US soldier stationed briefly in Germany, had died in Viet Nam. To my knowledge, Alex never knew him. Abandonment. Her mother worked to raise and support five children and died at fifty of cancer, when Alex was a late adolescent. Abandonment. Alex had to learn early to make it alone. Her assortment of last names always confused me. She had used several last names over the years, yet Sara's birth certificate read Porter. Since Duncan's name was Miller, I assumed Porter was Alex's maiden name. She was always elusive about her past, and I sensed she was trying to move away from it. No matter what their stories, the names spelled *abandonment*.

Dishonest or honest, when Alex was with me or I with her, we always had an honesty between us on a deeper level. Alex's face could never lie to me, and neither could mine to her. When I looked into her soulful eyes, a lifetime of mistrust and innocence overshadowed her street-savvy demeanor and Generation X nonchalance. Perhaps I saw the inner child Alex tried so hard to hide from the world. Perhaps I saw the little girl who was actually putting herself up for adoption—a lost, wandering orphan woman, so like the child I saw when I looked in a mirror. Or perhaps I simply saw Sara: funny; cute face; laughing eyes, both childlike and ancient. Whatever the truth, I was drawn to this woman, for I recognized a connection buried deep in our collective unconscious. We recognized one another: fellow liars.

What was the upside of total honesty? No business deal would ever be reached. No one could keep a job. No friendship would last. No marriage would reach its Golden Anniversary. I wanted to rewrite the ninth Commandment to read:

Thou shalt not bear false witness unless:

1. You might hurt someone.
2. A higher purpose would be served.
3. You can spare a friend grief.
4. The trouble it would generate would outweigh the purity of the principle.

I would have lied any day to save my marriage; I would have lied any day to keep Sara or protect any of my children; I would have lied any day to spare myself an argument that had no resolution; in short, there were some things one just didn't want to say or hear. Besides, God was never married.

That was my rationalization for being less than honest, for living as I did. Part of me bought it, and the rest of me knew that it had to change. If only I believed that I would be acceptable to Jason if I told the truth. But then, that was my demon, not his. I was not perfect, far from it. It was so hard to change.

§

The years went by so fast. Sara was four, and I was beginning to forget how she was as a baby. I tried to conjure images of Christian, Liam, and Daniella in my mind, too. If only I could get them back as toddlers for one day; how I would love to gaze into their innocent faces before the grief of the adult world placed filters of pain in their eyes. The guilt demon was on my shoulder. *Go away! I need to think of something good, something happy. Sara.*

Everyone told me to write things down when Christian, Liam, and Daniella were little. They claimed I would someday forget the cute, bright utterances and occurrences that filled my life in those days: the firsts, the profound comments "out of the mouths of babes." I maintained at the time that I could never forget a single word, yet there I was, having forgotten most their expressions, and I didn't want it to happen again. Now Sara was four, and although I was certain that I could never forget how adorable she was and the things she did, I was a little wiser this time. This time I would sit down and take the time to document her so that one day I could relive her through my words. Nothing could be left to chance or be dictated by fatigue this time around.

So, I attempted to describe this child—this Sara O'Connell—who was named at the restaurant in Seattle long before we made our first contact with Jack Hartnell, the adoption attorney. These are the words I wrote in my journal to describe her:

Sara! The name itself says a lot. You know that any girl named Sara has to epitomize charm, and Sara does, but I am getting ahead of myself. Perhaps it's easier to begin with what she hates, because Sara knows exactly what she likes and what she hates, and never the twain shall meet.

Sara hates to have her hair washed. She is as tender-headed as I am; I have come to pity my poor mother trying to scrub my head when I was little, because Sara is just like I was. Every bath is a negotiation; every comb-out is a trauma. I have to bribe her, cajole, and sometimes threaten in order to get her cleaned up.

Once she is dry, she takes on a completely different persona. She loves to dress up, and she especially loves dresses. No girl has ever loved dresses as much as she does, and jewelry, too. In fact, Sara has quite a flair for style. She dresses up all the time, concocting outrageously creative and stylish getups. Headbands, belts, wing-type capes, and so on. But I am off track.

Sara hates transitions with a vengeance. It doesn't matter if what she is going to do is better than what she has been doing; she just hates moving from one thing to another. It's the principle of the thing, I guess. Once she gets her bearings, however, she slowly begins to take over, eventually becoming the center of attention. For example, a few weeks ago, we went on a picnic with a set of triplets, two boys and a girl. They were three weeks older than Sara. When Sara first eyed them, she immediately made a face and hid behind Jason. The parents of the triplets were anxious, worried that Sara wouldn't have a good time. I assured them, "Just give her ten minutes, and she'll be running the show." Actually, it took twelve minutes before she had the two boys chasing her, and in fourteen minutes, the girl was in tow and the four were off for the afternoon.

Sara is a born leader and entertainer, albeit a little on the dictatorial side. She gives orders with ease and resolve, and when she asks a question, she wants a quick answer. She will say, "Do you want to play, yes or no?" Patience is not one of her virtues.

Sara is not fond of big dogs, getting her face in water (God help her poor swimming teacher!), and sharing. She does not forgive easily. When Liam and Christian took a small box of sparklers left over from the Fourth of July (we had twelve boxes left; Sara was afraid of them anyway and had refused to touch them), she greeted the boys on their next visit with, "Where are my sparklers?" She also has not forgiven her grandma for altering the order of events for getting ready for bed when she babysat. At their last phone conversation, she picked up the phone and declared, "Grandma, you can't take my clothes off again when I go to bed." She has a memory just like Jason's, I swear.

On Sara's "In" list, she likes My Little Pony, playing monster, bacon, chicken, Disney movies, mangos, hearing Jason make up stories, imagining elaborate stories of her own, posing for the camera, German pickles, and anything sweet—especially chocolate. In fact, a chocolate chip cookie can make her do almost anything . . . except put her face in water. She can sing "Hoppa Hoppa Reiter" in German with her own dialect and perfect intonation. She loves to design gowns and put on makeup "like Mommy," and she admires herself in any reflection she can find: mirror, pond, window. She is fascinated with birth and loves to hide under my blouse then pop out, at which time she wails like a newborn and wants to be held.

On the Oedipal side, she still is madly in love with her daddy and just tolerates my presence most of the time. She is so lucky to be adored by her dad, and it shows in many ways. She loves all men, something that I am sure

Jason will live to regret. At school, she runs with the boys in lieu of playing house with the more tranquil little girls. She usually has five or six boys around her, catering to her whims—or should I say orders. Once, I arrived at school and found her in the center of nine little boys, all playing drums in a circle around her. She was in the middle, singing her heart out. I wish I had had a camera.

We cannot rely on Sara to do the right thing in public, as she has very little concern for what others think. She is who she is, feels what she feels, and does what she wants. If Jason weren't strong, we would have a time with her, because I am a softy. Once, on a bus in Mexico, a nice young man sitting next to us reached over and patted her on the knee, to which she replied, "Don't touch me! I'm still little!" He pulled away in embarrassment and said that we had certainly trained her well. The thing was, we had never said a thing to her about this; that's just her sense of herself.

I have a deep conviction that Sara was a sailor in a past life because of her expertise in tying knots. Maybe that's why she hates water now. Who knows? Anything that can be tied in our house is tied. Every string, belt, shoestring, rope—whatever—ends up tied together in an elaborate knot. She even ties herself to things, or us to her. It is incredible! She constructs pulleys and contraptions of intricate complexity. It's a bitch trying to untie her shoes after she's had a go at them. They are tied to stay tied.

Sara has an amazing imagination. She is constantly inventing scenarios and stories around her toys. She has make-believe friends, all of whom have creative names and are capable of intricate conversations with her. She can play for hours while Jason paints, content with her imagination and fantasy.

Sara is a loving girl. She knows how to receive affection and to give it. She is not fearful. If I ever feel tired or down, she puts her arms around me and comforts me with words like, "Don't worry, Mommy, everything is all right 'cause I am here, and I'll never leave you." It feels good to know that she has heard this so often from us that it's second nature to her. On a funnier note, she also has picked up some of my New Age jargon: "Do you want me to check your heart chakra, Mommy?"

Whenever I think about Sara, I think that one thing is certain: Sara O'Connell is a powerful life force. She emanates life, spirit, light, and passion. There are no walls or niceties to mask the real person that she is. As long as you don't try to comb her hair or ask her to jump into the pool, she's fine. If you look up the words *tenacity*, *charm*, *determination*, *affectionate*, and *individuality*, you will find a picture of a cute four-year-old with large, expressive eyes that say, "I'm Sara O'Connell, and I'm getting bigger."

The specifics of the various milestones that my first three children passed through, such as learning their ABCs and learning to ride a two-wheeler, although momentous at the time, were all but lost to my conscious mind. There were three of them, after all, born within a three-and-a-half-year span, and I was lucky if I survived the day, much less had the wherewithal to record the event. When they went off to preschool, they were the Three Musketeers, two little boys with a tiny sister in tow. There were no tears, no resistance, because they had each other. They began soccer together, and the boys played right up to their Interscholastic Federation Championship game in their senior years, fifteen years later. They climbed trees together, contracted lice and chicken pox together, threw up together. Raising them was a group experience.

Raising Sara was just as unique as my marriage to Jason was. The rules were different, the eating habits were different. Liam was almost nine pounds at birth, and Christian weighed in at thirty-one pounds when he was twelve months old, so having a thirty-five-pound (soaking wet) five-year-old was quite a change. What Sara lacked in girth, though, she made up for in *esprit de corps*. Her fifth year was as uniquely her own as each year before had been. That year, Sara discovered that there might actually be some advantage to playing with the other little girls. Before this, Sara had sought out the company of every boy at her preschool; girls were too sedentary for her. And what was this doll business, anyway? Sara liked to run, jump, climb, mix it up. I attributed her fearless pursuit of boys as a manifestation of her relationship with her idol, icon, and god, her daddy. I mean *Daddy* with a capital D, for he walked on water in her eyes. Once, though, when he rebuked her for a transgression, I heard her say sharply, "You're not my hero anymore!"

In her fifth year, Sara still abhorred water. At the YMCA, she held the dubious honor of having flunked swimming three times. At the end of each session, she received a certificate that read:

Sara O'Connell received training in Guppies.
Next class: Guppies!

Since her peers were moving on to Polliwogs or Tadpoles, I felt appropriate shame that my daughter relentlessly resisted any suggestion to put her face in the water. But she was unaffected by her status and always calmed me down with the assurance, "When I'm six, I'll learn to swim." With that, she would be off and running. I thought I had overcome pride and hubris, having finished the first round of kids. Unlike most twenty-something mothers whose conversations I overheard on the playground, I was no longer interested in how fast my daughter could do this or that. I had learned that none of it mattered in the end who learned what when. But traces of my ego did surface with this swimming thing, I will admit.

The truth was that Sara didn't care what people thought; enough of Jason's artistic nature had rubbed off on her. When I said, "You just have to be a good girl in public!" she would innocently respond, "Why, Mommy?" I never did have a good answer for that. "Well, because . . . because I said so," I would proffer weakly. What I really meant was "So I'll look like a good mother."

Sara was just Sara, wherever she went. No airs, no people-pleasing behaviors, just an opinionated little girl with eyes so bright and a smile so contagious that almost everyone in the bank, post office, cleaners, pet store, and grocery store knew her by name. "Oh, hi, Sara," a checker would say, and I would wonder where on earth they'd met. More from my journal:

> Aside from water, big dogs, and occasionally the dark, Sara is fearless. She knows no strangers. She sees the world as safe, a concept foreign to me because I think every stranger on the street is a potential child molester, but that's my life filter, not hers. No one has betrayed Sara.
>
> In the "Love" category are the following: angels and horses (by far numbers one and two), mangos, Disneyland, playing dress-up, and cats, although I don't think her four cats share her enthusiasm. They usually take for higher ground at the mere sight of her, probably because she hasn't figured out that being dragged by one's collar is not particularly fun for the cat. But these four felines tolerate her transgressions as they did Daniella's, who could frequently be seen wearing one of them as a cape.
>
> Sara is an expert on the subject of angels. She tells anyone whom she meets that she is Mommy's angel, and though they find her statement charming, she is dead serious. She wears an angel pin whenever she goes out, insists on angels to adorn her room, and talks to me about them as though everyone should be able to see them. Actually, I take her seriously. Her imaginary friends have always been angels, and she began many intimate conversations with me with, "Remember, Mommy, before you called to me in Heaven and I was still an angel?"
>
> I remember one day at the lunch table when she was involved in an avid conversation with someone next to her. She made a little plate and placed a cookie on it. When I inquired as to whom she was playing with, she said, "Oh, that is just my little sister Hope, my sister angel." I took no stock in her remark until the next day, when Alex called to say that the ultrasound had confirmed that she

was carrying another girl and that she was planning to name her Hope. I never questioned Sara on the subject again; I just listened.

Sara's belief, of course, is fostered by my own belief in divine guidance, but sometimes I am humbled by this child's beautiful connection to the spiritual realm. She, unlike most of us adults, has not forgotten who she is, and this inner knowing emanates from her dancing, carefree eyes. Once she said to me, "Don't be sad, because I was sent to love you." She is an old soul, a kindred spirit, and we speak a language that resonates in the harmony between us. Sometimes I wonder where and when our spirits have crossed before; she is so much my daughter. Except, of course, that she doesn't care if she passes swimming. But she has promised me that she would learn, because "now I am six."

Sara entered school at five years old, and from then on, many things began to happen for her. The funniest was on her first day in school. When I picked her up from school, we had the following conversation:

"Mommy, don't you just hate timeouts?"

"Yes. Did you get a timeout today?"

"Yes. Mommy?"

"Yes."

"I love you."

"I love you too, but why did you get a timeout?"

"Do you promise not to get mad?"

"Yes, I promise."

"For kissing a boy."

"How many boys did you kiss?"

"Mommy?"

"Yes, Sara."

"I love you."

"I love you, too, but exactly how many boys did you kiss today?"

"Mommy, promise me that you won't get mad!"

"OK."

"All of them!"

Sara took to school socially like a flea on a dog. However, we began to notice immediately that she was having trouble with her letters. All her d's looked like b's, and she seemed not to be able to see the difference. Regardless of the assurances we were getting at conferences that she would overcome this, I didn't believe them. This went on through kindergarten, first, and second grades. Sara's handwriting was reminiscent of a young boy's, not a little girl's, which were usually neat. She was having a lot of trouble learning to read.

I noticed that she wasn't paying attention during homework sessions. Jason worked hours upon hours with her. She would improve, but in the school setting, she would still do poorly. I talked to Alex about this and learned that she, too, had had the same problems and that she had been in Special Education. This explained her poor spelling in the letters she sent me.

Learning this kind of thing about one's child does wonders for one's humility. There is a certain grief that one experiences when one knows her child is struggling in school, and it was a new feeling to me. My ego had always been well greased by my other three kids' great accomplishments, but now I was learning what it was like to have a child who struggled instead of being at the top of the class. In the past, I had had very little to do with the children's homework, but Sara was unable to do hers without help. Jason took all of this much better than I did.

As a counselor, I had access to many intelligence tests. I gave Sara a few and discovered that she had an IQ of 120. Then why wasn't she achieving? Naturally, her school didn't accept my results, but when we asked them to test her, they came up with the same results. She scored poorly in the areas we had noticed and was placed in some special programs. Sara told me that when she saw that the other kids could finish their work quickly, she would just fill in any old answer so she could go to recess and play. As a counselor, I was beginning to understand the pained expressions on the parents' faces in my office who had kids who were not thriving. Now I knew.

With test results in hand, a sixty-page assessment, we handed them to her new school when we moved. They rejected the assessment, retested her, and said she was "just like all the other kids." As an educator, I was infuriated by this total lack of knowledge about Special Education criteria. Ultimately, we dismissed the new school's results and tutored her at home. Sara's schooling went year-round so she would not fall behind. She got better and better and learned to compensate for her weaknesses.

We looked at Sara's strengths, which were numerous. By now she was taking gymnastics and doing well. Her petite, agile little body made her a natural. And then there were horses. Sara had loved horses since she was a baby. Whenever we entered a toy store and gave her a choice to pick out a toy, it was inevitably a horse: big horses, little horses, red ones and black ones—it didn't matter; Sara had an insatiable love of horses. When she was eight, Jason began taking her riding, and that, as they say, was all she wrote. Now, every Saturday morning, she and Jason would take off together and ride for an hour. Her diminutive body atop a huge horse was quite a sight. Of course, since I was afraid of everything, I couldn't bear to accompany them on these outings because I was sure she would be killed. It took a couple of rides before I realized that watching her bob up and down on this massive beast was going to put me in my grave, so I stopped going to preserve my marriage and my sanity.

I was in awe of my now eight-year-old Sara. I knew that she and Jason had an uncanny bond, but I still liked to think that I played a role in her life, albeit a less fun one. I stood in awe of her spirit, and the connection I felt was real, even though at eight years old, Sara now refused to let me call her an angel. She no longer talked to angels or about Heaven, and she was looking forward to becoming a teenager about as much as I was not looking forward to it. She had forgotten those things we used to share, but I hadn't.

§

I touched your cheek tonight as you slept
Lying open-armed in your bed.
Your face responded to my
Whispers although
Your eyes remained closed.
Sleep now, dear one
You are safe with me
Your angel is here, too

So no harm can befall you.
Is that why your tiny arms are
Open wide
To embrace Heaven as you travel
Dream's trails?
No armor on your sweet face
No fear of monsters
No question of tomorrow
Sleep now, my dear one
For you have briefly returned to
Where you know who you are.
How I wish I could accompany you
On your journey
Just one more time
But my feet must grow roots here
Beside you so that you may
Fly free
Bring back a remembrance
When you return tomorrow, dear heart
A reminder that I, too, have made this trip
Before.

§

I closed my journal and tried to sleep, but that night I was transported back to the day that Alex got to see Sara when she was four years old. It was a day I will never forget, the day our pact was finalized, the day I had to start telling Jason the truth.

Dear Alex,

When I got the call today that you were in town, my heart stopped momentarily. Even though I know that you are no threat to Jason or me or our little family, and even though I knew why you were in Washington, I got that familiar twinge inside. It's probably some reptilian brain thing about self-preservation, territory, and the like. My rational mind knew that you wanted to visit me in my office and show Hope to me, that a big part of you wanted me to see how good a mother you had turned out to be now that you had your own little girl. I understood that completely on one level. But when I heard your voice, that optimistic lilt and tone, I responded with my guts rather than my brain. "Why don't you skip the office visit and come over to the house?" Your silence told me that you realized the importance of that remark. Sara would be there, and I had said four years earlier that the next time you would see her was when she asked to see you, and I anticipated that to be after she turned eighteen years old.

Our last visit was when Sara had just turned one and Jason and I had decided it was better not to confuse her with two sets of parents. Our situation was atypical, since most birth parents separate from the baby at birth. That had been your ace in the hole, remember? You had held out signing the papers until we promised to let you visit Sara once a month for the first year. We had negotiated a deal with your therapist at the time. Negotiation implies, however, that both parties have something to do with it, and in that case, you held all the chips.

We lived in terror that you would have a change of heart. You were no teenager. You were twenty-seven years old and had been abandoned by everyone you had ever loved. Your dad had died in Viet Nam. Your mom had died of cancer when you were just a teen. Your first husband was gone. Duncan, Sara's biological father, had left you, and now you were losing Sara. Maybe part of you wanted to know if we were going to drop you as soon as we had what we wanted, namely, Sara. I can understand that. Many birth mothers must feel that way.

Whatever your reason, you held us hostage for one year. Every month you'd make the trek to see Sara. You'd call her your baby and tell us how she looked like her daddy, and Jason and I would hold our breath. It was a hard time, a kind of adoption hell, which most people could never even imagine, much less agree to. But we wanted Sara, and so we agreed. For days before your visit and days after, Jason and I would argue over it, rage against the power you had over us, and proclaim our own feelings of total helplessness. Once you even threatened us over the phone, saying that if we weren't good to you, you would take her away. Many times I thought Jason was going to leap off the couch and shake you, and I had to pretend to be strong and wise when I, too, was scared to death and afraid to say the wrong thing.

And yet, a part of me felt for you, Alex. The part of me that is a mother understood what you were going through and made allowances for you. I understood how crazy you felt after birth, how emotional, irrational, unpredictable, how very fragile. For that reason, I tried to find a spot in my heart that could deal with the situation. I gave you my word on Sara's life that I would never abandon you and that I would never cut you out. I have never broken that promise to you, and I may well be the only person on Earth who hasn't.

After you drove away, I cried tears of relief and anguish for you and for myself. It was all so confusing. Life is easier when things are done in traditional ways. You know, Mama Bear, Papa Bear, and Baby Bear. But Jason will never know the safety of having his own child, whom no one can threaten or take away from him. Your needs stole that from him. I knew that feeling with the other three children. I could look around and say, "All this is mine." They came from my body. No one could lay claim on those children.

Over the last few years, friends have criticized me for sending you pictures and updates of Sara's progress. However, something in me always knew that we were linked for eternity and that someday Sara would need

you. And I had promised. As I have repeated a thousand
times, I never want Sara to think she was abandoned,
and that is why I have persevered in my correspondence.
It is a gift I one day will give to her when I explain how
deeply she was loved by two women.

The territorial part of me wants her all to myself, of
course, but another part of me knows that we humans
need all the love we can get. Statistics say that adopted
kids have more problems because they live with the
reality of that first rejection by their own mothers and
fathers.

I do know that you love her, Alex, even though
you couldn't raise her at the time. Naturally, there are
times when I curse you because you will someday be
the "real" mother. I am enraged when I see those talk-
show reunions that show a girl or boy embracing the
one who gave them away and the one who loved and
cared for them is nowhere in sight. Those shows, which
glorify the birth mothers, infuriate me. Suddenly, the
biological mother is the heroine. She has done none of
the work, but she assumes a mythical status, which is
usually undeserved. I sometimes see myself observing
Sara embracing you on a future *Oprah* show, and I see
that she finally feels complete.

But the term *mother* is a tricky one, isn't it? Who gets
to be called mother? I am Sara's mother. I am the one
who is here and now. You are, after all, the one who gave
her up. I am jealous and heartbroken that my lifelong
effort and commitment are dismissed by biology and
mystique. This is why there will be no search in our case.
When Sara wants to meet you, I will take her to you, but
still I am torn between compassion and rage, clarity and
confusion on the topic. Please forgive my truthfulness. It
is not meant to hurt you.

When you called, a tiny opening in my heart said
that it was OK for you to see her at this juncture in her

life, as long as you could play by some rules. You were to be my friend, not Sara's mother. You agreed, and I hung up the receiver, wondering if I had done the right thing. I knew Jason would not have agreed to your visit, or at least I thought so, so this would be an act of deception, and I didn't want to betray him more than I already had for the last four years. He guarded Sara with a religious fervor, which is both understandable and formidable. She is his only child.

I rushed home early to pick her up from preschool. I gave her a quick bath and dressed her cutely. I told her a friend and her baby were coming over and that we were going to have a party. Sara loves parties; she has the party gene. The mention of the word sends her into immediate compliance with any request, even brushing the tangles out of her hair. She was excited and I was nervous, though probably not as nervous as you were.

The doorbell rang, and I did a mental *Curtains up!* How were we supposed to act? Could we pull it off? Could you keep from crying? Could I? I was met at the door by a smiling face—two smiling faces, in fact, yours and Hope's. Camera in hand, you entered and extended your hand to Sara. "Hi, Sara," you said, and Sara lit up the room with her smile—your smile.

The next two hours seemed to play out in some kind of alternate reality, where rules were silently followed. Two women, two little girls, bonded by genetics, love, and destiny. Your energy impressed me, and several times I saw how my own fell short of a young woman of thirty-one. I am now fifty and am not the same kind of mom I was at twenty-six. I saw the difference. I felt it. I felt afraid and yet happy to see you dancing and playing on the floor with the two girls. I felt like an observer of the scene, watching two women who desperately wanted to do the right thing, where no words were necessary. To my amazement, it all seemed comfortable, and I felt at home with you there. Sara kissed and hugged little Hope, not realizing the tie between them, and you snapped away with your camera, trying to capture something you could take home with you to hold for the long winter ahead. I, too, was snapping photos and memories in my mind, making journal notes, looking at your features and trying to see Sara in you or Hope. *Actually, Sara looks like me*, I thought. And Hope looks like you. Funny, how Sara has taken on some characteristics from Jason and me. Or maybe, as I have often said, Sara is my natural daughter, lost to me and then found.

As the time neared an end, I sat next to you on the couch as we watched the girls play. I held your hand and listened carefully to the story of your healing. It wasn't easy for you to face giving up a child, yet Hope has become your salvation, your sign that God has forgiven you and that you have forgiven yourself. I felt it. I sat and held your strong hand, watched your large, dancing eyes fill with animation and laughter at your two daughters getting to know each other. The amazing thing of it all was that I was not threatened in the least. It seemed so natural. I know who I am. Sara knows who she is, and you know who you are, too. It's been a long road for us, Alex. I have loved you. I have resented you. I have been grateful to you. I have raged against you. Yet, here we were together, two women again. In the end, it was so simple and so beautiful.

Being an emotional woman, I felt my tears beginning to well up the moment you said you had to go. I wanted to ask you for dinner but felt that it didn't seem appropriate. I wanted to take you in my arms and cradle you, too. There was an eerie attraction to you: motherly, womanly, and utterly intimate. You wanted me to see how smart Hope was, and smart she is! I wanted you to see that Sara was OK with her fate, so I asked her to tell you, in her own words, how she came to live in our family.

She climbed up between us, looked straight into your eyes, and spoke with an honesty and beauty I have never before experienced on this earthly plane.

Well, once upon a time, my mommy and daddy fell in love and got married. They loved each other so much that they wanted to have a family. Now, Mommy already had Christian, Liam, and Daniella, but she couldn't have any more babies. Her baby maker was broken. So Mommy and Daddy prayed every night to God to send them a little girl to love. Every night, Mommy would stand over my little crib and call to me in Heaven and ask me to find them.

One night, they got a call on the phone. It was very dark outside and raining. It was a doctor, who said that he had a perfect little girl and asked if they wanted her. They said, "Oh, yes! We've been waiting for so long." So the doctor said that they could come and see me.

So Mommy and Daddy and Sister got in the car and drove a very long way to a hospital. They were very happy and nervous. They went up the elevator that led to a little room. There, in the middle of the room, was one little baby, all wrapped in pink. Mommy went over and looked at me. It was me, little Sara. She touched my little turned-up nose and picked me up and said to Daddy, "Here's your girl, the one you've been waiting for." Daddy was so happy. They unwrapped me and counted my fingers and toes: one, two, three, four, five, six, seven, eight, nine, ten fingers! Perfect. One, two, three, four, five, six, seven, eight, nine, ten toes! Perfect.

The nurse said, "Now, who wants to feed this little girl?" And Mommy said, "I do." And Daddy said, "I do." And Sister said, "I do." But I said,

"Mama!" So she fed me. We were all so happy. I looked at Mommy with my big blue eyes, and I recognized her as the little mommy I had been calling to. She was the one who had been calling to me, too. And I was happy.

When Sara was finished, there was a long silence. It was the kind of quiet one feels only in a church. Even little Hope had been quiet throughout the tale and sat mesmerized on the floor. My eyes were riveted to yours, and in them I saw an acceptance so profound, a serenity so sweet, and a love so great that I could not determine if we were two women or one; in that moment, there was no separation between us. I literally saw a wave of healing descend upon you, and I felt my heart open and my capacity to love expand, similar only to the moments just before birth, when I felt my body open in one single wave of surrender to life. "Thank you," you said without tears. "Thank you," I replied, and nothing else was required of the moment. We both knew that Sara was whole, that you were healed, and that I would never be threatened again by losing Sara to you.

Almost without words, you packed Hope's diaper bag and hoisted her to your hip for departure. You asked Sara for a goodbye kiss, and she resisted at first. I whispered into her ear that it would make you very happy if she would hug you. Her arms opened without hesitation, and she embraced you fully and kissed both cheeks in innocent abandon. I stood in front of you and held your face in my hands for what seemed a long time. I felt utter love for you, as I do now as I write. I saw Sara in your wide-eyed gaze. I saw peace and the magical bond that had brought us together five years before . . . or five centuries, for there is a timelessness to our relationship.

I will always remember your final words to Sara as she pulled away from your arms. "Sara, I live very far away, and I will probably not see you again until you are a very big girl. But I want you to know how beautiful I think you are, how smart you are, and how much I love you. You are so beautiful!"

"I know," she answered matter-of-factly, as if she hears that every day—because she does—and away she ran. You looked at me. I caressed you and said, " I will always love you. We are one in our love for Sara. I have kept my promise. I have kept my promise."

"You're the only one," you whispered as you walked away, and we both knew it was true.

Alaina

§

CHAPTER 23
Alex

I called Alaina at the end of February and told her I was planning a trip to Washington for three days in March to see friends. None of my Washington friends had met Hope, and I wanted to show her off. They were there when I went through the adoption with Sara, and now I wanted them to meet Hope. I really wanted Alaina to meet her.

I asked if we could meet at her work, but to my surprise, she suggested that we meet at her house. I was not prepared for that at all. I knew Sara would be there, and I didn't expect Alaina to let me see her at this point in her life. Was I ready to see her again?

When Alaina said it would be OK to come to the house, my heart started pounding. I really thought that the next time I would see her would be when Sara was eighteen years old. My mind started to race. How was I going to act toward her? How would she act toward me, a perfect stranger? Would there be a bond between us? Four years had passed since I last held her, and she had been only a baby. Now she was a little girl.

I thanked Alaina for this wonderful opportunity and thought how very brave it was of her to let me see Sara now. She did make it clear to me that I was only to be a friend of the family's and not Sara's birth mother, which I agreed to. I would never say anything to hurt Sara or Alaina. I knew that Alaina would tell Sara about me when the time was right and that it was Alaina and Jason's decision, not mine. I was so happy that she was going to let me see her that I would have agreed to anything at that point.

We flew in on Wednesday, and I called Alaina shortly after our arrival. She said that we could come over Thursday afternoon after she picked Sara up from school. The next day, Hope and I drove to their beautiful home. As I was driving, I noticed that the streets looked different, but maybe I was different. Maybe it was me who had changed. My life had been healing over these past four years. I was not angry or jealous anymore. The memories started coming back, those times of riding endless hours to visit Sara once a month, grasping onto a baby that no longer belonged to me. Now I wasn't alone during my drive; my little Hope was asleep in her car seat, and my heart had healed from the scars of the past.

As we approached their house, my poor heart was beating a hundred miles an hour, and my palms were sweaty. I parked the car down the street past their house and just sat there. It seemed that I sat there for an hour. Hope was starting to wake up, and my heart was in my throat. She started to get fussy, so I knew I had to get her out and walk up to the door.

How many times I had walked this sidewalk full of anticipation and hope. With little Hope in tow, I walked to the door. I looked down at my fifteen-month-old baby and smiled. This was the first time she was going to meet her big sister, and she wouldn't even know it.

I swallowed hard and rang the doorbell. Alaina opened the door, and there stood Sara. My eyes took her in. The first thing I saw was that she looked just like me. Her hair was cut short and was no longer a golden blond but a beautiful light brown. Her curls were gone, replaced with fine, thin, straight hair. Her smile and eyes were mine. Freckles ran across her nose. I bent down to shake her hand, and I saw my mother's hands. I said hello and introduced her to Hope. Her smile lit up the whole room and my heart, as well.

I stood and looked at Alaina; she still looked young and beautiful. She never looked her age. As I looked upon her face, all the love I felt for this woman came over me. This was the woman in whom I had entrusted my baby to almost five years earlier. I hugged and kissed her while tears filled my eyes and joy filled my heart.

Sara and Hope took to each other right away. Alaina took us on a tour of Sara's room, and I saw pictures on the wall of her when she was two. We went upstairs to the playroom, where Sara and Hope started to play with all the toys Alaina had left on the floor for them. I played with my daughter and watched Sara's every move. I took her in, savoring her sweetness and excitement. She told me about her school and the songs she had learned. I took pictures of Sara and Hope together, knowing that one day Hope would want them for herself.

Alaina and I sat across from each other on the floor. I remember Alaina saying that Sara's eyes had changed colors. They were blue when she was little, but now they had some green to them, just like Alaina's. I looked at her and said yes, they did look like hers, knowing sometimes my eyes were green, too. Then I realized just how much Sara has become Alaina's daughter and really did belong in her family. Sara never belonged to me; she was a spirit that just passed through my body, and Alaina was her guiding light to show her and help her choose the road of life. I am Hope's guiding light, but God did not choose me to be Sara's mother. I was just a soul to carry her here. Alaina was her mommy and always would be.

The love I felt for Sara could never change, but the way I saw her that day changed what she and Alaina meant to me. Watching both my daughters play with each other brought me indescribable peace. Everything Sara did, Hope would try to do, and it brought back memories of my childhood with my little brother. I was taken by surprise when Alaina asked Sara to tell me the story of how she was born.

As she told me her story, I was taken back in time to the day of her birth, and all the feelings came back. But this time I didn't feel the sadness and anger, only the love. After Sara finished her tale, I wanted to grab her and hold her to tell her how much I loved her, how much she meant to me, to tell her who I really was, but I knew that would have been the wrong thing to do. As she went on with her story of how her mommy and daddy came to get her, my heart spilled over with an overwhelming feeling of closeness. She looked at me with my eyes, and all I could see was total love and happiness. At the end of her story, my own eyes filled with tears, and I told her how wonderful her story was and how grateful I was that she told me.

Then it was time to go. I gathered up Hope, and we walked to the front door. I kneeled down and told Sara how beautiful she was. I told her that I lived very far away and wouldn't see her for a very long time. I asked her to give me a kiss on the cheek, but she refused at first. Alaina then asked her to give me a kiss on the cheek, and she did. I kissed her forehead in return, just as I had kissed her for the first time after she was born and again after our meeting when she was one year old.

I turned to Alaina. We embraced, and I thanked her for all that she had done. She was the one whom I had chosen to be Sara's mother. I did not regret my choice, because Alaina had also become my friend.

As I walked out of that house for the last time, my arms were not empty anymore, and neither was my soul.

§

CHAPTER 24
Alaina

*J*ason discovered what I had done just hours after my meeting with Alex. When he came home from work that night, the story was written on my face. Naturally, he was justifiably hurt and angry that I had deceived him for so long. He was angry that I had met with Alex without first talking to him. Trust had always been a major issue with Jason, and this situation had served to undermine his level of trust in me. I deserved his anger. I tried to explain why I had continued to correspond with Alex, but there are some things people just can't be expected to understand. Though Jason was the pivotal figure in Sara's life, he was not a part of the bond Alex and I shared. How, then, could I expect him to understand?

Sara was Jason's only child, and anything that even remotely appeared as a threat was magnified tenfold. I was ashamed of what I had done, of how I had deceived him. In time, however, our phone calls and letters no longer upset him. Once in a while, Alex and he would even talk briefly. I never lied to him about Alex again.

We had moved from our big home to a smaller one in June of 1998, a move to downsize our life in order to eventually move out of the city and into the country. Sara was now eight years old. One night, a few days after the move, Sara asked me, quite concerned, if her birth mommy knew our new address. I was taken aback.

"Yes. She knows where you are."

"How does she know? 'Cause if she doesn't, she might get worried about me." Sara's voice was determined. I realized for the first time that

Sara was thinking a lot about things, things that Jason and I had no clue about.

"Well, she always knows where you are, because I tell her."

"Does that mean she has my phone number?" she asked.

"Yes, she has your number and your address."

"Could I call her?" she asked innocently.

I was stumped. What should I say? Was she old enough to handle this? I didn't know what was right, but I was beyond the point of caring what the "experts" had to say on the topic, so I said, "If you want to call her, I'll dial the number. Do you want me to do that now?"

She hesitated and then answered, "No, not today!" I could see discomfort, a pause in her eyes, but there was also an honesty and trust, too. I knew she was OK with it.

A few months later, she approached me again with questions.

"Do you think my birth mommy misses me?"

"Yes, she does."

"Is my birth mommy pretty?"

"Yes, she is." The questions didn't bother me, but the word *mommy* hit a nerve. The questions got tougher as the months went on.

"Mama, you said my birth mommy was too young to be a mommy, right?"

"Yes, she was."

"Well, how old was she?" She wasn't letting this thing go, I could tell. I knew Sara.

"Sara, she was too young. She was just not ready to be a mommy. Being a mommy is a big job, and you have to be ready to do it."

"Was she like Daniella?" she grilled me. Daniella was twenty-four and not too young to be a mother, but I paused and just decided to say, "Yes, just like Daniella."

"Oh!" she answered and left the room. What was this child thinking? What was she processing in her little mind? I worried about her and the adult troubles she was trying to sort out.

One night, while brushing her teeth, she exclaimed, "I don't want to be special anymore! I am not an angel. I am a little girl. I just want to be normal!"

"Oh, Sara, you are normal. Are you worried about something?"

"I just want to be like all the rest of the kids at school; I don't want to be adopted anymore." Tears streaked down her face, and my heart broke. I sensed that kids at school had said something. "Sara, many children are adopted. All those other kids at school? Their parents had to take what they got—and what they got sometimes were little brats!" I knew that remark was not wise, professional, or educationally sound, but I said it anyway.

"Now, with you, we chose you. We chose the one we wanted. The best one!" A smile returned to her face for an instant.

"But I still just want to be regular!"

"I know. Me, too."

Sara trotted off seeming to be OK, but I knew that it wasn't over. The real world was encroaching on her, and it was just beginning. This was not the last time we would have this exact conversation. Not by a long shot.

§

Sometimes I hate kids. I truly do. One day I was reminded why Jason wished that we would never have to tell Sara that she was adopted. That day, I understood. Daniella was working as a Special Education aide at Sara's elementary school while she finished her MA in school psychology, and she was on yard duty during recess that day. That's where kids are the cruelest; I even remember that from my own school days.

Two little boys approached Daniella and got her attention. "You see that little blond girl over there?" they asked, as if holding on to a secret too good to keep. "Yes, I do, as a matter of fact," she replied. She didn't expect what came next. "Well, you see, her 'real parents' didn't want her, so they sold her for a lot of money to some people!" Daniella flashed back to a day in the second grade, when she was being bullied by a couple of kids at school. When she confided in her two older brothers, they ambushed the culprits and swore they would tear them to bits if they ever bothered their little sister again. They never did.

Daniella bent down so that her eyes met theirs. "Well, first of all, no one, but *no one*, bought Sara O'Connell. Second, I am her big sister, and third, if you know what's good for you, you'll get out of here!" When she told me about it that night, I felt akin to a mother lion whose cub had been threatened: I wanted to kill someone. I wanted blood. This was just the kind of thing I had feared would happen one day. When she was in second grade, Sara had proudly explained to her class that she was adopted and had even put her birth mother on her family tree. But this was the third grade, and things were different. I imagined that kids were saying things like that all day long to my child, and I wanted to see some heads roll.

When I questioned Sara that night as she brushed her teeth before bed, she said nonchalantly, "Oh, everyone knows I'm adopted. No problem!" I guess I was supposed to feel consoled, but I wasn't. Later, as we cuddled in bed, she asked if she could have a diary to write down her feelings. I gave her a little spiral notepad. She wrote: *Today was a bad day. Today I was sad. I wish that tomorrow would be better and I will be happy.*

The truth is, we can't protect our children. They are out there in the world, and the world can hurt them. I saw that Sara was protecting me when I wanted to protect her. Of course she wanted to be like everyone else. All kids did. Why should she be any different? My attempts at helping her didn't quite soothe the hurt that lived within our little girl, however. I tried to imagine what things went on in her head as she grappled to come to terms with being different. I knew it was time for Alex to start answering some of the hard questions. I had thought that those would come later, but it was time now. I couldn't let Sara think that someone had thrown her away. I couldn't stand it. I lay awake all night thinking about what to do. The next day at work, I called Alex.

"Alex, Sara needs you to call her and tell her that you love her. It's not enough coming from me anymore. She needs you to say it. She needs you. Kids are talking shit about her at school, and she needs to know you love her." "I'll call tonight after six," she promised.

At six o'clock, the phone rang. I let Sara answer it. I tried very hard to stay out of the room; however, I found myself tiptoeing to the door, trying to hear the conversation, trying to read her reaction. Sara stood straight and tall at the phone, a serious expression on her face. "Uh huh. Uh huh. Yes, I understand." How could she understand anything? Anything at all? She saw me watching and waved me off. I walked five steps away and returned, this time more quietly. "But Alex, I have one question. Why did you give me away?" There was a long silence as she listened to the answer. "But why were you so afraid to be a mother?" she asked. Alex must have been dying right about now. She had always dreaded having to one day answer these questions. How many times had she asked me how Sara would respond?

"Uh huh. Oh, that is sad. That must have been so hard." That was my Sara, always the little mother. She was mothering Alex. Finally, she asked, "Can I please have your phone number in case I have more questions?" In case she has more questions! If I live to be a hundred years old, I will never get over this child, her strength, her spirit, and her straightforwardness. After they talked, I spoke briefly with Alex. "Wow, what a kid! It wasn't as hard as I had always feared. She made it easy for me. I just told her the truth. Thank you, thank you for allowing this, Alaina." "Well, isn't that the deal? We will always do what's best for her, right?"

As Sara lay asleep and I was alone with my thoughts, I wondered what a psychologist would say about that little talk. No one really knows what the right thing to do is. We were trailblazers, Alex and I, and all those who opt for open adoption. We were constantly stepping into the darkness, hoping that we landed on terra firma. Sara's breathing promised sweet dreams, and that was all I needed in that moment. Sara was just eight years old. It was her birthday.

§

CHAPTER 25
Alex

*M*oving on with my life was a new experience for me. I was no longer ashamed of myself or angry at the world. I was no longer afraid to ask for help if I needed it. I had nothing to hide. My strength came from within, and I listened to my fears and faced them instead of running away from them. I now had a baby to take care of. I lived near my family in Arizona and worked in Scottsdale. Hope adapted to her new surroundings and started attending her new daycare. Being a mommy for the first time, I decided I wasn't going to date anyone. I wanted to devote myself only to Hope.

The first three years of living in Arizona were great, and I kept in touch with Alaina and Sara. After leaving our last reunion, my healing was complete. I had done the right thing for us all, but mostly for Sara. I would not have been a good mother to her. I knew that now. We can never see the outcome in the beginning; we can only feel the pain of loss and separation.

My relationship with Alaina continued to grow in leaps and bounds. Our trust was now sealed forever in our hearts. She let me talk to Sara on the phone many times over the years, and we continued the game of being friends from Arizona who called to talk. I had told Hope about Sara from the very beginning and why I couldn't keep her but could be a mommy to Hope. I kept my explanation very simple, and for such a little one, she seemed to understand. Up to this point, Sara didn't know she had a sister. I would let Hope talk to Sara many times, but I asked little Hope not to divulge our secret about her being Sara's sister. She did pretty well, but a couple of times she let it slip out. Sara didn't catch on until April 20, 1999.

It was her eighth birthday, and I called to wish her a happy birthday. I got the answering machine, so I sang "Happy Birthday" to it, then let her know it was from her friends in Arizona. I always remembered her birthday, as I remembered the moment of her birth. No matter where I was, she was in my thoughts when her birthday rolled around, and that day was no different.

When I returned home from work that night after picking up Hope from preschool, I got a phone message from Alaina saying that Sara needed me. At that exact moment, the phone rang. When I picked up the phone, to my surprise, it was Sara. This was the first time I had ever gotten a call from her. It was usually me calling Alaina and Alaina letting Sara talk to me. Her sweet voice surprised me greatly. We began our conversation with what she was doing for her birthday and how she was doing in school. Then, out of nowhere, she said, "I heard that you are my birth mother."

Oh, my God, she knows! Alaina had told her! I didn't know what to say. I couldn't believe it. *My baby knows.* I asked, "Did your mommy tell you?" She said, "Yes." Then I waited. What would the next question be? Would it be "Why did you give me away and not Hope?" But that question didn't come. I could hardly compose myself. I started to shake uncontrollably. Then I said, "I have a surprise for you."

"You do?"

"You have someone very special here who wants to meet you."

Her excitement exploded. "Who, who?"

"I have your baby sister here, who would love to talk to you."

I knew she had talked to Hope many times before, but this time she would be talking to her as a sister, not just a friend.

As I handed the phone to Hope, I just let go and cried hard, so powerfully hard. *She knows me now. My child knows I am her birth mother.* I scared poor Hope; she had never seen me cry so hard before, but I couldn't stop. Everything just came out. I tried to calm down, but it was no use.

Alaina must have heard my sobs, because after the sisters had been talking a while, she asked Hope if she could talk to me. Through my tears I said, "You told her! What made you tell her?"

Alaina was crying, too. She was so brave. "I have nothing to be afraid of anymore," she said. I cried even more. This woman, whom I once mistrusted and would never let me know my daughter, was now giving her back to me. She had let love and courage guide her to this moment. I never thought it would come, not before Sara was eighteen, but it came at eight, instead. It was so powerful.

After we all calmed down, we talked about the courage it took for Alaina to tell Sara and where we would all go from here. I thought about how Sara was feeling. Alaina and I had been through so much already; we were seasoned professionals, but Sara was only a little girl of eight. She had known nothing but love and safety, and now it was OK for her to know about me because she was safe and secure.

Alaina said that Sara had been asking many questions lately. She assured me that Sara was fine with the news, but I was a wreck. We talked for a long time that night, telling each other how this was the right thing to do. Now I would have a new relationship with my daughter. I would no longer be the stranger on the phone. After the call, Alaina showed Sara pictures of me and Hope that she had been saving. She told me that Sara's reaction to Hope had been uneventful, as if this was just ordinary information. It wasn't life-altering; Sara had just accepted the news the same way one would accept meeting a relative one had never met. It was more as if that sort of thing happened often.

A month later, Alaina called me from work and told me that Sara was having a hard time at school. Some kids were making fun of her, and Alaina felt that it was now time for me to talk to Sara and let her ask the big question about why I had given her up. I called that night and asked her how everything was going. She said, "OK." But then it came.

"Why did you give me up?" This was it, but I wasn't afraid. I had waited for this question for eight years. I told her the truth.

"I wasn't able to keep you because I had no money and no good home to take you to. I was all alone and scared. I loved your birth father very much, and through that love came you. I wanted to keep you, but I didn't know how, so I prayed to the angels to bring me the right parents, and they sent your mom and dad. Your mommy and your dad needed you more. And I made a promise to you when you were born." I read to her the words I had kept in my heart for almost nine years.

Today I am making you a promise, my beloved child. I will go out and find the right family to raise you. I will search this whole world if I have to in order to make sure you have the best mother and father any child could have. I will look for a home filled with love, music, and art, because these things matter to me. I want your world to be filled with song and dance and lots of sunshine.

When you look into your mother's face, it will not be mine, but a woman's who will love you as much as I love you now. When you wake up in the morning, her hands will hold and care for you. When you stumble and fall, she will be there to help you back on your feet. And when you cry, she will be there to wipe your tears from your eyes.

I will find this woman for you. I will always know where you are and how you are doing. I want you to know that even though I will not be there when things happen in your life, I will never be far from you. I will carry you with me always, until one day you will come to see me and know that I did it all for *you*.

Just know I love you with all my heart and soul. And I will keep my promise.

Alex Porter

Tears fell as I read this letter to my little girl. Long ago, these words meant so much to me, and now these same words meant everything to this little girl, too. I told Sara that I loved her with all my heart and that if she ever needed me, she could call me on the telephone. I gave her my number and told her I was going to send her a special gift in the mail. She said she understood why I gave her up, and she was OK.

Later that week, I bought her a locket and put a picture of Hope and me in it. I wrote her a short note: "Keep this locket close to your heart, and I will always be near." I had asked Alaina first if it would be alright to send this gift to Sara, and she had no problem with it.

Now our lives went on. I found a new love, and we shared a house in Summit County. We raised Hope together, and I finally came into my own at thirty-four years old. My life was good. I was grateful to Alaina because she never took my baby away from me. I had taken a hard road in life, but I learned so much about my worth and myself. I knew that one day I would come face to face with Sara as my daughter and that I would hold her and love her as I did the very first time I held her in my arms. God had blessed us all on this journey.

§

CHAPTER 26
Alaina

*O*ne day Sara asked me if I would be mad if she loved her birth mother as much as she loved me, if I would mind. She didn't want to hurt my feelings. I said, "No, of course not!" Then it occurred to me that had she asked me that question five years before, my response would have been quite different. I realized that a profound shift had taken place. Even when she received her locket from Alex and announced to me that she would never take it off, I was not threatened. It was all OK.

Now Sara talked monthly to Alex and Hope. It was natural; it was no threat. Sara wanted to teach Hope how to ride a bike and all the nuances of riding a horse. She asked me how far Arizona was from Washington because she wanted to go see her little sister and play with her. She was at peace with having two women as her mothers. She knew who her mommy was, but she also knew that there was another woman with whom she was forever linked, too. One day they will come face to face again, and it will be fine for all of us.

Over the past eight years, we had all changed. Sara no longer wore dresses; in fact, she wouldn't be caught dead in one. Her life was filled with dreams of having her own horse and moving to the country. She knew that she was adopted and talked about it without shame or fear.

Alex was now thirty-four years old and a strong, self-sufficient woman. She had come to terms with her decisions and had gone on with her life. She was a wonderful and devoted mother to Hope, who was now four years old, full of spirit and energy. She knew she had a half-sister and was proud of it.

I had changed a lot from the woman who decided to start over and adopt a child. Jason and I were in a complicated relationship, which meant it was a rollercoaster of learning. I had had to a take a hard look at my ability to deceive, even for a noble cause. My resolution for the millennium was to be unafraid to tell the truth, to be seen, to be enough. I had more wrinkles than I had eight years before, but I also felt more of a woman than ever before. My older children were all professionals and healthy, whole people. My relationship with each of them was evolving every day. They, along with Sara, were still my best teachers—they would let me know when I slipped off the track. The funny thing about it all was that I didn't regret anything that had happened.

People asked me almost daily what it was like having an eight-year-old at fifty-four and about having a relationship with the birth mother. Every time I sent off an envelope of Sara's newest pictures or received a set of Hope's, there was a sense of discomfort from those around me. "How do you do it? Aren't you threatened?" "How will Sara react to all of this later?" The questions revolved around a central theme: fear.

Fear was no stranger to me, because surely the past eight years had run the gamut of hope, fear, joy, terror, and acceptance. We lived in changing times, when there were no guidelines. We were the trailblazers of open adoption. We were finding our way, stumbling along with good intentions, but often as if blindfolded.

The courts at that time were ill-equipped to decide cases of custody on issues such as ours, which so touch the soul of a child and all those around her. Answers could not be found in books and certainly should not have been decided by old men whose adherence to the letter of the law had hardened their hearts to the needs of the child.

Even the wisdom of King Solomon would have been tested when we were breaking ground, because the role of parenthood is fuzzy and constantly changing. But the needs of the child have never changed, since the first human child looked up into her mother's face. Who that face should be is clear: the one who loves her, cares for her, has chosen her. When Jason and I decided to adopt in January of 1991, we had no idea what obstacles would lie ahead. I certainly had no idea that opening my heart to a child would mean that I would also begin a relationship with another adult woman and that our relationship would last as long as the one with the child—forever.

Alex and I began our relationship in an attorney's office, two women choosing their futures. I believed, though, that this relationship began long before February 14, 1991, that on some imponderable level of the soul, our individual fates had brought us together for a reason. Perhaps Sara chose us. Though the relationship between Alex and me began in hope, it had trekked through the darkest corners of our souls, incited rage in us both, confronted our demons, and forced us to question our roles as women and our relationship to one another. We had emerged as different women for the rest of our journey together, and someday Sara would reap the harvest of that sojourn. Maybe she already had.

Alex chose to give a child up for adoption because she knew who she was and that she could not give that child what the child needed at that time in her life. I couldn't even begin to comprehend the depth of that sacrifice. At first I thought I chose to raise another child to give Jason a family of his own. Later, I realized it was for me, too. I used to want Sara all to myself, for her never to know that she had been adopted or given away. I pondered this for countless nights in the darkness; yet because of how Alex and I had evolved, I could see that there was no black or white, no this way or that way, no right or wrong way of doing things. Sara would have the legacy of two women who loved her. King Solomon would not have to sever this child in half, because if asked to choose, Alex and I would both have said in unison, "No, let her go to the other so that she may live!"

We both loved our Sara. This love for her and our mutual understanding of one another had brought a wondrous forgiveness and healing. Wasn't it Gibran who said that we don't own our children? Sara was a gift on loan from a universe of love. She didn't belong to anyone but herself and God.

It has often been said that there are only two emotions: love and fear. Had I chosen fear in my relationship with Alex, she would not have been able to heal her own wounds and I would have chosen to live in fear for the rest of my life, just as my troubled childhood had directed. Somewhere along our journey, I changed my mind about love. Perhaps it happened as I looked into Sara's soulful eyes and saw the magnificent life force and unconditional trust she had in me, her mother. The only question we must ask ourselves is, What is best for the child? There is no other question, for in the answer, our fragile egos, delusions of ownership, and fear are dwarfed by the wondrously simple needs of every human child: unconditional love, safety, and respect.

In the end, two women had blessed me: Alex, a woman of extraordinary energy, life, and courage, and Sara, the daughter of my soul. My life now included two sons and three daughters. There are no accidents, only miracles.

On April 20, 1999, as Sara put down the receiver after having talked to Alex for the first time about her adoption, her simple response erased any doubt I had ever had about whether Alex and I had done the right thing. She looked up into my eyes and said without hesitation, "Today is the BEST day of my life!"

§

Epilogue

Alex

2017

How does a person revisit a story that began twenty-six years ago about two women in a lawyer's office in Seattle, Washington? My life has taken me to places I wish never to travel again, but if I had not traveled them, I would not be the woman I am today. All of the events that happened have led me to this point in my life.

Alaina and I were strangers meeting for the very first time. Fate was playing out her unseen hand, changing our lives forever. It was 1991, Valentine's Day, the day of love. Our story started there in that big, opulent office. Our journey took hold of us that day, leading us blindly, taking new, unexplored roads to this thing called *open adoption*. OPEN. That word has changed my life more than I could have ever imagined. Our journey began with two women, a promise, a poem, a hug, and an untold story about to unfold. Few books had been written about what we were about to do. We had only our hearts to guide us; no written word guided our hands or our fate.

I've learned so much about that word from my experience over the last twenty-six years. I grew as I learned about myself as a woman and daughter. I learned how to let go, to forgive, to accept, to deepen my spirituality, and to trust in faith, love, and always to have hope. Now, at the age of fifty-two and looking back twenty-six years, those events seem like they happened a lifetime ago. I was a scared young woman trying to do what was best for my baby. Unsure and alone, I was trying to be brave, trying not to second-guess myself. Open adoption was not very open in 1991. I couldn't find a single story to read or book to help us. I could only hope that the choices we made back then were the right ones for us and for Sara. Those choices taught me to let faith guide me.

Now, twenty-six years later, Sara stands as a strong, beautiful, loving, kind, and secure young woman. As I look back now, I reflect on how worried I was that Sara wouldn't understand why I placed her for adoption. I never wanted her to feel abandoned, and those fears never became a reality. Openness let us explore this new thing called open adoption. Did we have fears? Yes, many, but it all came down to what was best for Sara, and that is what has led us to the last chapter of this book.

My life changed when I moved to Arizona. My Hope was young, and I was finding my way and trying to support my small family. Arizona had amazing opportunities for me, and I looked to start my own business. Within two years, I was expecting my third daughter, Faith. I was able to purchase a home when Faith was a year and a half old and started my business shortly after. I worked hard to raise my girls.

I never tried to hide Sara from my children, as she was part of them, too. I told Hope and Faith about Sara from the very beginning, when they were little and could understand. Hope was thrilled when I told her about Sara's adoption. She knew she had an older sister, one she couldn't see but could talk about through pictures I had shown her. As she grew older, she asked more questions about Sara and her parents. "When can we meet? Can she come to visit us?" She had been too young to remember our early visits.

When Sara was eleven years old, Hope started asking more often about her sister. At that time, I had no answers. Alaina and Jason had relocated to a rural part of Washington to give Sara the opportunity to grow up in the country. They had bought a beautiful home on three acres and had horses. I knew Sara loved horses. I think Jason was the one to introduce Sara to riding. I remember getting pictures of her on a huge horse when she was twelve. I saw Sara as an infant, a toddler, and now as a young girl. Eleven years had passed quickly, and Sara was growing before my eyes, through Alaina's lens as she sent photos and letters to me. I cherished every photo and kept every letter that she wrote.

A few months after Alaina and Jason were in their new home, I asked

Alaina how they would feel if Hope and I came for a visit. Alaina wanted to talk to Jason about it first, and then talk with Sara to see how she would feel about us coming to meet her. She called back after a few days and said Sara would like us to come. This was huge!

We booked our tickets to Washington. Over and over in my mind, I tried to imagine what Sara was like now, at eleven years old. My mind kept me busy thinking and guessing. I knew I would be a stranger to Sara. Will she like me? Will she wonder why I kept Hope and not her? Will I feel maternal toward her like I feel for Hope and now Faith, with whom I was in my sixth month of pregnancy?

The day came, and Hope and I flew to meet Sara. This would also be the first time I would see Alaina and Jason since Sara was four. It was a reunion of great importance for all of us but in different ways. What would I say to Sara's mom, who had kept her promises to me for eleven years and who shared Sara with me? How would I thank her for this kind, loving gesture? And now she and Jason were letting us see Sara again.

I remember walking to the end of the walkway after landing and seeing Alaina first. She was just as beautiful as the last time I saw her. She never seemed to age. She was tall, graceful, beautiful, and professional. Sara was with her, and my heart skipped a beat. I remember seeing her from a distance for the first time. She had changed so much. She was tall and slender, with freckles covering her nose and cheeks. Her large, beautiful eyes—my mother's eyes—met mine. I hugged Alaina first. All these emotions came flooding out as tears ran down my face. I hugged Alaina tightly, just like the last time.

I tried to collect myself and bent down to meet Sara. I introduced myself as Alex and asked Sara if I could give her a hug. She smiled and said yes. For the first time since she was four years old, I held Sara in my arms. I looked up at Alaina and whispered "Thank you" as I held Sara. She was no longer a baby but a sweet little girl. Hope was over the moon with excitement. She hugged Sara and Alaina, and then we started to make our way for home.

Sara was very shy and quiet at first. I kept looking at her in the back seat with Hope. I didn't want to overwhelm her. We pulled into the driveway, and I saw that their house was surrounded by green hills. There was a small barn, fields with hay, and horses spread across their three acres. It was just beautiful and had a more bucolic feeling than Seattle, where we had all begun this story. What a beautiful home Sara had!

That night, I soaked her in. She watched me closely, and I watched her. I watched her talk, listened to her laugh, watched her interact with her parents and get to know Hope. She looked a lot like me when I was her age. I saw a lot of Duncan in her, also. She showed me her beautiful room. I met her sweet dog, Ginger, and we had a wonderful dinner. Hope and I got to meet her two horses.

We all stayed up quite late that night and got to know each other a little more. Sara was sweet, kind, and very smart. As the evening came to a close, I asked her if she would like to know how she was born, and she nodded. I told her her birth story in the most loving way that an eleven-year-old child could understand. It was simple and filled with love. I told her I loved her and wanted her to have the best life possible, and so I found Alaina and Jason to be her mom and dad.

She quietly listened to my story. At the end, I saw a light of understanding in her eyes; she was not judgmental or angry or sad but was a happy, well-adjusted, eleven-year-old child. She was OK with my story. She was OK with her story. She was OK with me. She was who she was, and I gave all the credit to her parents. They hadn't kept Sara from me or from her story. Instead of keeping secrets from her, they gave her openness. They gave her truth. That visit was great because I could see that Sara was where she needed to be, and I was where I was meant to be. Her parents were doing a wonderful job.

Later, Sara and Alaina showed us to the guest room. As we prepared to go to bed, Sara asked her mother if it was OK to sleep with Hope and me. I didn't want to make Alaina or Jason upset, because I respected them as Sara's parents and didn't want to step on or hurt their feelings. I was thrilled—and shocked—when Alaina said yes.

The following evening, we took pictures of all of us in the living room. Our visit with Sara and her parents was just completely wonderful. I left Washington a very happy woman, because now Sara knew who I was. She had a face for my name now. I was no longer a stranger to her, but a friend. I had given her life, but her parents, Jason and Alaina, *were* her life. If she needed a question answered, I was only a phone call away.

I could raise Hope and Faith knowing Sara was right where she needed to be.

Hope and I flew back to Arizona and waited for the arrival of baby Faith. She came into the world quite early, at thirty-two weeks. She was three pounds and one ounce—tiny, sweet baby Faith. Having a premature newborn and a six-year-old was no easy task, and my life was full. Alaina and I continued to send pictures and letters to each other. The promise Alaina had made all those years ago was never broken. *Thank you, Alaina!* The years flew by, and Sara grew into an amazing young woman.

§

The next time I saw Sara, she was eighteen years old. She had invited me to her high school graduation, and I was honored that she wanted me there to see her graduate. I knew her whole family would be there, and I wanted to be there for her, too. I was proud and happy for her. Meeting her extended family made me feel honored and special.

I wondered what I could give her for graduation that would have meaning. Many years earlier, when Duncan and I were together, I had bought him a pocket watch with thirteen jewels in it for his graduation from the university. You could see all the movements inside. I had saved money for a year to buy it for him. Right before his graduation, I gave it to him as a gift. A week later, we parted ways. He didn't feel he could keep the gift, so he gave it back to me. I had carried it with me for eighteen years and kept it very close, knowing that one day I would give it to Sara. Eighteen years later, I arrived in Washington for her graduation with the wrapped pocket watch in my hand.

I was so excited. The last time I had seen Sara, she was eleven years old. Now she was eighteen and a young woman. Her parents were throwing her a huge celebration and had invited her sister and one of her brothers, aunts, uncles, cousins, and Grandma O'Connell, Jason's mother. Everyone important in Sara's life was going to be there. No pressure, of course! *Nervous* is an understatement. I'm very much a free spirit and have always walked to the beat of my own drum, but I knew this trip was going to be a little more challenging. Everyone there was going to know who I was, so I pulled up my big-girl panties and went. What mattered was not what her family thought of me but what Sara thought of me. I got ready to fly out to Washington on a beautiful June day. I bought a dozen roses on the way to the airport; I wanted to give her something beautiful, and roses were perfect.

I met a sweet lady on the plane, and we shared stories. She said, "Wow! Are you nervous?" Well, sure—this trip was going to be different from the last. Sara had been eleven, just a little girl, and now I was going to meet a young woman, a whole new person.

I knew Alaina and Sara would be there waiting for me when I landed. I saw them both at the same time. Sara was standing beside her mother, and of course, she was beautiful. Blond, tall—a totally different person from the last time we met now stood in front of me, a stranger but yet so familiar. Alaina was beautiful, as always. There were no tears this time when I hugged her, only true happiness to see each other. I looked at Sara and was overwhelmed by her beauty. I handed her the flowers. Sara said, "You're shorter than I remember you!" "Really?" I replied. Maybe it was like returning to one's elementary school and noticing how small the drinking fountains are. We stood silent for a moment, and then we all laughed.

Alaina drove us to a wonderful restaurant in town, just us three. She had been to this restaurant before, so she ordered for us. We chatted a lot and talked about who was coming to Sara's graduation. I had my gift for Sara, wrapped in a box and tied with a ribbon. I had held on to this gift for eighteen years, and now it was going to its rightful owner. Sara sat between Alaina and me. I was so nervous.

I wasn't sure if we were going to be alone again, just the three of us, so I knew that this was the moment to give Sara her gift. I told her the story of its journey and how I held on to it for so long. I explained to her that it was hers to have. She slowly opened the box. Her eyes opened wide as she pulled out the watch and held it in her hands. She could see the beauty of this timepiece as I saw it all those years ago. I was so happy that it had found its way to Sara, because it always was meant for her. The watch was the last thing I had of Duncan's that remained of our relationship; now it was with Sara, and the door was closed to that part of my life forever.

Next, I handed Sara her story, the book Alaina and I had written for her eighteen years before, her story from her mother and me. I think it overwhelmed her. I, too, was overwhelmed with emotion. There was so much I wanted to say to her, but this was not yet the time. I was so proud of her and her accomplishments. The open adoption had given Sara wings to fly and soar because her mother and I loved her so much.

After we ate, we headed to Sara's parents' new house, and I checked in at a hotel close by. Alaina and Jason had sold their little ranch and now lived in a beautiful home in the suburbs. Jason greeted us with a big smile. He looked older now; his hair was whiter and he was balder, but he was still handsome Jason.

A lot was going on that day. Everyone was on a mission with a chore to run to get ready for the relatives to arrive the next day. I got caught up in the excitement. That evening, Jason, Sara, Alaina, and I sat upstairs and talked about Sara's birth. It was the first time that Jason and Sara heard my side of the open adoption. I shared my story of how hard it was for me to give Sara to them after she was born. I explained how I really didn't know what I was giving up until I had held her in my arms. Even though it was the right thing to do for my life at that time, and right for Sara, it still was bittersweet. After eighteen years, retelling this story now to Sara and her parents, I felt the pain of not being able to parent her. I went into detail about that day and the loss. It felt good to let out my sorrow to them.

Sara drove me back to the hotel that night, and she saw me now in a different way. After retelling those memories and feelings, I felt a huge lift. She knew I loved her but that I was not meant to be her mother. I knew Sara had a lot of things thrown at her that day, and having this big party and graduation on top of it was a lot for her to handle.

The next morning, everyone started arriving. The last time I had seen Alaina's children, they were teenagers. Eighteen years is a long time. I was nervous, but as soon as I met everyone, my fears were calmed. All of Alaina's children were grown and doing well in their adult lives. Sara was the last child at home, and she planned to go to college in Oregon. All of her family was there for her, and I felt honored to be there, too. Everyone was very kind to me, so I didn't feel out of place.

The night before the graduation, the whole family gathered for food and drink. We listened to Sara sing "The Wind beneath My Wings." She dedicated it to her parents, who had loved, guided, and showed her the way to adulthood. The whole night was wonderful and filled with love.

The morning of Sara's graduation, we all gathered and drove to where it was being held. She was dressed in her gown, and as she marched to the podium to get her diploma, she lifted her arm, and I could see the watch I had given her. She had worn it under her gown. That moment was wonderful; it meant so much to me that she wore it as she graduated. My heart felt so much happiness at that moment.

I was flying back to Arizona the next day, so that evening, I said my goodbyes. It was hard to leave because I wasn't sure when I would see Sara again. She was going to college soon. I hugged her goodbye and wished her all the best, hoping that we would meet again soon. It would be five years before our lives crossed again.

After returning to Arizona, I went about my busy life. I had a business to run, and raising two little girls to adulthood was a full-time job. Sara was in college and had decided to go into nursing school after graduating.

In 2011, I found myself falling in love and starting a relationship with a local homebuilder named Don. He had four children himself whom he was parenting. We have been happily together ever since. I have learned to trust.

Don started to build a home for our family in the summer of 2013. He had always known about Sara and had read a draft of this book when we first started dating. I started working with two adoption agencies. They had core classes on open adoption, and I would drive down once a month to speak to adoptive parents who were interested in open adoption. I would share my experience as a birth mother with these families and would take questions from them after my speech. I could tell when some of the adoptive families were uncomfortable with the open adoption concept. I have to admit that open adoption is not for everyone. No adoption is like another; every one is as unique as the individuals involved. This is why I am grateful to Alaina and the adoption that we agreed to. She could have changed her mind about being open with our adoption. She could have kept the truth from Sara, hiding or having secrets about Sara's beginning, but she went with her heart, instead. She kept every promise she made to me. I got to see Sara grow and flourish for eighteen years. I truly feel I was able to heal much faster because I never really lost her.

I am so happy I picked Alaina and Jason to be Sara's parents. They have done a magnificent job in raising her. Our adoption is made from love, hope, faith, and trust. I would not change our adoption experience for the world. I grew through it, and I learned to forgive myself. I learned to let go and to accept the things I cannot change. I learned to take responsibility for my own actions.

There is a stigma on birth mothers around the shame of giving up a child to adoption. In the old days, girls were sent away and disappeared for nine months to have the baby, and then the baby went to an adoptive family or a relative. The girl returned to her family and never talked about the baby or the adoption again. But that was the old days. I talked openly about my adoption because it gave me strength and because I am comfortable sharing. I enjoyed those speeches with the adoption agencies.

§

During the construction of our home in early January 2014, I got a phone call from Sara. I hadn't heard from her in a long time, so I was surprised and caught off guard. She asked how I would feel if she came and spent a week with us in Scottsdale in early February. I was deeply touched and deliriously happy that she wanted to hang with me for a week. I told her that I would be happy if she came. My Hope was nineteen years old and Faith fourteen. The girls were excited because this would be Faith's first time meeting her half-sister. Sara made her flight plans, and Hope, Faith, and I would meet her at the airport. I was excited because I would have all my children in my home for the very first time. My three daughters would be together for a week! *Heaven!*

Sara's plane landed, and I saw her right away as she walked toward us. She was a beautiful twenty-three-year-old blond. I hugged her tightly, then Hope hugged her, and then Faith. I felt like I was in a different world having all my daughters together.

We drove to my townhouse and got settled in, then we went to have dinner with Don and his children. Sara met everyone; she fit right in. That night we fed seven children, Don's four and my three. After dinner we talked, played cards, and just had a really great time.

The next morning, I gathered the girls together and took them to breakfast in town. Afterward, we drove to my land in Taos. I wanted to show Sara the land and look at art along the way. We were driving from my land to an artists' colony when I glanced at Sara sitting next to me. I saw a necklace around Sara's neck and thought, *I know that necklace!*

It contained a picture of me and baby Hope. I had given this necklace to Alaina more than twenty years before to give to Sara, and now Sara was wearing it around her neck. I didn't say anything then, but my first thought was, *Thank you, Alaina. Again you kept your promise.*

As we drove, we laughed, talked, and enjoyed the sights of beautiful Arizona. As we were wandering from one artist haunt to another, I said to Sara, "I love your necklace." She smiled and opened it, and I saw myself and baby Hope. For the first time in a long, long time, I became emotional, and tears sprang from my eyes. I simply could not stop crying. I said to Sara through my tears, "I'm so very proud of you, Sara. You're smart, beautiful, and most importantly, you are very kind." She looked at me with her large eyes and said, "Well, that's because I'm a lot like you, Alex." I pulled her into my arms and sobbed. My daughters put their arms around me and Sara, and we all hugged. Those words, that moment, meant everything to me. I was hugging my firstborn. She stood, a secure woman now, a kind, beautiful, caring, woman. Everything was right where it needed to be. Sara was in a good place, and so was I. It's funny how this road, this journey, this open adoption has turned we three women into loving, caring human beings. It was for the love of Sara; it's that simple. That's how I look at it. We were strong for Sara, and now Sara is strong for herself.

We drove back to Scottsdale to spend our last day together. We had lunch one last time before she was to fly home. We sat next to each other at the restaurant, and I wanted to stop time so I could look at Sara little longer, a little more, to smell her and hold her hand. But we said our goodbyes, and I wished her safe travels. Hope drove Sara back to the airport because I had to work. Sara's stay was wonderful.

Now, three years later, my other two daughters are growing. Hope is twenty-two now and has moved to Denver. Faith is a beautiful sophomore in high school. She would like to be a nurse just like Sara. I'm enjoying our wonderful new home in Blue River with my companion, Don, and am grateful for every day. Our story has no end but many, many new beginnings. I have found peace.

§

Alaina

2017

*O*f course, this story has no end. It is not a fairy tale. It is a living thing, and as with all living things, it continually evolves and grows. It is not a story of perfect people with no baggage. Some chapters don't have a happy ending. The truth is that life is messy and muddled with layers of perception and family baggage. In 2013, my twenty-five-year marriage came to an abrupt end, and with it, the end of a love story I very much wanted to believe. It can only be compared to the "overnight success" that takes years to create. Truth be told, it took many years to end suddenly.

I saw a statement on Pinterest the other day that said to simply write one true sentence. A true sentence—the thought is an intriguing one and not that simple when talking about one's own life. What makes a statement true? That you agree with it? That it syncs up with your life's narrative? That it is a fact? While proofing this story, I was stopped many times, not only by my own gratitude about my decision to adopt Sara, but also by deep emotion, because life looks different when we look back. I left out many details that would hurt too much to write, but I acknowledge the wisdom of giving this family story to Sara, for whom it was, after all, written. This tale is a love story; it just isn't the love story I thought I was writing. Ultimately, the truth of the story wrote itself.

I do have some facts: Sara is almost twenty-six years old. She is home, visiting from her advanced nursing program for a few weeks before returning to finish her degree. She had earned her BS in English only to change her mind about her goals after she graduated. She had to start from the beginning, taking all the science and math courses she had avoided in order to get into a prestigious accelerated nursing program.

She is no longer the blond I always wanted her to stay. Her long, dark red tresses make those huge, round, green eyes pop when she looks at me. How proud I am of this young woman who knows her own mind. She has the work ethic of my tribe, her brothers and sister, all of whom have beautiful families of their own. I am a lucky woman if judged by the success of my children. That is a fact.

Years have come and gone since my last entry into our story. We did move to the country. Sara did get her horse to raise and train and ride. In fact, she became quite a horsewoman in high school. Sara is still Sara, though, and she is still a young woman who hates change and mulls over every decision a thousand times, questions herself, and enters an obligatory funk when she must move to the next step. She still comes for comfort when she needs to "let the tears out," as she describes it. I stand speechless at her tenacity and sunny spirit.

Alex and I kept our promise to Sara over the years. She has visited us a few times, and Sara has gone to Arizona to spend time with her and her two daughters, Hope and Faith. Her first visit after moving to Arizona was when she was pregnant with Faith. With Hope in tow, she came to our small ranch-like place in Washington. I was the principal of a charter school at the time.

Alex was all smiles and gaiety, as I remember. A hippie at heart, she was dressed in flowing dresses and proudly showed us her big belly, stretched to make her stomach tattoo look as if it was designed specifically for a pregnant woman. Naturally, Hope zoned in on Jason immediately and wanted his attention. Sara, truth be told, was jealous of Hope's need for her daddy's affection, because she had never had to share him with anyone before. I had expected that they would be fast friends, but that was not the case. Sara continued to battle her jealousy issues throughout the visit and was frankly glad when it was over. Of course she had fun with Alex, but she was too threatened by Hope to be anything but jealous. No one noticed this but me.

Jealousy was not confined to Sara. I was a bit jealous that Alex was so young and playful; I seemed so businesslike and dull by contrast. The fact that I worked a twelve-hour day couldn't help but manifest itself in my lack of energy or willingness to get down on the floor and play. As I read those words now, I question whether I was really dull. No one has ever accused me of being dull, but it's hard to compete with youth. I had become the breadwinner, and my behavior was more serious than my true nature, which can be more Leo-like.

I envied Alex's high spirits on that trip, but I wasn't around much because I was always at work. She and Jason spent the days together, and I felt my old fear of the younger woman issue rearing its ugly head. Just when I thought I had conquered all the demons, they seemed to find a way back. Although the entire trip was a good one, I wished that I wasn't fifty-six and tired, but I was.

It's strange that the things we fear will happen are never the things that actually happen. It's also sad to look back and see my petty jealousy and fears. Why are we women pitted against one another all our lives? There was no reason to be jealous, but my jealousy had nothing to do with Alex. It had to do with the fragile nature of my relationship with the man I trusted with my life.

I look back now and have 20/20 vision, but then, I was still caught up in a mythology of my own. It would be many years before I came to terms with the saying, "Don't push the river." My life was in the middle of a strong current, and I convinced myself that by pushing in the opposite direction, I could redirect the flow of the river itself. I had pushed the river of my life for years, only to be knocked down and thrashed around in the rapids until I almost drowned. I lost myself long before Jason left. He loved Sara; he did not love me. And to be perfectly honest, I didn't much love myself yet, either. Sara was right—change is hard. But until inner change happens, we just keep on keeping on, digging the same ditch and falling into it, acting surprised that we are in a ditch. But change would come. I just wasn't finished digging in 2001.

Alex returned the following year, this time with baby Faith. Now Sara had to compete with Hope *and* a cute little baby. Jason was in his element, and I was again working most of the time. When I was home, I was cooking for everyone. I recall one conversation Alex and I had while on a walk down to the barn. She had been quiet around me for the first time. Intuitively, I sensed her dilemma. She had come to introduce her daughters to the first daughter she had given birth to, but her feelings toward Sara were not as intense as the previous year. I broached the topic with her carefully.

"Are you OK, Alex? You seem a little quiet, not your usual bubbly self."

"I know, right? I don't know why, though," she replied, tears welling in those famously huge eyes of hers.

"Are you feeling guilty that you love Hope and Faith more than you love Sara? It's just this feeling I am having."

Now her tears were jumping off her cheeks, the way they had when we said goodbye many years ago. "Yes. I feel bad because I love Sara, but I don't feel the same about her as I used to."

"Is it possible that this is because Sara is not your daughter, since she is my daughter and Hope and Faith are yours?"

"Oh, my God, it's true. She isn't my daughter, is she?" It seemed as if a huge boulder was lifted off her.

"She is your birth daughter, but that's not the same as what you've experienced with your girls. It's OK, Alex. It's OK." Things were easier for her after that conversation. We never spoke of it again.

After she and the girls went home, I asked Sara how she felt about the visit. She said she was happy but that she didn't need to have them visit for a while. I understood her more then than she understood herself. At twelve, she was absolutely unwilling to share her dad with anyone. I think everyone came to some resolution during that trip, which would have never happened had we not been open. *Open.* This word was becoming the *leitmotif* of our journey, the golden thread that connected us all. We had chosen open adoption. We had chosen to open our hearts to sharing this experience with each other. We were open to the possibility that one can be open completely amid very human fears and demons. Our openness was the key for a child to never feel given away.

§

The next step in our journey came at Sara's graduation from high school. She came to me one day and asked if we would mind if she invited Alex to her graduation. It was to be a huge celebration at our home, with the entire family gathering for a three-day visit. We, of course, agreed.

I met Alex at the airport with Sara. Alex emerged a trim, athletic young woman dressed in a low-cut sundress, a myriad of bracelets winding around her toned, tanned arms, and with long hair extensions that trailed down her back. Of course, the first thing I saw was Sara's big eyes and huge smile on Alex's face. We embraced, a homecoming of sorts. Jason had not wanted to come to the airport nor accompany us for dinner, so the three of us made our way to my favorite restaurant.

Sara was nervous. I was dressed in my work clothes and must have struck a drastic contrast to Alex's free-spirited demeanor. I recalled my days as a counselor, when I wore flowing dresses and my heart was soft and pliable. Now I was running a nonprofit for abused children and was always serious, overworked, and stressed. I saw in Alex the spirit that existed somewhere within me but had yet to resurface. It was that Alaina who had connected to Alex in the beginning. I felt a sad emptiness in my own soul, but it was not the time to examine it or the invisibility I felt at home.

I ordered a variety of tasty foods, and Alex talked. She had so much to say, as if she wanted Sara to know things she had stored inside herself for a long time. I listened, acknowledging to myself how important this moment was for Alex, but also knowing that Sara may not have been ready to hear all the details of Alex's relationship with the birth father, a topic we never spoke of in our household. Jason had become reluctantly comfortable with the open aspects of the adoption, but I always thought his view was that Sara had only one father, even if she had two mothers. Sara was a daddy's girl, so the topic of birth father was uncharted territory for her.

Alex chatted on and on about how much she had loved Sara's birth father, about their intimacies. I don't think she saw the look on Sara's face. Then Alex opened her purse, drew out a box containing an expensive-looking watch, and gave it to Sara. "This was your birth father's. I once gave it to him, but he gave it back to me when we broke up. I think it belongs to you." Alex was emotional. Sara sat still, more stunned than moved. I realized that we were once again in uncharted territory. Even eighteen years later, we were still experiencing new crossroads in this experience called open adoption.

As I looked at Alex and Sara from across the table, I saw two of my girls. On some level, I had indeed adopted them both. When I put aside all my crap and allowed unconditional love for this woman into my heart, I realized that Alex was being vulnerable, and in that respect, we were very much alike. The intimacy in that moment would change when I had to turn into hostess for the weekend. I am happy that we had those few moments together alone before complicating the dynamics with Jason and the whole family.

The noise of the restaurant quieted as the sun's rays permeated the window and us. Three faces, three women, three hearts trying to figure out once again where all the pieces fit. We still had so much to learn.

The weekend passed with one celebration after another, and many photos were taken. Plans were made for Sara to visit Arizona one day, although it would be several years before that day came. But on this occasion, I both rejoiced over our accomplishment of successfully living an open adoption and felt Sara's emotional landscape changing. She was now of an age where she could do what she wanted. Years later, Sara wouldn't request Alex's presence at her graduation from college, but she did eventually visit Alex and her girls in Arizona.

Sara is not the kind of person who would ever say anything to hurt another. This means she will bend the truth to keep the peace. The coincidence was not lost on me that Alex and I both had this very issue— open, but not that open. Truthful, but not that truthful. This tenuous fence-sitting plagued three generations. This is not a judgment; rather, it's a statement of the human condition we all shared.

I can't say that I fully understand what challenges Sara has faced in dealing with birth parents, adoptive parents, stepbrothers and a stepsister, half-sisters, and all the other stuff, but I know that she rises to any challenge in a loving and thoughtful way.

The words "adoptive parent" have no meaning for me, but people need to put labels on to organize their worlds. I have never viewed Sara as adopted; she has always been simply my child. I have found myself saying the word *adopted*, but I never felt the word. I have given birth to three biological children, and I have adopted one. I can say honestly that there was no difference—none. Others might find that hard to believe, but it is a fact. At least, it is true for me.

The idea of being open to loving another person is a choice that is made every day in a thousand small and big ways. Sometimes it takes great courage to stay open, and sometimes openness is a place to hide in plain sight. Things I believed in my twenties seem amusing to me now. Things I believed in my thirties, forties, fifties, sixties, and now seventies are often diametrically opposed. Maybe that is just what happens when you live fully. In fact, how our views and beliefs change throughout our lives is why I now gather people together to write. Holding a sacred space for people to write something true about themselves has given me perspective and taught me to be more tolerant and accepting of others and myself. When I look into the faces of my students and hear their life stories spoken in their own voices, I see that we all are not so different.

In the labyrinthine process of bringing this book together, I have discovered the real me, a woman who no longer fears everything. I have faced the worst challenges, the most surprising turns of fate, and have survived. My step is more youthful, and my heart is soft again, but wiser. I no longer seek validation from anyone else, just my own soul. I have learned to listen again to that inner voice that knows best what path I should take and which I should walk away from. All these things I had to learn alone. I am not taking any bows for it; in fact, I had to face cataclysmic losses before I was willing to open my eyes and heart and rethink my life. The good news is that I did it. The great news is that I am happy, but "happy" is an inadequate word to describe the wild-spirited woman I have become. I am no longer afraid of losing. I have embraced the joy of being independent and accountable to myself. I have discovered a daring, sensual side of my nature that has blown up everything I believed about myself. I am no longer the victim of my life but the heroine of my own story. In short, I am living on purpose, conscious and fully awake. The best news is that it was all a choice.

Someday, my children will run across the thousands of pages of thoughts and stories about their mother. Some of the stories will surprise them. Some of them will confirm what they already know to be true: that their mother was imperfect and thus completely human. They will find journals in which I question my decision to marry Jason and all the heartbreak that decision caused them. They will learn about the conflicts I grappled with as I tried this notion of a blended family. They will find their mother's private thoughts, the things they knew, suspected, and feared. They know my successes. They know my resiliency, but they will discover that I loved them more than circumstances around us would have had them believe.

We don't know who we are until we live on purpose. My role as a mother has taught me more than any college class, degree, or professional work I have done. My children have been my teachers, and they have taught me what it means to love someone more than myself. Jason is no longer in my life, but those who remain are the most important: Christian, Liam, Daniella, and Sara. My only regret is that they had to live with my choices. Isn't that how all of us feel as parents? I certainly don't speak for everyone, but I know there are a few out there who have not always met every life challenge with perfect grace. I certainly did not handle with any semblance of grace Jason running off with a younger, richer woman. My older three told me before we married that he would one day do exactly that, and I always lived in fear that he would. My worst fear was realized not when I was forty-five but when I was sixty-eight. Now I realize how that event allowed me to grow, to truly love myself, and to attract men into my life who really want a fiery, self-actualized woman. I learned how to play. Maybe I simply learned how to be unapologetically human.

§

I called Alex the other day and told her I had spent the last two days reading all the things we had gone through together. I wanted to remind her that, though we are in totally different places now, our story changed the very course of our lives. I still believe that our destinies crossed for a reason. I still believe that Sara was meant to be mine. I still believe that our decision to have an open adoption was the right thing to do for Sara. I still believe in the power of a love that defies understanding. Yet I also am saddened by how threatened we women often are with each other. We compete for everything: attention, praise, jobs, friends, and of course, men. It's not usually until later in life that we begin to see other women as allies, the only group that will ever know what it means to be a woman in this world. Alex and I struggled with all these things, and the miracle of it all is that we overcame them through our openness with one another and our desire to make things work for something greater than ourselves: Sara.

I see the beautiful human being that Sara has become, and in her I see Alex and Duncan and Jason and me. I see the stubborn, determined, grounded human being who has weathered life very well so far. I know she will be an incredible, compassionate, and capable nurse. I also know that she never had to wonder who her birth parents were. She never had to secretly seek them out. She never had to wonder if she had been loved. Sara has solid relationships. She knows how to love, and she has vast inner resources that she hasn't even seen in herself yet. I see the best of myself in her. I see the unique human in her that has nothing to do with any of the players in her story.

I see another woman, too. Alex is no longer a lost little girl. She is an accomplished businesswoman with two grown children. I hear a secure, resilient voice on the other end of the line when we speak. I see a person who has grown up, and I am proud of her. I am happy for her. After all, she is my daughter, too.

Finally, I must look in the mirror. The woman looking back is seventy-one years old and has lived a full life. In many ways, this last chapter has nothing to do with children or mothering at all. For the first time in my life, I am just me. I am more than the sum of my experiences but have been shaped by all of them. I am not so serious anymore, but I still live intensely. I have a deeper connection with myself, maybe for the first time. I have a deeply satisfying relationship with all my children and have come to a place of peace.

Nothing has turned out as I thought it would, but everything has turned out exactly as it should. I have learned to live with the ambiguity that is life. I regret that I have been so hard on my looks, my body, and myself. Why do we do that? All the years I condemned myself were folly. I now feel authentic and open, and I feel people sensing it when I walk into a room. I have accepted the gifts that have been given to me and hope that I have used them to be a better person in this often-confusing journey we call life. Change is as powerful as water. We are no match for it. It's life. Although I have gone kicking and screaming through some of the changes I have had to live, I see now how necessary every single one was to fulfill my personal destiny.

Recently I was thinking that mortality is becoming more real to me now that I am seventy-one. Perhaps this feeling is exacerbated because I spend a lot of time at retirement facilities with people who are in their final act of life. Once I awoke to a bad dream about dying and began to shiver. I just sat straight up in bed, grabbed my phone, and texted Alex. I was half asleep but very clear about what I wanted to ask:

Dear Alex,

I had to write you at this late hour because I want to ask you a great favor. Twenty-six years ago you gave me the greatest of gifts. I love Sara beyond mere words. But I am not young. One day I will pass from this Earth. Since both of our mothers died in their fifties, we know what a loss that is. It's a forever loss.

My request is simple: please promise me that when I am gone, you will be Sara's mother again. Sara must always have a mother. She's that kind of girl. Promise me, Alex, that you will take this gift back, and our lives will have come full circle. Yours and mine. Sara was on loan to me. She changed my life. Let's do this one last thing for her.

Alaina

Alex' response was immediate.

Dear Alaina,

I promise that I will always be there for Sara. I promise you as you once promised me.

Alex

One thing has never changed for us. I kept my promise to Alex that, no matter what, I would never keep her from Sara. I proved myself worthy of that trust. I see that in keeping that promise, both of our lives helped support a wonderful young woman. This experience has left me completely O P E N.

§

Sara
2017

*L*ast night was a big night for me. Even though my adoption has been open all my life, I knew very little about my birth father. I knew a lot about Alex because I got to talk to her on the phone and she visited us in Washington a couple of times when we lived on the little farm I so loved. She also came to my high school graduation and met all of my family and friends.

Alex was a household name, but Duncan was another matter. It's not that anyone kept him from me; I just didn't have many questions about him when I was little. I had my dad and I had my mom and I had Alex. They were just always there. When I finally read the book Mom and Alex made for me, I was in my twenties. I realized there was a lot going on behind the scenes that I hadn't known. Maybe part of me hadn't wanted to know, but it took me until now to sit down and read the story. It was a story about me, and it was a story about the two women whose lives affected mine in huge ways. I don't know if anyone sees their parents as real people, but after reading their story, I began to see both of them differently. When I finished reading, I realized why I am a strong woman: I come from strong women.

Last night, however, I was nervous. I was going to meet Duncan for the first time. This man was a complete mystery to me. Alex was part of my life, but Duncan was not; he was never mentioned. For most of my life, he lived in Costa Rica, and contacting him was never something I wanted to do. Once I turned eighteen, he sent me a friend request over Facebook. Now I had access to get to know him without the awkwardness of having actual human contact. Hey, I'm a Millennial; this is how we communicate.

Soon afterward, he started messaging me, and we began a dialogue of sorts. It only moved to another level when he and his wife were going to have their first baby. This must have brought up a lot of stuff for him. He sent me a photo of a baby nightgown that he had bought for me. What touched me the most was that the photo he sent showed this wrinkled, worn, stained nightshirt that he had carried with him from college to

New York to Costa Rica. He had always kept it with him. That simple act moved something in me that I couldn't exactly name.

When he was coming to the United States to visit his family for Christmas, he said he wanted to meet me. I was happy—and nervous. We were to meet at local hotel in Seattle where I had spent many a luncheon when my mom was giving speeches for her work. This visit was different, though.

When I first saw him, there was just this overwhelming feeling of awkwardness. For me, it was awkward that he was a father now to his own daughter, Emma. I didn't know how to act. His wife was very kind and really helped me feel calmer.

I thought we would spend an hour together and then I could slip away, both of us content. Duncan had other plans. He wanted to spend the whole day with me, so we all went to a mall. As we walked around, I could see that he had a sweet little family, but I also felt that he wanted something from me. Wasn't I supposed to want something from him? It was just a feeling I had.

As the day drew to an end, his wife took Emma back to their room to give Duncan and me some alone time before dinner. I sat across the table from him in the lounge. I looked into his eyes, and in a way, I was looking at myself, because we actually looked a lot alike. With the exception of my eyes, which definitely are from Alex, everything else was Duncan, my birth father. He had a serious look on his face, and as I listened to his questions and tried to answer them, my mind drifted back to the letter.

§

A few years ago, my big sister, Daniella, handed me a letter from Duncan, which he had written about the time he had signed over rights to my parents. The letter had never been opened. Daniella said that Mom had told her to keep it for me, that it was important. She had hauled it around from college to grad school to her first apartment, then a condo, and finally to her beautiful home where she is raising her family. She had kept it for me all those years. The letter itself looked yellow, almost like parchment. I took it but didn't look at it right away.

Eventually, I did get up the nerve to read it. It was definitely written in a guy's handwriting. His cursive was very tiny and precise, and there were erasure marks in some places. I tried to imagine a twenty-three-year-old writing it. I was twenty-three at the time. What would I have done? I was not sure I even wanted kids. So many thoughts went through my mind.

In the letter was the great sadness of a young man. He talked about being too young to be a father. He talked about not knowing what to do. He said he wanted the best for me. He said he was sorry. He poured out his heart to me in that letter.

Now I was looking into the watering eyes of that young man, now in his mid-forties, a father, but not my father. He talked about how he and Alex had met and how scared he had been when he learned that she was pregnant. He was still angry with her because he felt that she had not taken responsibility for having tricked him. I was glad that I had read her writings, because I was able to tell him that she *had* admitted all that and how sorry she had been. He was different after that. He talked about being a confused graduate student who was just trying to figure out life. He was just a kid who was not ready to be a father. He started to cry when he told me that he had changed my first diaper. I tried to imagine how he must have felt.

I didn't know what to say. So much pain was pouring out. I thought about how Alex's openness had allowed her to move forward but that his absence had made it hard for him to have closure. His body and his hands were shaking a bit, so I did what my parents would have done to me: I took his hands in mine and told him the truth. "Duncan, I have never once in my life felt abandoned or unwanted. Even though we're just seeing each other for the second time in our lives, I can say that I love you."

Duncan squeezed my hand and thanked me. I felt a love for this man for creating me and letting me learn about him. I told him that I have never once blamed him or Alex for putting me up for adoption and that I loved my family and my life. "Duncan, I am happy."

When Mom asked me to write the last chapter of this book, to "have the last word," I wondered how to begin my contribution. I knew it was time for me to weigh in. After all, the story is about me.

Hello, my name is Sara O'Connell, and I am adopted. I have always known that there was my mother and there was the woman who gave birth to me. There was never a confusing distinction. The first time I ever told my friends that I was adopted, they asked me, "Do you know who your *real* parents are?" I was confused by that question, because never in my life had I referred to Alex or Duncan as my parents or thought that my mom and dad were not real. It was always, Alaina is my mother, and Jason is my father. These were the faces I remembered putting me to bed, blowing bubbles in the bath, teaching me piano. They were the ones I cried to when I was sad or scared, and the ones who punished me when I poured a glass of milk on purpose into the fish tank, thus killing all the exotic fish. (Sorry, Mom!)

Explaining this to my friends and to anyone who asked was easy, but I sensed that not everyone completely understood. Alex and Duncan became people who were like distant relatives—they were people whom I could always contact and ask questions of or just say hello to. Another question people asked was, "Are you mad at your real parents for giving you up?" I told them, "Absolutely not!" Never once in my life did I feel abandoned or unwanted. I grew up knowing that Alex and Duncan loved me so much that they wanted me to have a better life than they could give me. I know that they worked very hard to find good people to be my parents, people who would love me and give me a wonderful life. And they did.

I can't remember the exact moment my parents told me about being adopted, but I know that I was very young. I'm pretty sure that I thought it was super cool at the time. It made me different and stand out from my friends. "*Two* mothers! How cool was that?" is what I thought when I was young. At some point, I had a need to meet this unknown woman. What was she like? Was she just an older version of me? Did she like horses as much as I did? I have met Alex four times in my life. She lives in Arizona with my half-sisters, Hope and Faith.

The first time I remember meeting her, she was still pregnant with Faith, and Hope was six. I had asked myself what I would feel when I met her. Would something click and I would feel a maternal attachment? When we met, my first thought was how young she was. Compared to my mother, who was older and more of a no-nonsense mom, Alex was a cool, exciting, fun woman who loved to snowboard and surf and travel. But what struck me the most was that when I tried to put Alex in a mom role in my head, that fun young woman just didn't fit. Looking back at it now, I realize that I didn't feel maternal comfort with the woman who gave birth to me but rather with the woman who raised me.

Meeting Hope was actually the interaction I was the most nervous about. For my whole life I had been the little sister, and now here was my chance to be a big sister. But I had no idea how a big sister should act. I made a dumb move of trying to kiss her on her forehead, because I thought that that's what big sisters do. She gave me a strange look, and so I deduced that it was not the right thing to do. Had my sister Daniella kissed me on the forehead? No. She did hug me a lot and called me "little fart." She didn't like it if Mom called me Bobitz, because that was Mom's special word for her. My dad called me "Princess," but Mom called me "Sweetness," "Baby," and "Sara Sue."

My favorite visit was the one I made to Arizona to visit Alex, Hope, and Faith in 2014. I was twenty-three, Hope was almost twenty, and Faith had just started high school. It was wonderful to travel around Arizona, just the four of us. It was during this visit that I felt for the first time a sense of family with them. I felt special when us three girls, all with different dads, stood side by side and Alex introduced us as her three daughters. That moment didn't mean that I had found a new family, but that I had finally found a connection that bound all four of us into a relationship.

Perhaps all parents want their own child, an extension of themselves, something precious whom they created. But even when a child doesn't come from his or her mother's body, that child is still someone the mom created. The child whom the parents raise does become a part of and an extension of them. People even say that I look like my mom, and I do.

From an adoptee to potential adoptive parents, I say, don't be afraid. Even though there won't be that blood connection holding you and your child together, there will be something even stronger. Open adoption takes a lot of courage, I have learned. I am a strong believer that being open helps the adopted child naturally accept things from birth on. No secrets, no invented stories, no questions, no mysteries.

Open adoption has shaped who I am. I have always been comfortable in my skin. My brothers and sister have always treated me like one of them, and they made sure my mom didn't change her rules just because I was the baby. They always paid attention to that kind of thing.

I think I am one of the lucky ones. I know not everyone gets a story like mine. I am just grateful that I have always been loved. My parents are not perfect. They don't agree on everything—well, not on very much at all. But they do agree that they both love me. Isn't that all you need to make it?

I am grateful Alex gave me life, and I am grateful she had the courage to let me go. I am grateful that there was an open adoption so I didn't have to wonder. I am grateful that I am a combination of all of them. I have Alex's big green eyes and her compulsion to bite fingernails and Duncan's love of bugs and reptiles (which no one else has except me). I have my mom's strength to reach my goals and the belief that failure is never an option. I know from her that being a mother is a big, big deal. I have my dad's positive outlook and humor. Then there is the me that is just uniquely me. No one owns me, and no one has ever tried. I think it takes great love to raise a child like that.

I hope that people looking for their birth parents don't forget the parents who loved and raised them. I wish people had faith that there are no accidents, as my mom always says. I was meant to have the parents I have. Mom and Alex have shown me that no matter how hard it is or how scared you are, doing what is best for the child is always the right way. They taught me to be open. They taught me what it means to love.

§

49346626R00152

Made in the USA
San Bernardino, CA
21 May 2017